MODERNISM, THE MARKET
AND THE INSTITUTION
OF THE NEW

ROD ROSENQUIST

CAMBRIDGE
UNIVERSITY PRESS

CAMBRIDGE UNIVERSITY PRESS

Cambridge, New York, Melbourne, Madrid, Cape Town, Singapore, São Paulo, Delhi

Cambridge University Press
The Edinburgh Building, Cambridge CB2 8RU, UK

Published in the United States of America by Cambridge University Press, New York

www.cambridge.org
Information on this title: www.cambridge.org/9780521516198

First published 2009

Printed in the United Kingdom at the University Press, Cambridge

A catalogue record for this publication is available from the British Library

Library of Congress Cataloging-in-Publication Data

Rosenquist, Rod, 1974–
Modernism, the market, and the institution of the new / Rod Rosenquist.
p.   cm.
Includes bibliographical references and index.
ISBN 978-0-521-51619-8 (hardback)
1. English literature–20th century–History and criticism.
2. Modernism (Literature)–English-speaking countries.
3. American literature–20th century–History and criticism.   I. Title.
PR478.M6R666 2009
820.9′112–dc22

2008033469

ISBN 978-0-521-51619-8 hardback

MODERNISM, THE MARKET AND THE INSTITUTION OF THE NEW

Modernism remains deeply connected to ideas of innovation, and this has created problems for successive generations of writers. For example, how does one create an original work when the 'new' has already been established, marketed and institutionalized? Rod Rosenquist's study focuses on the writers and poets who emerged after modernism's high-water mark year of 1922, in which *Ulysses, The Waste Land* and early *Cantos* were published. Seeking to refine our understanding of the high modernists through the frequent difficulties encountered by the generation that succeeded them, this study discusses issues of cultural value, the relationship of history to innovation, and the market for new works in an era already dominated by the likes of James Joyce, T. S. Eliot and Ezra Pound. Containing illuminating examinations of Wyndham Lewis, Laura Riding and Henry Miller, this book will be invaluable reading for those interested in modernism and its complicated legacy.

ROD ROSENQUIST is Senior Lecturer in English at Newbold College.

For Maria & Rye

Contents

Acknowledgements

As with any book, there are many people who deserve credit for helping to shape it. Tim Armstrong should be mentioned first as a constant source of advice, commentary and feedback. Warwick Gould, Robert Hampson, Michael Bell, Helen Carr and the anonymous readers enlisted by Cambridge University Press all provided very helpful responses to various drafts of this study, for which I would like to thank them. Brad Haas has always been willing to offer dialogue on modernism and has unearthed some of the more obscure sources for this work.

I am grateful to the ORSA Scheme and to the Royal Holloway English department for the funding that enabled me to undertake the doctoral work in which this book had its beginning.

Past and present members of the Humanities department at Newbold College deserve mention for their support throughout the writing process: Penny Mahon, Peter Balderstone, Sandra Rigby-Barrett, Kay Traille and David Trim. Other colleagues, especially staff in the Newbold College Library and the members of the senior management team, have also provided much-needed support.

The editors at Cambridge University Press have been invaluable in the final preparation of the work and I am indebted to them for their patience and expertise.

This study would not have been completed without the support of several significant others: my parents, Roger and Kathy; my brother, Todd, and his family; my parents-in-law, Johnny and Seka; the Kohtzes, the Nilsens, the Becejacs and the Balderstones; but especially my wife, Maria. If there is any merit in this book, it is hers.

Abbreviations

The following works are cited parenthetically within the text as abbreviated below:

ABR   Wyndham Lewis, *The Art of Being Ruled*, ed. Reed Way Dasenbrock (Santa Rosa, CA: Black Sparrow, 1989)

AG   Wyndham Lewis, *The Apes of God*, ed. Paul Edwards (Santa Rosa, CA: Black Sparrow, 1997)

BB   Wyndham Lewis, *Blasting and Bombardiering: An Autobiography 1914–1926*, revised edition (London: Calder, 1982)

CS   Laura Riding, *Contemporaries and Snobs* (London: Jonathan Cape, 1928)

LE   Henry Miller, *Letters to Emil*, ed. George Wickes (Manchester: Carcanet, 1990)

LWL   W. K. Rose (ed.), *The Letters of Wyndham Lewis* (Norfolk, CT: New Directions, 1963)

NCZ   Jenny Penberthy (ed.), *Niedecker and the Correspondence with Zukofsky: 1931–1970* (Cambridge: Cambridge University Press, 1993)

PAA   Laura Riding and Robert Graves, *A Pamphlet Against Anthologies* (London: Jonathan Cape, 1928)

P/Z   Barry Ahearn (ed.), *Pound/Zukofsky: Selected Letters of Ezra Pound and Louis Zukofsky* (London: Faber and Faber, 1987)

SMP   Laura Riding and Robert Graves, *A Survey of Modernist Poetry* (London: Heinemann, 1927)

TWM   Wyndham Lewis, *Time and Western Man*, ed. Paul Edwards (Santa Rosa, CA: Black Sparrow, 1993)

Introduction:
The modernist latecomer and 'permanent novelty'

'Literature is news that STAYS news.'

Ezra Pound, *ABC of Reading*[1]

At the end of 1922, Ezra Pound announced to Margaret Anderson, 'Intelligent reviews of my last works, of Eliots Waste Land, and even of that olde classicke Ulysses wd. be suitable features for an up to date annual.'[2] While there is an evident employment of irony in the use of the word classic to describe these fairly recently published works, Pound's statement reveals a contemporary acknowledgement of a tension in early twentieth-century literature that critics of the twenty-first century still find perplexing. That a work of art could be considered simultaneously well established, even 'classic', as well as 'modern' or 'up to date' is perhaps a peculiar problem in studies of the movement we still call, nearly a century later, 'modernism'. Those critics focusing on the period have done much to make this paradox a central element of the character of the movement, revealing the methods modernist authors used to make careers for themselves out of constantly reinventing the new, all the while consciously positioning their works within an older literary tradition.[3] We cannot know, of course, whether Pound could foresee the future literary histories which would confirm 1922 as the *annus mirabilis* of modernism, as well as making *Ulysses, The Waste Land* (both 1922) and Pound's poems of this time into what we call, perhaps oxymoronically, 'modernist classics'.

But the modernists themselves, of course, did have their own pronounced views on the relationship between the new and the classic works of art. T. S. Eliot's essay 'Tradition and the Individual Talent' (1919), a significant statement which still forms a central pillar in monolithic views of the modernist period, first illustrated the view that the 'really new work of art' takes its place among the 'monuments', thus changing the structure of the literary tradition and taking its own place as a classic.[4] The emphasis

I

here is placed on the work being 'really new', which might translate as a work which (paradoxically) breaks with tradition before it then reenters or reshapes it. Likewise, Pound places the emphasis on the new when discussing his own definition of a classic in *ABC of Reading* (1934): 'A classic is not a classic because it conforms to certain structural rules, or fits certain definitions (of which its author had quite probably never heard). It is classic because of a certain eternal and irrepressible freshness.'[5] This idea of eternal freshness – Wyndham Lewis, as we shall see, would use the phrase 'permanent novelty' – clearly characterizes the paradoxical emphasis modernists would put upon the new finding its way into the establishment. The key here is that these high modernists were aware of the paradox that this break with tradition often meant simply the remaking of it or, to put it otherwise, that a work taking on the qualities of the really modern often involved it becoming, in time, a classic. Modernist literature aimed to be new, but also to *stay* new, to paraphrase Pound's significant dictum.

This study will aim to show that the writers of the modernist period were highly aware of the paradox involved in a simultaneous focus on the advanced or up to date and on the already established tradition, and that it resulted, in the late 1920s and after, in a reaction by a group of writers we might call the modernist latecomers within the context of the historicizing efforts and institutional manipulation of modernism's more established writers, those who are sometimes called the 'high modernists'. Yet before we can discuss the latecomers, we must first define what it means to be 'on time' – to characterize those who first established modernism as a historical period. Any group of writers we might designate 'high modernist' will necessarily be based on a later historical configuration, since there was no such label at that time; yet I would like to suggest that authors and commentators during the period shared the view that, even without an agreed label, certain authors stood out from the others as epitomizing what 'high modernism' now represents to us. The term seems often to be used in two subtly distinct ways, though both normally involve the same authors: one is used to designate those modernists who were devoted to an autonomous or art-for-art's-sake aesthetic, or those who were perceived to pursue 'high art'; the other is used to represent the writers establishing their careers during the 'high modernist' period, when the early revolutionary spirit was for the first time formalized and brought into cultural prominence, from roughly 1914 to 1925. While some writers might fit into one of these categories but not the other, it seems that an overwhelming majority of critics agree that Eliot, Pound and James Joyce form a central core to this specific strand of modernists. Even more importantly, though, than the academy's later (re)construction of the historical period, these writers can be considered high modernists because, as I aim to reveal, they at one time or another held respective positions of cultural power within the period itself, and found ways to establish their newly modern works as more permanently modern*ist* icons.

This shift from the idea of the modern to that of the more enduringly modernist was to some extent, of course, due to the work of historians, but the period has always received attention as one which highlighted the rules for belonging to the movement, largely through manifestos and critical essays. The period's synonyms for 'modernist' – including 'advanced' or 'up to date' – did not, as we shall see, simply include *anyone* writing during the period, particularly since there were numerous contemporaries of the modernists who were considered to be passé in their literary efforts, or simply writing within a different aesthetic. Chris Baldick makes this the central theme of his volume of *The Oxford English Literary History,* 'The Modern Movement', choosing a broader understanding of the period than many critics have traditionally chosen. But while discussing his inclusion of more popular writers and alternative traditions, Baldick acknowledges that the current tendency to celebrate the 'triumph of the revolution' of high modernism is partly due to the actions of the high modernists themselves as they turned their revolution into an enduring cultural dominance.[6] This meant that writing in a modernist manner usually involved conforming to the characteristics of the period as defined by certain authors – particularly the blend of tradition and innovation exhibited by the high modernists in the late 1910s and 1920s. One could choose to ignore these high modernist tendencies, and many did, but those authors – as some openly acknowledged – were often aware that they were counting themselves out of the prevailing movement of the age.

This raises obvious problems in defining what is modern for any given age, especially within this specific period when, for a significant proportion of literary producers, writing 'good' literature came to mean writing 'modern' literature – two highly relative terms depending on each other for their definitions. W. B. Yeats, for instance, when compiling his influential *The Oxford Book of Modern Verse* (1936), had to face just such questions. Does one define the modern according to the age of the poets to be included, or their dates of publication, or rather according to the display of the characteristics of modernity? And if the latter (which seems more common, at least within the period), who is to decide which characteristics are modern for each new generation? Yeats may not answer these questions for us, but he implies that being modern involves more than simply writing in one's own age when he states, 'I too have tried to be modern.'[7] In defining what it means to 'be modern', Yeats is suggesting it has little to do with simply writing or publishing in a specified period but rather with putting in an *effort* to represent or reflect the age. The irony of the sentiment here revealed is that even one of the most central modernist poets at the height of his career expresses anxiety over qualifying for a period identified, even then, with advancement and innovation. This study concerns itself with individual writers coming late to this period characterized by the up to date, particularly once the modernist movement had already been to some extent established, when all that was left was to choose to belong to one's age – as it had come to be defined by those who had gone before – or to opt out.

But first we must examine to what extent the writers of high modernism managed to institutionalize the notion of the 'new'. By 1922, the individual careers of these modernist writers were still capable of complete transformation; but for the most part, as will be shown, modernism as a *collective* movement had come into its own. *Ulysses* and *The Waste Land* had successfully attracted enough attention in the press to be recognized even beyond the select circles of readers that modernist writers had until then found for an audience. As Lawrence Rainey suggests, the year marked the transition from an audience made up of coterie circles and publication in small circulation journals into the more widely recognized literary institutions.[8] Certain prominent modernists found their reputations growing within a limited but highly influential literary field and, though they could not rightly be considered 'popular', they managed to acquire a certain element of cultural celebrity, as Aaron Jaffe has observed.[9] Looking back on the period from a historic vantage point, many critics conclude that an ascendant or 'hegemonic' strand of literary modernism emerges about this time, a dominant mode of critical values led by the cultural and institutional power of, most obviously, Eliot and, to varying extents, Pound, Joyce and others.[10] While such a term as 'ascendant' is necessarily relative, rating the group's 'dominance' within the context of exclusivity in which they positioned themselves, it remains a useful designation for the few authors who managed to make a name for themselves within the various constructions that literary historians have built out of the period.

One of the central questions of ascendant modernism, however, concerns the source of the perception of this group's centrality or dominance.

High modernists had gathered, even during their own age, a reputation of detachment, even to the point where they were considered aloof to critical or popular reception. For example, when writing about the modernist artist in general, Richard Aldington would say, 'He writes for an audience equipped to understand him, and is indifferent to popular success.'[11] This may have been a view modernists encouraged of themselves or simply a misconception, but it now appears increasingly outdated, as more critical attention has been given to modernists within the marketplace. It is now recognized that the high modernists did not entirely resist the commodification of art, but took part, albeit hesitantly, in what Pierre Bourdieu has called 'The Market for Symbolic Goods'.[12] High modernists were aware that literary reputation and cultural value are forces which can be shaped and formed by any number of different factors. This was even acknowledged by their contemporaries, such as Louis Untermeyer, who in 1923 identified 'a group, in attempting to do for Mr. Eliot what "Ulysses" did for Mr. Joyce', that had displayed 'some of the most enthusiastically naïve superlatives that have ever issued from publicly sophisticated iconoclasts'.[13] The key here is the recognition, even by the high modernists' contemporaries, that there was a concerted effort to publicize and market certain works as the important literary texts of the age. Most high modernist artists were not reluctant to engage in the active manipulation of public opinion or institutional and cultural histories in order to ensure the best reception of their work by both contemporary readers and future literary historians alike. This is rarely disputed, but the consequences of these engagements with cultural institutions and historical formulations remain debatable – and it is the consequences arising that this study takes as its subject.

Examples of this group negotiating their own cultural reception can be readily found in the various collections of correspondence of high modernists such as Eliot, Pound and Joyce. With *Ulysses*, to take one illustration, Joyce proved himself to be an avid executor of his own public relations programme – one which made the novel a cultural monument long before it had a substantial readership.[14] According to the biographer of Sylvia Beach, the American expatriate who founded the Shakespeare and Co. bookshop and first published *Ulysses*, the author would spend every day at her shop, suggesting methods for getting his novel reviewed, even when the reviewers were reticent.[15] One reluctant reviewer of *Ulysses* was Ford Madox Ford, who claimed in *The English Review* that he had been 'pressed to write for the English public something about the immense book of Mr. Joyce', going on to say, 'I do not wish to do so;

I do not wish to do so at all for four or five – or twenty – years.'[16] But Joyce and his supporters were not sufficiently patient to allow opinions of the novel to form of their own accord. A letter from Joyce to Harriet Shaw Weaver, his patron and publisher, reveals that it was she who 'dictated' the substance of Ford's article, with Joyce continuing, 'I am glad you have taken to writing the favourable criticisms. It seems to me I wrote most of them so far – I mean I see my own phrases rolling back to me.'[17] Another letter reveals Joyce encouraging Eliot to 'use or coin some short phrase, two or three words' for the benefit of the English reading public, despite the fact that copies of the book were largely unavailable in Britain, having been seized and destroyed at Folkestone customs.[18] Here we see an example of a high modernist helping to compose catchphrases and favourable reviews of his own novel, encouraging opinions to be formed from his own dictation rather than waiting for them to form in their own time.

This is not only a manipulation of literary consumerism, I will argue, but in a way a preemptive strike against literary history. But before the case is made, the example of Valéry Larbaud is similarly instructive. Not only was Larbaud the first to use the phrase 'interior monologue' in regard to *Ulysses*, he was also the first to discuss publicly what is variously called the 'key' or 'schema' behind the structure of the novel. Larbaud became an admirer and close friend of Joyce a few months before the book publication of *Ulysses*, and he was shown the schema which Joyce had used to construct the novel, an elaborate outline of each chapter in terms of its specific Homeric episode, technique, organ, architecture and various other categories. It was, in effect, a reader's guide to the structure of the novel, but paradoxically was not intended for the general reader, as Joyce made clear to Carlo Linati, the first person to see the plan.[19] Yet Joyce encouraged Larbaud to use it for a starting point in his public lecture on *Ulysses* at a special 'seance' held in Paris in Joyce's honour in December 1921, and for his follow-up essay in the *Nouvelle Revue Française*. Although *Ulysses* had already been printed by *The Little Review*, it should be remembered that there would have been few readers of the novel by the time Larbaud was stressing the way it should be understood. By April, he was writing, 'If one reads *Ulysses* with attention, one cannot fail to discover this plan in time.'[20] Yet Larbaud had not 'discovered' the key himself independently. Joyce admitted to Weaver that the purpose of the schema in the first place was 'in order to confuse the audience a little more'.[21] In so doing, Joyce had constructed a closed circle of interpretation, providing complications to his novel which only his own 'key' could unlock. It was when Jacques Benoîst-Méchin wrote to Joyce demanding to be given the entire schema that Joyce famously answered, 'If I gave it all up immediately, I'd lose my immortality. I've put in so many enigmas and puzzles that it will keep the professors busy for centuries arguing over what I meant, and that's the only way of insuring one's immortality.'[22]

While this strategy may not involve the manipulation of commercial institutions, like marketing a novel in literary reviews, it has everything to do with the institution of a *historical* modernism. In other words, we are not only forced to come to terms with a high modernism involved in marketing itself, but with a group at the core of a notional modernist canon who were involved in the formation of, not just the new texts of the period, but the structure of the literary field and the history that would come to be written of the movement – in fact, investing time and energy in the institutions that would make these new works endure beyond their immediate novelty. Michael Whitworth, introducing the period in a section entitled 'Modernist Self-Construction', suggests that 'As the modern movement began to become established, various author-critics attempted to secure its group identity by writing first drafts of its history, and, in particular, by defining epochal dates or moments at which "the modern" was born.'[23] This hints at the modernist link between the creative and forward-looking artist, devoted to the new, and the traditional and historically minded critic, concerned largely with endur-ance and institutions. In fact, awareness of how literary critical studies led to a type of immortality was growing throughout the late nineteenth and early twentieth centuries. The rise in historical self-consciousness that was infiltrating the minds of writers in the 1910s and 1920s closely parallels the rise of professionalization in the literary vocations of the time, as well as the development of modern 'English' as taught within academic institutions.[24]

Likewise, there is evidence that academics in the third decade of the twentieth century were aware of an emerging movement based on innova-tion and experimentation with form and language, and that certain writers could be identified not just as subjects for study but as contem-poraries or allies. I. A. Richards went so far as to confront Eliot with an open position in the faculty at Cambridge.[25] His colleague, F. R. Leavis, proposed as early as 1926 to make the banned *Ulysses* a textbook for an unspecified undergraduate class, a full ten years before the novel would be allowed in Britain and only four after its publication as a book.[26] The eagerness of the academic establishment to adopt the latest figureheads of a contemporary movement served only to reinforce the positions already held by these writers. As contemporary literature grew more common material for the classroom, the modernist writers themselves grew more aware of their position within academic institutions and their prospects of entering an 'immortal' historical narrative.

Louis Menand has traced the reactions of modernist writers to the general professionalization of late nineteenth-century culture by looking specifically at Eliot's career and context. He describes how the various poetic associations of the period, as characterized by the anthology and the -ism, managed to institutionalize the new poetry immediately within more traditional and professional organizations. Menand writes:

> The task of the usurping practitioner is to make his discourse seem not new, but in fact the traditional discourse, and to make the language of the amateur he is supplanting appear to be an aberration. And this was exactly the procedure modernism followed in distinguishing itself from and claiming superiority to the established literary culture of its time.[27]

That Eliot succeeded in gaining considerable cultural and professional authority through his stylistic experimentation and concurrent assimilation of tradition is illustrated clearly by Menand. Although the modernists would become known for their experimentation and 'newness' – it was, in fact, what gave them their name – it was their ability to be simultaneously traditional that made them endure. In seeking to highlight their connection to the past, many high modernists, as Menand suggests a few pages later, aimed to acquire the status of the institution.[28]

Most of the authors writing within high modernism were dedicated to making their past visible in this way. Any casual reader of Pound's collected essays will come across numerous examples, usually in footnotes, of his reminders of the dates when he first developed or made public the ideas he promotes. This technique is identified by Stan Smith – who outlines many of the problems referred to above – as one which keeps Pound's criticism continually up to date by positioning his 'new' observations within a historical time frame.[29] With significant essays entitled 'The Tradition', 'A Retrospect' and 'Date Line', it is easy to judge how important historiography was to Pound's own assessment of the movement. Instructively, his 1934 volume of criticism, entitled *Make It New*, rather than beginning with any really new pronouncements, commences with 'Date Line', containing a type of *curriculum vitae*, complete with the dates of his major publications and those of his associates, alongside evidence of, in his own words, his 'capacity to pick the winner'. 'Let it stand', Pound states, 'that from 1912 onward for a decade and more I was instrumental in forcing into print, and *secondarily* in commenting on, certain work now recognized as valid by all competent readers, the dates of various reviews, anthologies, etc., are ascertainable.'[30] Here Pound is cashing in his cultural credit as one who correctly judged the newly established authors years before they had grown established so that his readers might believe him regarding the next new thing (in this case economic theory).

But in setting out his past cultural triumphs, Pound is making an institution of himself, rather than 'making it new'. Like many of the modernists, Pound considers himself a step ahead of the tastes of the general reader, viewing the present as if from the position of a future historian, able to fit the immediacy of the 'modern' into the wider concept of a past tradition. This strategy, though, often leads the high modernists into playing simultaneous roles as literary artists, critics and historians, helping to institutionalize the creative work of their contemporaries, even their own, as it is produced. As Pound's phrasing illustrates, the modernist 'work now recognized as valid by all competent readers' was first 'forced' into print and then affirmed as 'valid' by Pound himself. The question that remains is whether this is because of his foresight, as Pound would have us believe, or because the conditions for literary validity were established by Pound as cultural arbiter in the first place. To phrase this another way, what best explains the eventual acceptance of modernist works as 'valid': the innovation and inherent aesthetic appeal, or the influence on publication and public acceptance that certain high modernists were capable of using? This latter explanation carries a whole new meaning for the phrase 'make it new', whereby the literary work is '*made* new' almost simultaneously through the artist's creative faculties and through the institutional work of publishers, commentators and journalists, and where the quality of 'newness' is measured by the literary work's relation to history as a whole – extending into both the past and the future.

Joyce and Pound were not the only modernists to formulate the position of their works while keeping firmly in mind the literary critics and historians of the future. Pound's forward thinking when it came to *Poetry* magazine, aiming for 'the files of this periodical to be prized and vendible in 1999', is echoed by Harriet Monroe, his editorial partner, who questioned as early as 1912, 'How will twenty-first century critics rank artists of the present day?'[31] This general concern over a future posterity's perception of the period almost certainly led to the active, though often unpremeditated, attempts by high modernists to historicize themselves. These attempts could be either implicit or explicit. For example, Pound's often-quoted narrative account of how he and Eliot came to be linked within the movement comes as a response to Eliot's own much less obvious attempt to assimilate a history he never actually took part in. In 'Harold Monro' Pound tries to make the whole story clear:

[Eliot] displayed great tact, or enjoyed great fortune, in arriving in London at a particular date with a formed style of his own. He also participated in a movement to which no name has ever been given.

That is to say, at a particular date in a particular room, two authors, neither engaged in picking the other's pocket, decided that the dilution of *vers libre*, Amygism, Lee Masterism, general floppiness had gone too far, and that some counter-current must be set going.[32]

But just before this narrative of the 'counter-current', Pound takes issue with Eliot for labelling Monro's brand of poetry – as distinguished from the other common brand of that time, Georgian poetry – 'our own'. He writes, '"Our own" is too generous a term. And it might be of more general, critical service to point out how few of "us" have survived from a pre-Eliot decade, how few of the people who were there at all, in 1911, would still be admitted to Mr. Eliot's "our own".' Pound and Eliot were both intent on establishing their own versions of tradition, even when they conflicted, often focusing on that which survives the currents and counter-currents of successive modernist novelties. The struggle for the high modernists was not always to be the first or the newest but also to be the most enduring – survivors of the advances of innovation.

This is what leads Art Berman to distinguish the high modernists from the avant-garde modernists, stating, 'High modernism is modernism become self-conscious of itself as a historical event, decades into its progress, rather than as the new event announced in the early modernist manifestoes.'[33] This distinction perhaps ignores the fact that many high modernists were first avant-garde in approach, and that the two positions can, at times, be held concurrently. But there is a key recognition here that the historical development of modernism as a movement, particularly as viewed self-consciously by its participants, is a major reason for the complex nature of the period's relation to past and present. The idea can be found in an earlier work by Michael Levenson, who divides the earlier radical modernists from the 'counter-current' of the mid- to late 1910s, emphasizing tradition and authoritarianism and gaining dominance only once the early modernist visual artists and theorists, including

T. E. Hulme, Henri Gaudier-Brzeska and Lewis, departed for the First World War.[34] The distinction is important since it applies specifically to modernism the general tendency for every radically new movement to eventually seek to establish for itself a position of cultural authority and historical certainty, to move from what Levenson calls provocation to consolidation. Pierre Bourdieu, perhaps the best theorist of the phenomenon, recognizes this when he says:

> The ageing of authors, schools and works is far from being the product of a mechanical, chronological, slide into the past; it results from the struggle between those who have made their mark (*fait date* – 'made an epoch') and who are fighting to persist, and those who cannot make their own mark without pushing into the past those who have an interest in stopping the clock, eternalizing the present stage of things. 'Making one's mark', initiating a new epoch, means winning recognition, in both senses, of one's difference from other producers, especially the most consecrated of them; it means, by the same token, creating a new position, ahead of the positions already occupied, in the vanguard . . . Each author, school or work which 'makes its mark' displaces the whole series of earlier authors, schools or works.[35]

This last statement clearly echoes Eliot's description of the way a 'really new' work of art enters and displaces the tradition of established monuments.[36] The modernists' own self-conscious understanding of this interaction rests at the heart of the relative success of high modernism, and would provide an awkward position for those artists coming after this group's rise to cultural authority.

In this respect, Bourdieu's phrase '*faire date*' is an important one, supporting translations as diverse as 'to make a mark' or 'to establish an epoch' or 'to mark out a place [for oneself] in history'. There are a number of metaphors used throughout this study which perhaps require brief discussion. In particular, such phrases as 'to make a mark' (which suggests surveying, inscription or branding) and discussions of cultural 'positions in the field' (which has military overtones) – both of which are borrowed from Bourdieu – can be useful for illustrating the high modernist efforts during the period, but they also somewhat obscure the true context in which they are used here. There is an attempt in the next few pages and beyond to use as many direct examples of problems of 'cultural space' and the 'cultural field' as well as what it means to 'make a mark' or 'make a date'. What is at stake here is a study of 'the structure of objective relations between positions occupied by individuals and groups placed in a situation of competition for legitimacy', particularly in the high and late modernist period.[37] An example of this within the period is provided by

Edmund Wilson, describing his attendance in the early 1920s at 'The Coffee House' where other writers would gather. He describes how 'Ezra Pound was then a kind of bugaboo for those mediocre novelists, drama-tists and journalists . . . such people sometimes baited us with some such challenge as, "I suppose you admire Ezra Pound."' Here Pound's name becomes a symbol of artistic pretension towards modernist legitimacy, a representation of, in this case, Wilson's position within the modernist cultural field, despite the fact that Wilson claims to care little for Pound.[38] Pound had at this point made his mark and begun to represent the established notion of 'advanced' literature in the period.

The high modernists followed Bourdieu's pattern nearly perfectly, first creating a new, avant-garde position for themselves by breaking with the earlier, specifically Victorian tradition, creating their own distinctive marks (names, programmes and group formations); they then set about preserving their works through their own historical efforts and making their own tradition. Already by the mid-1920s, *The Waste Land*, *Ulysses* and Pound's contemporary poems seem to have been considered 'classic' enough to allow their respective authors a place at the centre of a dom-inant strand of modernism and worthy of a place in history as such. For example, Monroe would write of Pound in 1925, 'As a leader, a revolutionist in the art, he will have a place in literary history; as a poet he will sing into the hearts and minds of all free-singing spirits in the next age – and perhaps in the ages beyond reach of our prophecy.'[39] Written nearly five decades before Pound's death, this seems to us premature, but not untypical of the historicizing efforts of the high modernists' contem-poraries. High modernism had, in Bourdieu's phrase, already established an epoch by the mid-1920s.

To what extent this is true, however, depends on how far a notional 'high modernism' represented something at times larger than the sum of its parts. While it has been suggested that high modernists were successful partially because of their own institutional efforts and historical self-consciousness, individual authors followed career paths that varied greatly from one to another, growing and diminishing according to minor changes in their fortune, their work, their reception and the nature of the literary field they were helping to form. For instance, even with such seemingly automatic candidates as Eliot and Pound, it must be pointed out that Pound's sphere of influence was much more widely recognized in the 1910s than the 1920s, when Eliot's influence was growing dramatically. Similarly, it should be remembered that Pound had a greater impact on American writers and Eliot on the English, or that Pound's poetic development was carried out in public – with each development being published – unlike Eliot's.[40] Joyce may be considered an ascendant or 'dominant' modernist owing to his reputation during the period, or because of his covert publicizing activity, but clearly he did not contribute to the kind of critical formulation of modernism that Pound and Eliot helped to publish and propagate in literary journals, manifestos and editorial work. As this suggests, any attempt to characterize this group of ascendant modernists uniformly is bound to lack some definition and come across a number of exceptions in any case.

For these reasons, in this study the definition of high modernism will not be formulated according to recent academic interventions, nor according to documented evidence of 'height' or 'dominance' for each individual writer included. Rather, it must be recognized that it often fell to those either on the margins or completely outside of high modernism to begin to offer definitions and descriptions of the dominant movement – revealing an awareness of defining characteristics of high modernism of which the high modernists themselves were ignorant, as Whitworth suggests.[41] We have, therefore, a conception of modernism that is defined in part by the activities of the artists included, in part by the institutions that supported them – including the small presses, the editors and the academies – and finally (and most importantly in this context) by those rival artists who felt disenfranchised by the trends that were coming to define the movement. Even if it is not the whole picture, a significant conception of high modernism appears only when examining the literary field with which the latecomers believed they had to come to terms. As Menand notes, 'Writers are compelled to deal not with their predecessors, but with their predecessors' reputations.'[42] We can add that this is true even if those predecessors are still alive and presiding over the cultural domain in which the successors must find their place. The complicating factor in this respect, however, is that successors also have a hand in forming the reputations of their predecessors, meaning that both the established modernists and the latecomers – whether antagonistic or cooperative – each played a role in shaping the way the period is viewed.

As is often the case, Eliot provides a useful illustration of how the group can be defined in this way. For instance, David Chinitz has described how far the term 'high modernism' has come to stand for the 'institutional, elitist and aesthetic' side of modernism, particularly lamenting that 'the rediscovered variety and vitality of early-twentieth-century writing does not extend to "high modernism"'.[43] He adds, 'Eliot remains, of course, the public face of this discredited movement, however designated', before going on to reveal just how far Eliot should be seen as a simultaneously popular writer concerned with mass culture, playfulness and political engagement. This is an important statement to acknowledge, particularly in a study such as this, which does not seek to reaffirm the sometimes reductive perspective that colours the high modernists. But even if it is a vital critical endeavour to reclaim Eliot and other high modernists from a narrow view of a 'discredited movement' – to remind ourselves of their creativity, energy and eagerness to facilitate innovative work by other writers – we cannot pretend that this is the only high modernist contribution to the period. We must also ask ourselves: if this reductive view depicts high modernists as overly autonomous, hegemonic or elitist, where does it come from and when did it emerge? Was it projected by the high modernists themselves? How pervasively was it felt by those contemporaries who did not themselves feel qualified to join the movement? Thus far it has been suggested that the ascendant writers were themselves responsible for the image of high modernism that evolved from the period. But even when these authors are not responsible for this conception, we shall see that writers who felt excluded from high modernism often assist – following the lead of the high modernists, and preparing the ground for later critical views – in formulating the identity of the group and its position of cultural authority and autonomy within the period.

For these reasons, we turn our attention to the writers coming after modernism had reached its height to examine how far responsibility for the conception of high modernism as centralizing, ascendant and exclusive lies here. It is often remarked that one of the first instances of poetry receiving the label 'modernist' was in the title of a book written by Laura Riding and Robert Graves, but less often discussed that these two poets were themselves excluded from the until then unnamed movements associated with modernism. It is significant that an early work like *A Survey of Modernist Poetry* (1927) considers a broad range of poets that more or less matches our own canon of modernist poetry, despite the fact that they are highly critical of more than half of those they select for comment. Riding and Graves discuss such central figures as Eliot, Pound, Yeats, Aldington, H. D. (Hilda Doolittle), William Carlos Williams, Edith Sitwell, Wallace Stevens and e. e. cummings, while adding a few more peripheral figures who they think deserve more attention, including Isaac Rosenberg and Riding herself.[44] What is instructive is that two poets writing towards the end of the 1920s are capable of identifying a more or less coherent group of writers who had 'made a name' for themselves, even if that name is assigned by those already excluded from it – those wanting to break open the canon they felt to be rather rigidly completed soon after the works were first published. Riding and Graves were not the only ones who identified this epochal movement, and modernism was not the only name attached. Wilson's *Axel's Castle* (1931) famously labels Eliot, Yeats, Joyce and Marcel Proust, among others, symbolists. Although this gives a different name and a slightly different canon, there is still an identifiable movement, one which could be discussed as a coherent project destined to be assumed into literary history.

Other modernist writers, acting neither as historians nor as literary critics, identified Eliot, Pound and Joyce as the foremost representatives of an established movement. For example, Henry Miller, who boasted in 1934 of being free of 'all cults, isms, movements, countries, latitudes, and philosophies', cited these three modernists in the same letter as a specific example of a coherent group formation from which he was proud to remain independent (*LE* 152). Frank Swinnerton, writing an early critical survey of the period just two years later, entitled his book *The Georgian Literary Scene: A Panorama*. But rather than this suggesting that, during the 1930s, the high modernists were not the dominant group and did not in fact define the epoch under discussion, Swinnerton is hoping to play down the actual centrality of the high modernists and their emphasis on writing new literature to represent the period. As he says of Eliot's restricted range of emotion, 'In this respect he is of his age. Admirers of the age will say, properly; doubters will question contemporaneity as a virtue.'[45] Swinnerton is among the doubters rather than the admirers of the age, but even then implicitly acknowledges that the period belongs more to Eliot and others who are 'of the age' than those who simply write *during* the age – i.e., those who do not consider a literary work to be good simply because it is up to date. In seeking to reclaim the period for the Georgian group, Swinnerton identifies that definitions of the literature of the modernist period are written too quickly and, in some cases, too narrowly, based upon the institution of a literature of the age associated with a few prominent practitioners.

Similarly, Richard Aldington both begs to be excused from defining 'twentieth-century literature when it is only beginning to emerge', and also goes on to say that 'one may note a certain homogeneity in the writings of M. Marcel Proust and Mr. James Joyce, of Miss Sitwell and Mr. Huxley, of Miss Moore and H. D., of Jean Cocteau and Paul Morand and T. S. Eliot.'[46] Again, the canon is slightly different, but it still emphasizes the position of the high modernists in defining the century's new literature. Perhaps more significantly in the context of this study, Aldington goes on to suggest, 'The typical modern poet whose affinities are chiefly with the writers above mentioned is something extremely unlike the conventional idea of poet.' Aldington highlights here the significant distinction that was evident, even in the period, between being a 'typical' poet (as in belonging to the newly established 'modern' movement) and the merely *conventional* one (i.e., not modern-ist). Contemporary authors, critics and readers were aware, then, that the relatively small group of authors we here call 'high modernists' were the exceptional few – as Baldick makes clear in his history of the period. But in identifying these exceptional few with a select 'type' of poet – a type distinguishable from the merely 'conventional' poet, with which others might share 'affinities' and therefore belong – Aldington hereby highlights why a group with limited popular appeal and exclusive mani-festos and critical formulations might still manage cultural dominance. These authors, signifying the typicity of 'the modern', were drawn into definitions of the period, perhaps even against their will, and often at the expense of those who remained conventionally outside.

Therefore it is not enough merely to illustrate that there was an ascendant strand of high modernists readily apparent to their contempor-aries. The effects of their dominance on other writers is part of the subject of this study, and affects our understanding of it. For example, in the same year that Miller recognized Eliot, Pound and Joyce as three central established authors, Malcolm Cowley published his *Exile's Return*, a memoir of literary life in 1920s Paris and New York. He relates the process by which a younger writer might encounter an 'established author', a relationship which is based not only on the published works of such an author, since

there is also to be considered his career, the point from which it started, the direction in which it seems to be moving. There is his personality, as revealed in chance interviews or as caricatured in gossip; there are the values that he assigns to other writers; and there is the value placed on himself by his younger colleagues in those kitchen or barroom gatherings at which they pass judgment with the harsh finality of a Supreme Court – John X has got real stuff, they say, but Jonathan Y is terrible . . . until they [the younger writers] begin to form a picture, vague and broken at first, then growing more distinct as the years pass by: the X or Y picture, the James Joyce, Ezra Pound or T. S. Eliot picture. But it is not so much a picture when completed: it is rather a map or diagram which the apprentice writer will use in planning his own career.[47]

Cowley's position, though it should not be taken as representative of all modernist latecomers, is clearly built in relation to the formulations of high modernism that have been discussed thus far. It is instructive that a few select high modernists frequently form a central group considered to be 'established', and that through their establishment they provide the younger authors with a historical pattern upon which to start to build their own place in history. Certainly, by 1934, and seemingly already in the mid-1920s (the time Cowley is recalling), there seems to have been in existence a group of modernists whom we may call ascendant or dominant because they were the ones who formed the 'map or diagram' for the younger generations to build their careers from.

So while it is accepted that our own vision of high modernism is largely based on historical reconstruction, there is also evidence that the contemporaries of the high modernists viewed them as forming a coherent and dominant group of writers – in fact, that the historical configurations were begun by the high modernists themselves and their immediate literary contemporaries and successors. This leads us to wonder about these contemporaries, particularly the authors among them, who were writing from a position outside the hegemonic movement. The high modernists' success in fashioning their own reputations and consolidating their own positions created a sometimes hostile environment for those unable to establish their own positions within the movement or unwilling to join the company of successful artists. Levenson attributes this hostile environment, into which some authors found themselves forced, to the high modernists' activities in outlining new rules and criteria for the production of up to date art. He writes of the ambitions of the high modernists 'to set the terms by which they would be understood, where this often meant setting the terms by which others would not qualify for understanding. The circle of initiates was closed not only against the unwashed public, but also against rival artists who were excluded from the emerging narrative of Modernism triumphant.'[48] This implies, perhaps, a high modernist scheme to become exclusive, which is no doubt true in certain cases but misleading in others. The causes of the institutionalizing of high modernism are less important, perhaps, than its effect. True, those who first managed to attract cultural capital in the modernist period found themselves in a position where their durability as artists was maintained through the existence of rules under which they and their contemporaries were to be judged. But it is these contemporaries – Levenson's 'rival artists', who fell outside the dominant high modernist camp – to whom we will turn our attention as we explore the alternatives to the 'emerging narrative' most commonly associated with the modernist period. Those who found themselves marginalized by the establishment of high modernism are the ones who speak most clearly of the nature of the literary field in the modernist period and the sometimes unique problems that arose from it.

The search for alternative narratives in modernist literary history has been continuing for several decades. The problems raised by the ascendancy of high modernism and the inherent contradictions within its self-historicized framework, in fact, lends itself particularly well to many of the critical theories now in use. Feminist, Marxist and Cultural Materialist critics might all, at times, use the modernist period to focus on writers who are marginalized by the success of the more dominant group. This has led to a fortunate recognition that there is no single conception or narrative of the modernist period, and to a description of the variety of 'modernisms' which existed.[49] Many careers of 'underappreciated' writers – including those who received little recognition during their lifetimes as well as those who have been 'forgotten' since – have been resurrected during the past few decades in the attempt by such critics to correct the injustices of both former and contemporary arbiters of taste, including historians, critics, publishers and anthologists. It should be emphasized that the basis for these studies has not been to seek out the marginalized because there is anything inherently noble in marginality, but often to question the very idea of how literary tastes are formed in the first place.

The process by which a work of literature attains its 'cultural value' has formed the basis of several important critical texts since the 1980s. Jane Tompkins, for one, recognized that, while aesthetic value should be the only criterion for canon selection, this value was not an unchanging quality, and that it could be taught and learnt, instilled and modified by numerous factors.[50] While Tompkins focused on institutional modifiers of public taste, such as publishers and anthologists, other critics recognized the artist's own role in the struggle for establishing a text's literary value, as well as in 'the making of the reader' – the title of David Trotter's book on this topic.[51] The implications of this idea – that the critical tools by which we judge the literary merit of texts have been, at least in part, instilled in us by the authors of these same texts – have yet to be fully worked out, and make up what Bourdieu has called the struggle to 'impose the dominant definition of the writer and therefore to delimit the population of those entitled to take part in the struggle to define the writer'.[52] There is little doubt, when applied to the period under discussion, that our idea of the 'modernist writer' has been defined, to a large extent, by those who themselves best fit the definition. Likewise, the texts produced within ascendant modernism often complete a self-reinforcing circle, as illustrated by the early imagist movement, proving their authors to be capable of fulfilling the criteria they themselves have established as the prerequisites of modernist literature. Works of literature, especially ones endorsed with great literary capital, have immense power over the shaping of thought, and will always maintain this power (in the form of 'literary value') so long as we think them 'great' for producing the literature which has so long formed our definition of greatness.

   This study, similarly, has little to do with the desire to resurrect marginalized writers – though most of the writers discussed could be considered so in some way or another – but rather to investigate the effect an ascendant modernism had upon writers coming after this initial dominance had already been achieved. In other words, having established that such a thing as a dominant strand of modernism had to some extent established its centrality within specific literary circles by 1922, the question must be addressed of the effect this centrality had upon writers whose careers were only beginning (or in some cases coming into a new maturity) in the subsequent two decades. Unquestionably, the obstacles presented by a monolithic vision of hegemonic modernism would have appeared differently to each individual artist, depending on their literary objectives and their respective involvement in literary journals, institutions and cultural circles. Still, even such established writers as Eliot, Aldington and Ford found *Ulysses*, to take one example as discussed in the conclusion, to be such a mammoth achievement that each of them wondered what could possibly be written after it. Likewise, Pound, in trying to secure publication for *The Waste Land*, attested that 'Eliot's poem is very important, almost enough to make everyone else shut up shop', going on to argue that it was in its way as important to 'literature' as *Ulysses*.[53] In discussing Pound's meaning, I think Rainey is right to suggest that the poet, rather than implying that these two works were similar in tone or theme, was trying to establish that each represented their respective genres within the wider context of modernism's establishment of itself in a cultural and institutional sphere. These were not merely typical works of the movement, but nonpareil monuments – as they still are, in certain contexts – each establishing itself within literary culture as a paragon of the modernist novel and poem respectively. In personal letters Pound went so far as to suggest that *The Waste Land* could stand as 'the justification of the "movement," of our modern experiment, since 1900'.[54] While this opinion may not have been universally agreed, nor even available to many, the conviction Pound maintained as to the value of the poem was passed on to active shapers of poetic tastes (in this case, the editors of *The Dial*, who helped establish Eliot permanently as an icon of modernism with a major award) and ensured the poem's positive reception within publishing circles. Indeed, the general reaction to the modernist monuments of 1922 seems to have been pervasive enough to force any subsequent writer who wanted to be considered 'up to date' to be aware of these dominant works and the respective positions of their authors.

   Starting from this hypothesis, the late modernist period becomes a rich field for the literary historian. According to Bourdieu's model – and the model is supported consistently by the period in question – those writers seeking to establish a position for themselves in the late 1920s or early 1930s had a limited number of options for how to engage with the existing literary field. Again, it is Cowley who spells these out, represented as a series of questions the young writer must ask him or herself:

1 What problems do these authors suggest?
2 With what problems are they consciously dealing?
3 Are they my own problems? Or if not, shall I make them my own?
4 What is the Joyce solution to these problems (or the Eliot, the Pound, the Gertrude Stein, the Paul Valéry solution)?
5 Shall I adopt it? Reject it and seek another master? Or must I furnish a new solution myself?[55]

This reveals the challenges facing any later generation within any literary field, but applied specifically to the decisions a late modernist had to make: should the younger writer adopt the problems and solutions of the previous generation, or search for new problems and new solutions? Yet we can take the problem even further, beyond the anxieties (in a Bloomian sense) of whether a literary 'father' should be embraced or killed off, to investigate the complication of succeeding generations within a distinct literary context of modernism.[56] Joyce, Eliot and Pound provided not just generational problems to engage with, but in having helped characterize and institutionalize the period in terms of newness, compelled the modernist latecomer to embrace or reject innovation itself. To leave the period of modernity behind often meant not moving forward at all, as we shall see.

   The one option which does not even seem possible, at least in Cowley's account, is to ignore the earlier generation of high modernists altogether.

It is difficult simply to ignore those who are already established as 'important' authors. For example, Conrad Aiken, in his negative review of Pound's *Pavannes and Divisions* (1918), suggests that 'the book is without value. If one is to examine it carefully, one does so for quite another reason; namely, because Mr. Pound is himself an interesting figure . . . and without any doubt a poet who has (sometimes severely) influenced his fellow poets.'[57] Since the writers of influence had already established themselves as the institutionally dominant mode within the high-cultural literary marketplace, to ignore them might be to risk attracting even fewer readers than the selective circles surrounding the high modernists – readers whose interests would rather be focused either on the already-established or on some new revolt against that establishment. This is not to suggest that ignoring the ascendant group was impossible, and some would certainly have found it easier to ignore them completely than others, depending on a number of factors – geography, target audience, involvement in literary institutions, even perception of who made up the previous generation and how hegemonic it seemed to them. Yet a large number of modernist latecomers who wrote from a position aware of the high modernist tradition had to choose between either joining the already existing movement, or finding some way to subvert or actively oppose those who had already made their mark, even if neither incorporation nor opposition to the dominant modernists appealed to the new candidate. This is not an unusual situation within the general context of literary generations, as Bourdieu makes clear. Artists who once had to establish their own positions in respect to the former dominant group of artists eventually make their own mark and become the field within which the next generation have to find their place. But by the third and fourth decades of the twentieth century, the normal pattern of displacement of older artists or assimilation of new ones was becoming increasingly complicated in several ways.

For one thing, literary generations were becoming briefer and briefer, and any single writer may find four or more 'generations' passing within their lifetime. Even within the relatively brief high modernist period, a significant number of new movements surfaced and then vanished – putting more pressure on artists to keep up with the 'modern'. Yeats, for one, seemed to feel the pressure of this phenomenon when defending the older representatives in his anthology, asserting, 'Even a long-lived man has the right to call his own contemporaries modern.'[58] Such progression of literary development soon led to a backlash against avant-garde posturing, evident even in the 'counter-current' which Eliot and Pound set in motion during the war years. The search for a more 'timeless' art, entrenched in tradition and classicism, meant that those artists who wanted to remain independent of the modernist orthodoxy were forced to appear in the role of transitory rebels, opting out of the traditional position to take an ephemeral interest in revolutionary charlatanism, even when this was their own criticism of the high modernists. Within Bourdieu's dialectic framework, the advancing of each succeeding movement is dependent upon a type of artistic insurrection. Yet the length of time from high modernism's own insurrection to its effective achievement of classical status was so short that yet another insurrection might have appeared unnecessarily abrupt and even counterproductive.

Secondly, the label now attached to the period of modernism is representative of another complication facing many late modernists. As has already been discussed, the word modernism puts simultaneous emphasis on the radically new and the traditionally established, so that the success of modernism might be seen as the institutionalization of innovation. While this is a fascinating development in its own right, it brings forward new problems for the artists who must invent themselves within the context of this aesthetic. Hegemonic modernists succeeded in drawing out their careers into a continual reinvention of the new within a context of classical tradition (as in Eliot's 'really new work of art' taking its place among the previous monuments), thus establishing an always newer new with which all other works must be compared. Because modernism was so readily associated with all that was modern, a quality which was by definition always changing with time, they cornered the market in change itself, and anyone intent on a new direction would then be required, in Lewis's phrase, to try 'changing the changing'.[59] That work which seems most 'new' or 'advanced' is, at least in the modernist epoch, the most representative – the 'best' – work of the period, and consequently the most likely to endure beyond its newness. This means that the characteristics of being modern for any given period are normally established by a select group of writers and all other writers are either 'of their age' or not according to how far they match up to this idea of modernity.

A third problem complicating the natural progression from one generation to another involved the iconic status of the modernist masterwork. It has already been said that the high modernists thought in terms of classics, monuments or masterpieces. But it should also be mentioned that with the birth of the modernist period came a renewed interest in the epic form. While Eliot established the critical model for the new monumental works of art, Joyce and Pound were the writers who most clearly pursued the monumental form, each contributing their own epic works. *The Cantos* perhaps especially typifies the modernist notion of the monumental, attempting as it does the collection of all aspects of history: political, economic, social and spiritual. Glenway Wescott, in a contemporary review of *A Draft of XVI Cantos* (1925), describes their first appearance: 'From time to time a canto, like a block of cumbersome, streaked marble, has appeared in one of the few brave magazines, as if on a pedestal of temporary stucco and obscured by scaffolding.'[60] This is a suggestive remark, commenting not only on the poem's scale or perceived permanence, but also on its unfinished quality, emerging decade by decade as the 'latest' or 'newest' contribution to an ongoing, lasting innovation. This is true of many modernist monuments, appearing in varying forms and reinventing themselves – editorially, structurally, stylistically – in an open-ended form of the epic that is not characteristic of any other period.[61] The high modernist reinvention of the epic in a context of both 'weighty' and permanent literature that was simultaneously mobile and open-ended produced its own problems for those writing after, even sometimes at the same time as, these epics were being produced.

There is one further complication to the natural progression of literary generations encountered by those coming after the high modernists. If insurrection was an awkward choice, and joining the 'movement' distasteful or impossible, the logical option for late modernists might be to simply build on what the high modernists had begun and encourage some form of development of the previous revolution's principles. This position involved accepting the modernist revolution as a genuine advance which remained relevant, but dissociating these advances from any specific writers or 'isms' – in other words, to generalize 'the movement' and take away the trademark that the ascendant writers maintained. Some late modernists succeeded in this to some extent. However, many writers beginning to write after 1922 struggled with the idea that high modernism could be added to. It has already been mentioned that soon after the publication of *Ulysses* and *The Waste Land* there was a general feeling that little more could be done within the mode that each work employed. Many of the contemporary critics, Edmund Wilson among them, classified these radically new texts not as a fresh start but the final 'culmination' or winding down of an earlier literary epoch roughly associated with the modern.[62] The high modernist texts produced in the early 1920s seemed so carefully wrought and critically accepted that it seemed to many that little more could be done to further the cause of experimental modernism. After all, it is impossible to build upon that which is already completed, and any further developments seem a waste of time.

It should be made clear in later chapters, if it is not already, that the contemporaries of the high modernists recognized certain texts – and to a smaller extent, certain cultural positions of authority – as inescapably established within an institutional structure or history. One critic has suggested that literary modernism had 'nothing comparable to the Seagram building' – that is, no clear-cut example or monument to symbolize or sum up its contributions to literary history.[63] Yet within the academy today, *Ulysses* and *The Waste Land* seem to be used in just this way. To some extent, the characteristics of literary modernism have been defined by decades of idolization of high modernist texts and critical essays, to the point at which very few literary histories of the period can get away with no mention of these texts. But my point remains that these works were used in their own time, just as they are today, to epitomize modernist literature and were considered the products or 'justifications' of the modern movement. Anyone who came after, whether they admired or condemned it, had to work with or around the existence of a new 'modernism triumphant' – in just the manner spelled out by contemporary writers as diverse as Lewis, Aldington, Miller, Cowley, Wilson, Aiken, Riding and Graves, and contemporary publishers and critics like Harriet Monroe and Swinnerton.

The formulation of a 'late' or second-generation modernism has been receiving more attention since the 1990s. Perhaps the first critic to subcategorize the larger period systematically was Levenson in *A Genealogy of Modernism*, where he outlined the difference between early modernism – the avant-garde forays of prewar artists – and the counter-current of Eliot and Pound during the First World War, which established a tradition for itself.[64] This model was sufficient for half a decade, until questions were asked about what came after modernism had become 'traditional'. Matei Calinescu pursued the idea of a 'late modernism' to help illustrate the shift from high modernist devotion to the new and the postmodern recognition that there is nothing new.[65] Further categorization came in 1994, with Art Berman's *Preface to Modernism*, where the period was divided into four distinct phases. Berman is careful to avoid rigidity or outright historical definition, but manages to designate the period up to 1905 as early modernism, from 1905 to the end of the war as mid-modernism, and high modernism as belonging to the 1920s. Late modernism, for Berman, arrives just prior to postmodernism, in the 1950s and 1960s. Berman notes that in late modernism 'it becomes clear that modernism, too, will have a history . . . Young artists sense that they have arrived toward the end of the celebration. Modernism can no longer be created, it can only be joined . . . They can, however, undertake the project of closing modernism, finishing it.'[66] This is a useful description of how modernism (in a narrow, aesthetic sense) worked its way towards closure, but there is evidence that the beginning of a modernist ending occurred much earlier than Berman suggests. If late modernism was created at the moment when high modernist works had become recognized as lasting monuments in history and their authors had found their place within cultural and commercial institutions, there is evidence that it had begun almost immediately for some texts at publication. Even high modernists, as has been mentioned, were aware that the artefacts they were creating were bound to become historical fixtures (as well as material commodities) and that modernism had to some extent established itself.

The historical construction of late or second-generation modernism has gradually infiltrated the academy, but a major contribution to a fuller theoretical model was provided by Tyrus Miller in 1999. Miller mentions other critics, such as Charles Jencks, Alan Wilde and Brian McHale, who first introduced the idea of late modernism, but goes further to specify a historical period, beginning around 1926, which exists 'in tandem with a still developing corpus of high modernism'.[67] This model seems more appropriate to me than Berman's because it recognizes a shift in the mid-1920s, as does Wilde's essay, which posits a late-1920s transition from modernism towards postmodernism, examining the writing of Ivy Compton-Burnett, Christopher Isherwood, W. H. Auden, George Orwell and Jean Rhys.[68] However, if we are to agree that high modernism and late modernism coexisted for a number of years, there seems little point in limiting ourselves to a commencement date of 1926, since high modernists had set the context under which late modernism might operate even earlier than that. Miller's theoretical framework is useful, discussing certain commonalities held by the late modernists in their responses to the dominant group, using the illustrations of Lewis, Djuna Barnes, Samuel Beckett and Mina Loy.

Yet the main characteristics Miller chooses to investigate have little to do with his proposition that late modernism was born of the successes – even the completion – of high modernist endeavours, focusing rather on more general themes of deauthentication and dislocation, grotesqueness and automatism, and self-reflexive laughter and play. These discussions, when applied to Miller's chosen authors, are valuable, but never quite take up the challenge Miller himself puts forward: that is, to determine the common reactions shared by late modernists when faced with the newly complicated cultural field they inherited from the high modernists, as outlined above. This present study, in aiming to investigate the shape of literary history, must establish broader characteristics of late modernism in order to highlight the problematic relation it bears to the dominant strand. In that respect, it attempts to follow up some aspects of late modernism described in Fredric Jameson's *A Singular Modernity*, even though Jameson positions his notional 'late modernism' in the postwar period, somewhat later than the recognition of an overlapping strand beginning in the late-1920s. For Jameson, the earlier modernists focused solely on innovation but without any consistency in ideology, whereas late modernists, because innovation had been somewhat formalized by the high modernist experimentation, could go beyond experimentation. Jameson asserts:

the first modernists had to operate in a world in which no acknowledged or codified social role existed for them and in which the very form and concept of their own specific 'works of art' were lacking. But for those I have been calling late modernists, this is no longer the case at all; and Nabokov is unlike Joyce first and foremost by virtue of the fact that Joyce already existed and that he can serve as a model.[69]

In a way, Jameson's assertions simply build on the observations of the contemporaries of the high modernists themselves, including Cowley as illustrated above or Lewis in the chapter to come. And it is to the views of these particular authors that we must turn our attention to fully appreciate the complex relationship between the construction of high modernism and the beginning of its end.

The end of modernism currently appears a less fashionable topic than its resurgence – yet the two, we must acknowledge, share a close relationship. Marjorie Perloff, for example, has identified the modernist revolution as 'one of deferral', abandoned in the context of two world wars and the subsequent Cold War.[70] But, she points out, poetics have not permanently abandoned the new, and a 'second wave' of modernism blossoms in the twenty-first century. There is no reason to disagree with Perloff's manifesto here, particularly as the innovative qualities of Eliot, Gertrude Stein and others are given new context within a narrative of the avant-garde that extends to the present. But the question of modernist 'deferral' is a complex one, depending on one's definition of modernism. It is not easily attributed to any singular cause, even one so disruptive to aesthetic experimentation as a century of war. How far the high modernists themselves are responsible for the deferral of avant-garde modernism is one important consideration; how far the belated modernists helped question the progression of an institutionally endorsed aesthetic revolution is another. To some extent, the question for the generations following the initial twentieth-century avant-garde revolution must be how far perpetual innovation is possible. For modernism to be resurgent in the twenty-first century, there has to be a period of consolidation, a reconceptualization of the place of the new within literary development. The late modernists play an important role in this reconceptualization, seeking to engage with the successful revolution of high modernism dialectically – two sometimes overlapping groups of writers equally complicit in bringing about a deferral of the modernist project.

Anyone attempting to trace an outline of this kind of complex historical development will be faced with a difficult task of identifying shared characteristics. In the chapters to follow, individual cases are presented rather than broad themes or shared politics, authors being selected with the intention of representing a broad spectrum reflecting more than one genre, nationality, gender and cultural background. It is appropriate, therefore, to establish some concerns shared by most modernist latecomers at this point, as they will be illustrated in the following chapters. The following characteristics – identified only after careful examination of a number of varying positions – can be applied mainly to those writers who felt there was a problem with the cultural field they had inherited. This does not constitute *all* writers post-1922, but the group revealing these identifying marks cannot be called a minority, or if so, at least not an insignificant minority. In other words, I do not want, by complicating the sometimes oversimplified vision of the modernist period – with subdivisions of early, high and late – to merely create a more complicated oversimplification. One must expect exceptions and nuances to appear. Yet I have found these characteristics to be generally true of those I have called modernist latecomers:

1. There is evidence of a pervasive distrust of literary groups, movements, cliques and coteries. While this is perhaps not the most significant of the traits of late modernists, it is the most universal, accounting for an oftentimes vehement reaction to the early and high modernist tendency of formulating programmes and -isms. Late modernists to a large extent recognized the marketing aspect of these formulations and groupings, but rejected them as irrelevant or even contrary to progressive writing. While openly targeting the 'individualist' reader, a fundamental institution of high modernism like the magazine *The Egoist* simultaneously represented

a homogeneous grouping, bringing together all those writers that a small editorial group decided were progressive and individualist. Late modernists recognized this paradox within high modernist institutions and called for each writer to be judged solely on his or her own merits rather than on the quality of the group to which they belonged or its proclaimed programme. This principle led to a lack of cohesion among late modernists writing in English and eventually hindered their careers more than it helped. Rather than forming their own successful institutions and cultural support groups, late modernists were forced to choose between accepting audiences ready-made by existing high modernist institutions or struggling to print their own work, often for extremely scarce readers.

2. There can also be seen a late modernist return to an avant-garde distaste for autonomous works of art based solely on form or style and a corresponding desire to see art more firmly integrated into the praxis of life – even in the late modernists who did not join avant-garde move-ments. A common reaction to this among narrative writers, as we will see, was to suggest the literary arts were becoming too intent on stylistic revolution and too detached from the potential revolution in the streets, which some believed in the middle of the 1920s to be still possible. In effect, the late modernists criticized what they perceived to be the high modernist belief that artists could remain autonomous, detached from reality while focused on the craft of their literary techniques.[71] Clearly, any group of writers considered to be 'latecomers' would take an interest in questions of innovation and progress, but late modernists tended to emphasize stylistic experimentation less frequently, and more frequently the effects of civilization, social revolutions and what was happening in 'real life'. For late modernists, the duty of the writer was not simply to reflect life through the prism of varying styles and structures, but to infiltrate nonliterary reality and actively change it.

3. The modernist latecomer can also be characterized by a conspicuous self-consciousness, inherited no doubt from the high modernists, who were also very aware of their own positions as literary artists and the literary field in which they sought to make their mark. Eliot's image of the new work of art taking its place among the monuments of the past marked a major change in the perception – an open recognition – of how the literary field functioned within an institutional framework. The modernists were fully aware of their own modernity and simultaneously conscious of becoming future classics. May Sinclair, as Tim Armstrong reveals, was one of the earliest modernists to recognize this paradox in

her 1917 novel *The Tree of Heaven*, where the revolutionary poet rejects the 'masters' who can be imitated, meanwhile ignoring the fact that he, too, is imitated and, if successful, destined to be seen as a master in turn.[72] The late modernists were the first generation to come to maturity acknowledging that their own contemporaries had tried to reconcile revolution to their own place in tradition – and criticizing them for it. There is a distrust during the late modernist period of those who historicize the present prematurely, particularly of a group of artists who find their own place in a literary history by identifying how their production of originality fits into a larger institutional framework. It is this self-awareness and self-affirmation that characterizes the high modernist period, but also leads to conflict with the emerging, or belated, artists who come after.[73] Late modernists reacted in different ways, some taking this self-consciousness to new extremes – often through satire or parody (like Lewis), at other times by openly addressing the issue of fame and marketability (like Miller) – while some found their self-consciousness to be almost crippling and paralyzing, leading them to detest the methods which might have procured an audience for them (Riding and, to some extent, Lorine Niedecker).

4. Almost all the late modernists I look at distrust explicit historical categorization or generational models, even when these writers sometimes engaged in their own categorizing. While this may be similar to their reaction against literary groups and -isms in that it derives from the hope that the artist might be viewed only according to their work rather than according to their position in a wider field, it is a reaction to the ascendant modernists' historical formulations rather than personal or political affiliations. In particular, the writers who first came of age (in a literary sense) after the success of the modernist revolution found the tendency of their peers to think in terms of literary generations or epochs as irrelevant, and sometimes even counterproductive. Late modernists seem to prefer a conception of history not as a series of stages or stepping stones, but as a more fluid development of individual writers in different contexts, as can be seen in Louis Zukofsky's relationship with Pound in the final chapter of this study. I, too, am guilty at times in the following pages of calling this group 'the second-generation modernists' even while this also derives from a formulation of the period inherited from the high modernists. This formulation led some late modernists to actively criticize the high modernists for their fatalism in working with a closed concept of history and progress; others were content simply to exist in and of their time, allowing the forces of history to play themselves out – so long as

they did not have to be involved in the historicizing process, like the high modernists before them.

5. Finally, late modernists commonly appear uncomfortable with the increasing institutionalization of art that they witnessed creeping into the market-oriented tactics of their high modernist precursors. This once more ties them, perhaps, to the earlier continental avant-garde movements, with their avid distaste for academies, museums and other centres of official culture. But unlike the radical avant-garde, late modernists refrained from actively opposing the existence of these institutions, choosing instead simply to remain on the outside of them as far as possible. Where late modernists did find themselves engaging with official culture, they typically aimed at some form of domestication of the institution, making it their own (as we will see in the case of Niedecker and her self-built version of 'the University of Texas' on her Wisconsin property). While both high and late modernists wished to remain aloof to official or high culture and retain their artistic detachment, there was a general recognition that a career could not be maintained entirely independent of marketing and promotion. Where the high modernists often promoted themselves behind the scenes, the late modernists preferred to foreground their engagements with the institutions they sometimes openly disdained. Owing to the uneasy institutional relationships that resulted (along with other factors), many of them were less successful in attaining the levels of recognition in literary culture that their immediate forebears enjoyed. This only intensified their distrust of cultural institutions and problematized their associations with them when, at some point in their careers, they were bound to make some attempt at widening their audience with institutional support.

These five characteristics present a loose generalization of what will be illustrated in the following chapters in detail. None of these late modernists seems to deal with common issues in precisely the same way. This is necessarily a broad view of a number of authors, and must therefore at times summarize entire segments of careers quickly, and at other times deal with certain works only in part, which I find unfortunate. This study partly arises from the belief that there is a depth to modernism misrepresented by the more rigid and superficial canonical formulations of the period, and the main purpose here is to trace the shape of a historical transition within a larger literary period. Partly for this reason, as much attention is given to critical texts, letters and memoirs as to the poems and novels which make these authors appealing for such a study. Essentially, my research is directed towards questions of late modernist self-perception and their varying perspectives of the literary field in which they wrote rather than towards their individual themes and styles. There is undoubtedly much more that can be said about how these are connected, and future inquiries might be undertaken into the wide range of critical and readerly responses to the work of these authors, but in this case I have tried to strike a balance between the particulars of texts deserving detailed attention and, on the other hand, the more general paths towards which these individuals directed their careers. Some of the questions arising from the nature of this investigation are addressed in the conclusion.

Each chapter is devoted to either a single author or a small selection of associated writers – each chosen as representative of a larger group and as an illustration of various reactions taken to high modernism. Wyndham Lewis is the first, though for many he will seem an unlikely candidate for a book on second-generation modernism; his open criticism of high modernism, however, is used as a theoretical bedrock upon which to lay down the later chapters. In fact, each subsequent author is seen to engage, in at least some small way, with Lewis's *Time and Western Man* (1927). This first chapter views Lewis as a rather paradoxical counter-revolutionary in the context of his postwar career, aiming to restore value to a devalued modernist conception of revolution by resurrecting the priorities for real change. The second chapter follows the early career of Laura Riding, particularly her critical works of the late 1920s investigating the dominant modernist culture, and especially that represented by Eliot and *The Criterion*. In setting herself distinctly in opposition to such a successful institution, she reinforced her own lack of audience. Having dealt, then, with both a novelist's and a poet's openly critical response to high modernism on a more theoretical plane, in the third chapter there will be a minor shift to view more opportunistic responses to the high modernist position. Henry Miller, while not one of the first names associated with any form of modernism, fits well with other subjects in this study. Miller's early career is significant for having developed largely as a reaction to the literary atmosphere created by the high modernists. Miller often deliberately adopts high modernist forms, in particular certain Joycean motifs of the artist as hero and obscene subject matter, but takes them to extremes until his texts parody the finished work of art. The fourth chapter then approaches a selection of those poets who have taken for themselves or received from others the name 'Objectivists'. Basil Bunting, Louis Zukofsky and Lorine Niedecker are chosen to represent a range of reactions to the influence of Ezra Pound, whether directly or indirectly felt. The Objectivists, it seems, were linked closely enough to Pound's enterprise to be considered by some as partially derivative or even subordinate. Yet they were not allied quite closely enough during the time Pound was at the height of his cultural power to have their careers made for them.

Clearly, this study must be somewhat limited to taking up authors who, while often uncomfortable with the high modernist legacy, still exist very much in the framework of a high cultural modernism. There are many writers not included here who add a great deal of depth to the modernist period but exist somewhat independent of the tradition examined here and therefore cannot be placed in a structure based, as this study is, upon reaction to ascendant modernism. For example, writers of the Harlem Renaissance, or authors of popular or genre fiction, are capable of wholly ignoring the existence of high modernism because they may work within differing aesthetic, political or cultural aims. So while there are additional authors who would fit into this study if there was space to devote to them, there are others, worthy of attention in their own right, who fall entirely out of the scope of this investigation.

In my conclusion I look at one more element linking all these writers; at some point in each of their careers, these late modernists gave up or suspended their involvement in the literary arts, taking a significant step away from the literary field upon which, I hope to have shown by then, so many struggles for recognition and independence from institutional entanglements had taken place. While there are many factors involved in the subject of late modernism, I believe the basic question being asked in every chapter, through discussions of self-consciousness, institutional histories and literary politics, is how far it was possible to conduct a literary career in the first half of the twentieth century while ignoring one's own marketability, one's reputation within contemporary cultural institutions or one's position in the literary field. Each writer I discuss struggles implicitly with these questions, and though each one of their careers provides their own often different answers, they all contribute significantly to a general understanding of the period, particularly to the literary field that the late modernists inherited in the latter part of the 1920s and throughout the following decades.

CHAPTER I

'Changing the changing':
Wyndham Lewis and the new modernist
ascendancy

> 'And, as to "progress" or "change", there are millions of extremely
> different forms available. You should . . . *wish*: and you should steadily
> oppose what you do not wish.'
>
> Wyndham Lewis, Paleface[1]

In the early 1940s, as Wyndham Lewis found refuge from the Second
World War in North America, a young acquaintance named Marshall
McLuhan began to find portrait-sitters and lecture appointments for the
ageing modernist. Regarding one of the first engagements, a lecture for
the Wednesday Club in St Louis, McLuhan would write:

> As for topic at the W.C. – 'Personalities in the world of modern art and letters.'
> Yes, frankly, they want anecdotes about 'Long-haired people I have known.'
> You can please them completely, simply by making it a chat about familiar
> names – Yeats, Joyce, Eliot, Picasso, Augustus John, T. E. Lawrence etc. Let it
> embrace more than one field. A musician wouldn't be amiss.[2]

McLuhan would prove himself to be a valuable ally for Lewis, generating
'publicity' and organising receptions for the artist – complete with
suggestions to turn *The Vulgar Streak* into an 'American bestseller' by
getting Basil Rathbone to play Penhale in a not-yet-existent Hollywood
production. Lewis himself was not unaware of the complex relationship
between his own high cultural artistic position and the mass culture
forms that intrigued McLuhan. But it is the legacy of high modernism
that is significant here, as Lewis trades on his position near the centre
of high modernism through stories of famous writers he knew rather than
speaking on issues more pertinent to the late modernist beliefs he had
developed in his writing for nearly two decades.[3] We find in Lewis a figure
who is pushed into poverty and disgrace through negative reactions to
his 1930s works and forced to survive through selling anecdotes of the
life that these works satirized and criticized.

33

Even now, Lewis is remembered for his early role in the movement yet judged by his later works. With more than one distinct phase to his career, Lewis was first an avant-garde painter, prewar revolutionary, 'man of 1914', author of *Tarr* (1918) and editor of *Blast*; then after burying himself for several years in the British Library, he was reborn as a critic, polemicist and enemy.[4] Although Lewis's most prolific period began in 1926, and most of what critics consider his best works were published after that date, it was the period *up to* this date which afforded Lewis contemporary recognition and which still finds its way most readily into the literary histories. Arguably, one of Lewis's most successful works is *Blasting and Bombardiering* (1937), a product of his late modernist position yet one which takes for its subject the more popular Lewis 'character' in the high modernist narrative, the energetic artist who helped orchestrate a new movement in literature and art. His name is perhaps inextricably linked to our picture of the high modernist period, yet there is no escaping the reputation of another Lewis: the author of books sometimes supporting fascism, racism, sexism and an intense criticism of all the other major characters in the story of modernism.

The two Lewises are difficult to reconcile. How might we fit this writer into our history of modernism? Is he included in the movement, being there at the beginning, or is he outside it, standing – as he did later – so much in opposition? Critics often attempt to find a place for him both inside and out. Hugh Kenner, one of Lewis's earliest critical defenders within the academy, places Lewis most squarely within the modernist construction, suggesting that 'No historian's model of the age of Joyce, Eliot, and Pound is intelligible without Lewis in it.'[5] Fredric Jameson seems more likely to take the model of Lewis being *in* the modernist world but not *of* it, distinguishing throughout his analysis between Lewis's position on one hand and what he terms the 'modernisms of the mainstream' or 'conventional modernism' on the other.[6] SueEllen Campbell considers Lewis to be 'as much a post-modernist critic as he is an exemplary modernist'.[7] While one critic will argue that Lewis needs to be returned to his place among the high modernists, another will claim that 'Lewis represents a strain of post-aesthetic writing that differs significantly from what has come to be defined as "modernist"'.[8] Yet none of these claims, despite their differing views, appears inaccurate or misleading. Lewis's position in the modernist canon has always been uneasy, less from uncertainty as to his significance than from disagreement on how he should be positioned in the literary map of the period.

The aim of this chapter is to show that Lewis's presence at the beginning of high modernism had direct influences on his critique of it and led to his prophecy of its end. As we will see, the fact that Lewis, in 1937, invents the label 'the Men of 1914' has less to do with establishing his own name alongside Ezra Pound, T. S. Eliot and James Joyce than it does with separating his own later career from these writers who went on to become the Men of 1922 – the year that saw masterpieces by Eliot and Joyce and Pound announcing the end of the Christian Era at the high-water mark of the period some call 'The Pound Era'. In that year the Lewis of 1914 was as good as dead – by his own account 'buried' (*BB* 5). He would rise again only at the point he labels the *end* of the postwar period – but only as 'The Enemy'. To understand how this highly essential artist – who describes himself in relation to 'this movement' as being 'at its heart. In some instances I was *it*' (*BB* 255) – then came to become its most tenacious critic requires a careful analysis of the two phases to his career, one high and one late. Even more, it demands an investigation into how the modernists saw themselves, often self-consciously, within a construction of history that they knew would be written. Lewis, acting as critic, philosopher, memoirist and, most important-antly, as modernist artist himself, is the perfect individual to illustrate the dilemmas of a movement which saw its end nearly as soon as it began.

In order to provide an idea of Lewis's developing sense of ascendant modernism and its inherent problems, this chapter will seek to investigate a number of texts to establish how Lewis's thinking might be mapped against the period in which he is writing and theorizing. There is much detailed work available on Lewis's individual texts; this chapter will serve its purpose much better by focusing on one strand of Lewis's complex thought to follow its progression throughout the transition from high to late modernism. It should be mentioned that Lewis's inclusion in a study focused on the modernist latecomer needs to be explained further than by the simple reason that there was more than one phase to his career. Lewis, as we will see, felt compelled to begin a new campaign in relation to the emerging high modernism he had first taken part in establishing; but even more crucially, Lewis provided a theoretical argu-ment known and acclaimed by many of the late modernist writers with which this study concerns itself. Therefore, in surveying Lewis's changing career, we might find not only the emergence of one of the first 'late modernists' but the earliest formulations of an argument vital to the position of the modernist latecomer, a category Lewis himself fits into only problematically.

In 1914, at what might be considered the beginning of the most revolutionary phase of modernism, Lewis was still primarily a painter who sometimes wrote short stories. His career, up to his first book publication in 1918, is highlighted by major works which are all paintings, including *Timon of Athens* and *Kermesse*. The one early effort which allowed Lewis to exhibit his entire array of talents was the editing of *Blast*, the official journal of vorticism, which brought him new levels of recognition. Although vorticism was a movement dominated by the plastic arts, the prominence within it of Lewis and Pound still draws the group into literary histories, and the wider artistic posturing similarly drew its members into more fashionable circles. Lewis recalls that around that time 'publicity had been accumulating about my head. *Blast* gave the finishing touch' (*BB* 46). Lewis's name could be found in the newspapers, *Blast* could be found in every 'fashionable drawing-room', and invitations to potential patrons' homes were found every day in the post. His time, Lewis suggests with some retrospective tongue-in-cheek, had come. By 1914, it seemed Lewis had already made his mark.[9]

But Lewis's mid-life autobiography reveals that this was not entirely the case, even while it describes him as a 'man of 1914', the year of his breakthrough in terms of critical and popular success. Instead of being the beginning of a successful career, the approaching war filled these years with a mixture of anxiety and hysteria. Lewis's comparison of war to modernist art stems at least partially from the positive reception he received in these prewar years – from the fact that, in the approach to war, modernist art was taken as a substitute for war. The antibourgeois, oppositional stance of the avant-garde artists was actually solicited by the masses they confronted, resulting in a mutually agreeable hostility during the military build-up. The best summary of such consensual dissent comes from Lewis himself: '"Kill John Bull with Art!" I shouted. And John and Mrs. Bull leapt for joy, in a cynical convulsion. For they felt as safe as houses. So did I' (*BB* 36). Lewis, without perhaps realizing it then, was caught in the machinery of an age requiring the scandal, outrage and militaristic fervour of avant-garde, or *avant-guerre*, art. He writes, 'Really all this organized disturbance was Art behaving as if it were Politics. But I swear I did not know it . . . I mistook the agitation in the audience for the sign of an awakening of the emotions of artistic sensibility.' The comparison to politics is also evident when Lewis notes, almost bitterly, 'I might have been at the head of a social revolution, instead of merely being the prophet of a new fashion in art' (*BB* 32).

In *Blasting and Bombardiering*, Lewis encourages the view of his prewar self as a fashionable character, an artist 'figure', by recounting his skirmishes with F. T. Marinetti, or his meeting with Prime Minister H. H. Asquith. At the time, however, he took himself seriously enough. *Blast*, while described in 1937 as 'light-hearted mockery', was still understood in 1915 as claiming a permanent place in literary history, as he writes to Augustus John: 'That you will enter the history books, you know, of course! Blast is a history book, too' (*LWL* 70). He wrote to Kate Lechmere in the summer of 1915 that 'the War has stopped Art dead' (*LWL* 69). But what this simple equation ignores is the role of a society which had turned his brand of art into 'Art', since the war, rather than stopping artists from working, had changed the conditions which, up to then, had been favourable for the more radical movements. David Peters Corbett outlines how the war destroyed the complicity between the artists and their public, who agreed to be outraged by the shock of the new in art before the war but later grew simply resentful.[10] Describing how critics changed their view of vorticism once the war had begun, he cites C. H. Collins Baker in a contemporary *Saturday Review*, where he offers Lewis's group a hint of sympathy:

In having degenerated so suddenly into such a bore, the Vorticists, or whatever they used to call themselves, have been a little unlucky . . . Life decreed that something serious should come to the rescue of a costive world, whose ennui was barely mitigated by all sorts of ingenuity and elaborate bright notions. So in August, to our horror, we were tipped right into things that really mattered. And now, when we have opportunity to look again at those old ingenious notions, our nerves still tingling with the impact of reality, we simply wonder what on earth was up with us that we should ever have been entertained by them.[11]

That war had come and tastes had changed is termed 'unlucky' for the vorticists, which only serves to emphasize the notion that modernist art in the years immediately before the war was dependent on whims of fashion and circumstance. But if it was unlucky for Lewis's popularity that tastes had turned against him, we will see that it was exactly this supersession which pushed him onward with his career. If Lewis had never gained, then lost, the appreciation of fashionable London, he might have continued simply performing his role in Art (as he saw so many of his contemporaries continue to perform), never realizing that so much of it was, in his revised view, merely 'entertainment'. Only once the joke was no longer funny, in the face of the horrors of modern warfare, did it become clear to Lewis that so much of what he had been engaged in had been little more than that: a highly involved joke.

But it was the threat the war carried for him, as well, that made Lewis realize just how fleetingly *Blast* alone could maintain his reputation as an artist. He remembers, 'All Europe was at war and a bigger *Blast* than mine had rather taken the wind out of my sails' (*BB* 85). It was with concern for his more lasting artistic reputation that he rushed to finish *Tarr* before the anonymous bombardier was sent to the perils of war. During an illness from which he seemed always on the verge of recovering, he finished the novel 'so that the world might have a chance of judging what an artist it had lost' (86). Lewis's glance towards posterity – 'under the circumstances a not inexcusable vanity' – places him firmly alongside other high modernists busy ensuring their own literary endurance, even those who were not bound for battle in Europe.

Lewis of course survived the war, but *Tarr* remained the work by which he was to be judged for the next ten years. His reputation, first established as editor of *Blast*, fared no worse as 'Author of *Tarr*'. He remembers that it 'brought me much attention as a writer' and 'was hailed as the first book of a new epoch, "a date in literature"' (*BB* 86). Quoting several reviews of *Tarr*, Lewis keeps assuring his readers in *Blasting and Bombardiering* that he is not simply boasting since each phrase he uses, 'as you can see, is literary history'. This acknowledgement of history, though, is inevitably revisionist, since the history of the literary epoch he is discussing had been mostly established by 1937. By revisionist, I mean that Lewis arrives late in the historicizing game, and must work with a preexisting historical narrative when discussing the place his own work takes. That Lewis portrays *Tarr* as the first book of a new epoch, for example, seems a deliberate dismissal of Joyce's 1916 *A Portrait of the Artist as a Young Man* – a book always seemingly a step ahead of Lewis's. The two novels share more, as many critics note, than the subject of an artist struggling against social and cultural forces. Lewis's novel also followed in the steps *A Portrait* took towards publication, only with difficulty finding a publisher and eventual serialization in *The Egoist*, with a later book publication under the same imprint. That the two novels shared most of the same supporters, among the press and the publishers, only links them closer together.

Joyce must have seemed to Lewis always a step ahead in literary matters. This would have mattered less to Lewis while he was primarily a painter, but it would matter more as the years led Lewis further into his literary career. Lewis, in fact, in looking back to the period of *Tarr* and quoting reviews as 'literary history', excises the many comparisons of his book to Joyce's *A Portrait*, which serves only to emphasize that Lewis wanted *Tarr* to stand without predecessors. For example, immediately after pronouncing that *Tarr* was the 'first book of a new epoch' in *Blasting and Bombardiering*, Lewis removes through ellipsis one of several comparisons to the earlier *A Portrait* in a quotation from Robert Nichols's review of *Tarr*.[12] The war would only heighten Lewis's sense of being a step behind in literary matters, as he would state in 1937: 'The War, of course, had robbed me of four years' (*BB* 213). While Lewis was trying to read philosophy in the trenches, and while *Tarr* was only just being read for the first time as a book, Joyce was already publishing chapters of *Ulysses* in *The Little Review*. And Joyce was not, of course, the only writer continuing to produce while Lewis was being robbed of opportunities. Tyrus Miller describes Lewis as finding himself just another author writing in the shadow of the monumental *Ulysses* and *The Waste Land*.[13] That it is the authors of these works that Lewis identifies with his 1914 self is surely significant, since neither of them went to war and so were subsequently able to continue developing their careers – both aesthetically and institutionally – while he was left behind.

It is with this notion of revising a prewritten literary history, therefore, that we must examine what lies behind the label 'the Men of 1914'. Lewis points out that 'four people more dissimilar in every respect than [Joyce], myself, Pound and Eliot respectively, it would be difficult to find. There is only one sense in which any such a grouping of us acquires some significance – we all got started on our careers before the War' (*BB* 294). There is indeed much significance in this affinity, but it cannot be left there. Lewis notably excludes T. E. Hulme and Henri Gaudier-Brzeska from 'the Men of 1914', both of whom had played significant roles for Lewis before the war, but had died in battle. The men labelled 'of 1914' include only those still alive in 1937, those who, at least by reputation, could still make literary headlines and, subsequently, literary history. But Lewis gives another clue as to why these four are chosen: they are all men of an 'age group', 'all born of women about the same time' (*BB* 293). We can see that other writers would fit these characteristics, including Virginia Woolf, though she belonged, of course, to the Bloomsbury Group so antagonistic to Lewis. There is one more criterion, then, for entering the group, one of social or institutional bonds, since the men of 1914 are those found 'within the critical fold of Ezra Pound – the young, the "New", group of writers assembled in Miss Weaver's *Egoist* just before and during the War' (*BB* 292). Still, others might be included in this category, such as Richard Aldington, but then Aldington in 1937 does not maintain the cultural capital of Eliot,

Pound or Joyce. These are the writers Lewis takes as his subject as literary historian: those young and 'new' writers from the height of revolutionary modernism, but – importantly – those who had survived the revolution to grow old, to extend their importance beyond the revolution itself. The level of detail required for this categorization serves only to highlight the problems Lewis faced in constructing his own preferred version of the epoch.

In fact, incorporated into Lewis's criteria for the label 'the Men of 1914' are indications that he believed such a grouping to be a false construction – albeit one he is credited with inventing. He speaks of 'the vanity of classification' in these terms: 'And if being born in a stable makes you a horse, why then being born in the same years is liable, perhaps, to make you an identical human product. A mechanical theory at the best, for the purposes of the literary pigeonholing of a complex society this method is useless' (*BB* 293). This revisionist history of the early modernist period – first proposed then termed useless – is constructed in the same year that Lewis would write, 'My mind is *ahistoric*' (*LWL* 246; emphasis Lewis's). However, in his memoir it is his own career and 'epoch' obsessively separated into periods. Lewis has the habit of labelling everything by date, and the autobiography itself takes the years 1914 to 1926 as 'the opening years of the present epoch'. Not only is Lewis playing historian, he is, in this case, describing a stretch of years that is primarily significant in defining his own career, and little else. As the title of the chapter tells us, this is 'The Period of *Ulysses*, *Blast*, *The Wasteland*' – another awkward temporal definition. *Blast*, placed in this configuration between the two modernist masterworks of 1922, seems either to pull itself forward in time or drag *Ulysses* and *The Waste Land* backwards. *Blast*, it seems, begins the 'period' of high modernism, while *Ulysses* and *The Waste Land* are perhaps its culmination, its completion. The authors are brought together in this way, but also divided. Whichever the case, it is notable that Lewis makes no distinction in this instance between prewar, wartime, and postwar, rather establishing a dividing line at his own resurrection date of 1926 to separate 'the beginning of the present' from simply 'the present' – a distinction between what is termed in this study 'high modernism' and 'late modernism'. In order to understand the reasoning behind this distinction in Lewis's revisionist history, we must look to the author's writings after the war, particularly his critique of the time-cult and the 'mainstream modernists'. We must begin, though, by looking at Lewis's sole book publication during the period he labels 'strictly private' – 1918 to 1926.

The 1919 pamphlet *The Caliph's Design: Architects! Where is your Vortex?* showed Lewis ready to pick up where he had left off in 1914, uncon- cerned or unaware that the high modernist revolution was becoming established. This is expressed most clearly in an article Lewis wrote for *The English Review* a few months before *The Caliph's Design* was pub- lished, entitled 'What Art Now?' Lewis begins, 'The war drove . . . all the arts underground. They now come up: a little wan and blinking, some of them. What are they going to do now? we are asked.'[14] The answer Lewis gives is surprisingly conservative for a former revolutionary: 'The war has not changed our industrial society or the appearance of our world; nor has it made men desire different things, only the same things harder still.' For perhaps the first time, we see Lewis in a position of defence, an artist who had achieved enough prestige before the war to claim nothing should change. Lewis perhaps considers himself to belong still to the ascendant brand of high modernists, and so opposes the view that art fashions should change every month, concluding the article, 'So, because you had a revolution six years ago, you need not expect another next month. The revolution in painting of the few years preceding the war has thoroughly succeeded.'[15] This suggests that Lewis believed his prewar position to be fully recoverable.

But if the war was hard on Lewis's career, the postwar period (1919 to 1925, according to Lewis) proved even harder. In a letter to John Quinn setting out his hopes for the postwar period, which include a new volume of *Blast* as well as multiple shows of his paintings, Lewis summarizes the content of *The Caliph's Design* as 'an appeal to the better type of artist to take more interest in and more part in the general life of the world' (*LWL* 110). In *The Caliph's Design* Lewis is generally affirmative of modernist painting, especially that of Pablo Picasso, Henri Matisse, André Derain and Giacomo Balla, but suggests that the modernist artist generally confines himself too much to the studio, which encourages 'an almost purely Art-for-Art's sake dilettantism'.[16] Lewis wants artists to take more interest in life on the street, rather than the 'congested' life of the studio, the dealer and the press. While Lewis certainly took the stance of an avant-garde artist before the war, *The Caliph's Design* signals his desire to get away from simple stylistic posturing and the beginning of his campaign to call attention to the modernist focus on mere formal experimentation. Toby Avard Foshay, for one, sees *The Caliph's Design* as the first example of Lewis's coherent cultural criticism, built upon the modernist revolution, but pushing for more fundamental change.[17] Foshay in particular employs Peter Bürger's distinction between the aestheticist focus of modernist writers and artists and the avant-garde's more political engagement, as outlined in *Theory of the Avant-Garde*. Bürger's further thesis – that autonomous art had established itself as an institution in the early twentieth century and that the first recognition and critique of that institution came from the avant-garde of that period – is also highly applicable to Lewis's career.[18]

Much of *The Caliph's Design* is devoted to the subjects of artistic style and fashion within the *Zeitgeist*, particularly how artists should deal with the contemporary 'mode'. In a chapter entitled 'Fashion', Lewis writes, 'Fashion is of the nature of an aperient.'[19] Each period has its own particular fashion, which keeps art moving from period to period. But Lewis – like many modernist latecomers, fascinated by fashion in the arts – goes on to say that the nature of this movement is not necessarily always progress, but simply some form of change. In the following passage he simultaneously adopts the modernist stance against the former age, but predicts an age to come which will similarly correct the errors of his own time:

The Victorian age produced a morass of sugary comfort and amiableness, indulged men so much that they became guys of sentiment. Against this 'senti-mentality' people of course reacted. So the brutal tap was turned on, and for fifty years it will be the thing to be brutal, 'unemotional.' Against the absurdities that this 'inhuman' fashion does inevitably breed, you will need some powerful corrective in due course. And so fashions go, a matter of the cold or the hot tap, simply. The majority of people, the Intellectuals, the Art World, are perpetually in some raw extreme. They are 'of their time' as a man is typically of his country, truculently Prussian or delightfully French.[20]

This is an instructive statement, especially at this stage in Lewis's career. It identifies what Renato Poggioli would later call 'the dialectic of move-ments'.[21] The 'unemotional' reaction to Victorian sentiment is an expli-citly modernist trait, fundamental to the movement, evident especially in Pound's and Eliot's theories. That Lewis no longer wants to be merely 'of his time' comes out clearly in this (implicit) critique of the other writers labelled 'of 1914' – even while the advertisement on the back of *The Egoist* edition, as a type of institutional branding, places his name squarely alongside Joyce, Eliot, Pound and Aldington.

Much that Lewis will later theorize in *Time and Western Man* (1927) is said more clearly in the sixty-page *The Caliph's Design*. Although there is no mention, as yet, of the time-cult, Lewis is already calling for individuals to stand up against the fashions of thought, and to force their own thoughts on the fashions. Lewis, always the individualist with strong beliefs, laments that 'Fashion is the sort of useful substitute for conviction.'[22] While an inadequate substitute, that fashion is still called *useful* shows Lewis is not yet ready to discount artists who are merely reflecting the *Zeitgeist*. Under the chapter title 'The Uses of Fashion', Lewis goes on to describe exactly how far new fashions or movements, especially the movement not yet labelled modernist, can be useful:

> To a good painter, with some good work to do in this world, the only point of the new movement, or whatever you like to call it, was simply that it changed the outlook and pre-occupation of the living section of art from one mode to another. To look for anything more than the swing of the pendulum would be an absurdity. That *more* is supplied at the moment of every movement by the individual . . . Still, the individual, although ideally independent of and superior to the flux and reflux, is beholden to conditions and to the society in which he finds himself for the possibility of the full development of his gifts. So the 'movement' in art, like the attitude of the community to art, is not a thing to be superior about, though it is a thing you may be superior to.[23]

Lewis again proves himself to be simultaneously more moderate than some of his contemporaries, yet more dedicated to 'real' revolution in the postwar period, suggesting that any 'mode' of painting (presumably including the vorticist) is only a reflection of fashion, resulting from the *Zeitgeist*, while anything *beyond* fashion or style in painting results from the individual, regardless of the time he or she lives in. The *manner* of painting, we could say, is a useful indication of the age, while the *matter* deserves something more permanent, labelled 'conviction'.

The result is an uneasy partnership between the artist and the *Zeitgeist*, often resulting in a struggle for domination. The general critique Lewis was to make throughout the next decade was that, when faced with contemporary fashions or philosophies, the majority of people, even the majority of artists, lacked the conviction required to remain individuals. Lewis, as early as 1919, calls for a reversal: 'What we really require are a few men who will *use* Fashion, the ruler of any age, the avenue through which alone that age can be approached to get something out of it, to build something in Fashion's atmosphere which can best flourish there, and which is the best thing that therein could flourish.'[24] Lewis had already witnessed artists who were used by fashionable prewar society as cultural capital. Art had been too much associated with the *style* of the age, and in response the style of painting (or any art) had taken precedence over the content.

Lewis leaves his chapter entitled 'Picasso' for the end of the pamphlet, as perhaps his finest illustration. Again, Lewis praises Picasso's ability and vitality. The Spanish painter is described as 'one of the ablest living painters. It would be impossible to display more ability. In addition to this he is extremely resourceful and inventive.'[25] But an implicit criticism infiltrates the acclaim by the next page; Picasso is 'a very serious and beautiful performer' and 'definitely in the category of executants'.[26] If Picasso's ability cannot be questioned, his purpose can, since Lewis finds little justification of the art-for-art's-sake position. Lewis sounds genuinely baffled by Picasso's lack of direction, questioning the reader over Picasso's apparent dabbling. 'Has he got bored with a thing the moment it was within his grasp? . . . He does not perhaps *believe* in what he has made. Is that it? And yet he is tirelessly compelled to go on achieving these images, immediately to be discarded.'[27] Picasso, for Lewis, is a stylist, an inventor of fashions in painting, but he does not *believe*, and therefore leaves no lasting mark on the *Zeitgeist*. Although an innovator, Picasso is still only a product of his time.

We have already seen that *The Caliph's Design*, while focusing on painting, begins Lewis's critique of his fellow literary modernists. The analysis Lewis makes of Picasso can be compared with similar analyses in 'The Revolutionary Simpleton', especially of Joyce and Pound. Like Picasso in The *Caliph's Design*, Joyce is criticized in *Time and Western Man* as a dabbler in styles and historical periods, and also for failing to escape his time. A section of the pamphlet on 'the primitive' anticipates Lewis's later views on Pound and Joyce, though these writers are not mentioned by name. 'There is the *Primitive* in point of view of historical date, the product of a period. And there is the *Primitive voulu*, who is simply a pasticheur and stylist . . . the pasticheur merely, en touriste, visits different times and places, without necessarily so much a readjustment of his mind as of his hand.'[28] Lewis, as we saw in 'What Art Now?', sees no need for a reinvention of the *manner* of art, since the prewar revolution he helped to instigate had already succeeded. In the postwar years Lewis's quarrel was with his former allies who excelled at modernist style, but required 'a readjustment' of the *mind*, and a new approach to the matter of art. This would lead Lewis into a new phase during the next decade, struggling against art as an institution, including but not confined to the institutional position of his modernist contemporaries.

The silence stretching from *The Caliph's Design* to *The Art of Being Ruled* (1926) is broken only, apart from an occasional article in the English reviews, by Lewis's own journal *Tyro*. It reveals Lewis, during this transitional phase, believing in the revolution of 1914 but still wanting a new start. The discourse in the first number of *Tyro* is marked by these desires. 'We are at the beginning of a new epoch, fresh to it, the first babes of a new, and certainly better, day . . . No time has ever been more carefully demarcated from the one it succeeds than the time we have entered on has been by the Great War of 1914–18.'[29] This demarcation was necessary to Lewis, who would appreciate, in 1937, the circumstances which had created 'the obligation to make a new start . . . I might never have submitted myself to the disciplines I did, if I had not been thrown back on myself. In a rather silly way, I had been too successful. So in the long run the War helped my career; but it was a long run all right' (*BB* 213). This evident fear of success is an important factor in Lewis's career. But by the second number of *Tyro*, there were already those suggesting that the war had marked the end of Lewis's type of art. In that issue of his journal, he writes, 'When people assert, therefore, that the movement in painting about which I am writing, is *dead*, you only have to ask yourself what is going to take its place, and you see the unreality of the position occupied by the speaker.'[30]

This somewhat cryptic comment, requiring an understanding of how Lewis defined 'the movement' yet also assuming the answer to his question will be obvious, marks an important moment in Lewis's contribution to modernism. Lewis is clearly speaking in more general terms in referring to 'the movement' than the specific strands of vorticism or cubism, rather referring to the yet unnamed modernist movement in painting which encompassed them all. And in forcing his readers to ask what could possibly come after the modern, Lewis is, perhaps for the first time, facing the complexity of the period in art to which he belongs. Lewis appears to ask: if you are suggesting that the current movement in art, emphasizing experimentation and revolution, is over, simply ask yourself how the revolutionary can ever be overthrown without a new revolution? The answer is it cannot. As long as 'the movement', therefore, commits itself to the new and the revolutionary, it can never be labelled 'dead'. At this transitionary point, Lewis still felt comfortable enough with his own role in the modernist revolution of painting to see this as a healthy situation. But in his literary career, even by the following year, with the appearance of *Ulysses* and *The Waste Land* (and a few years later *A Draft of XVI Cantos*), Lewis began to recognize that *being modern* was a quality which could be made more permanent than even he envisioned. It seems likely that Lewis was one of the first to recognize that these works might become known as modern for all time. And, as we will see, he spent much of his career fighting the idea.

Knowing as we do that 1922 was a turning point in the establishment of modernism, it is remarkable that Lewis was still introduced, in the 28 April 1922 *Evening Standard*, under the 1914 label, 'The founder of Vorticism'. The Lewis article being introduced is on the subject of fashion, entitled 'The Long and the Short of It', strangely enough concentrating on the fashionable length of women's skirts. Yet it is in this unusual context that Lewis first portrays his desire, which would be elaborated in all his books of this decade, to 'break up the world-uniformity that the snobbishness of fashion imposes'.[31] That Lewis finds the style of women's dress to be a useful illustration of fashion in general is perhaps most clear when he says, 'All women must dread the arrival of an unbecoming vogue – unbecoming to them. There should be at least three alternative fashions; or, if you like, the *exact opposite* of the fashion should be recognized as being as fashionable as the fashion itself.' That certain fashions do not flatter the shape of certain women Lewis takes to be an injustice easily remedied, one which applies, presumably, just as well to fashion in art. This shows Lewis, for the first time, attempting to rectify his change in fortune by taking up 'the exact opposite of the fashion', a stance he would later adopt as 'The Enemy'.

It is important to remember that while Lewis was buried in the period 1918–26, he was not inactive, but 'incubating'. Lewis mentions his 'little treatise, "The Man of the World"' as early as October 1923, in a letter to Eliot (*LWL* 136). The little treatise would grow into a 'megalo-mastodonic masterwork', half a million words long, which, after the publisher Cassell rejected it on the grounds that 'it was too expensive to print, too heavy to lift and too large to store', was broken up and reworked into six large volumes, all published between 1926 and 1930.[32] Although Lewis might always be remembered first for his prewar avant-garde posturing yet judged by his works of the 1930s, it is the *Man of the World* books in which Lewis first outlined his central philosophies and extended them on a broad socio-political level, and it is these books which form the basis of Lewis's critique of high modernism.

The Art of Being Ruled appeared in 1926, his first book in seven years. Coming from a once well-known avant-garde radical painter, the book would have been surprisingly political to its readers. There were few of these.[33] From the beginning, though, Lewis knew the appeal would be limited. In an 'Author's Introduction' Lewis describes his potential audience: 'Most books have their *patients*, rather than their *readers*, no doubt. But some degree of health is postulated in the reader of this book'

(*ABR* 13). A text which implies that nearly the whole of society is sick but is intended solely for the healthy has little chance of selling well. But then, as Lewis goes on to say, 'A book of this description is not written for an audience already there, prepared to receive it, and whose minds it will fit like a glove . . . It must of necessity make its own audience' (*ABR* 13). In this respect, *The Art of Being Ruled* was a failure, continuing even today to find a relatively small readership, when compared to, say, *Time and Western Man*. By the time this latter book was written, Lewis announced he had already 'modified' his views from the former, thus dooming *The Art of Being Ruled* to a slight readership for years.[34]

Still, the book is typical of Lewis; we might say it is typically radical, if a book can be called radical that begins by doubting the worth of revolution. We once more see Lewis in the conservative role at the exact moment he is playing the radical, enveloping himself in politics only in the hope of protecting his position in art. But Lewis leaves discussion of art until he has announced his political theories. In *The Art of Being Ruled*, he reveals a distaste for what he terms 'democracy', openly researching the alternatives. For this reason, the book is often cited in studies of Lewis's fascist tendencies, even though of all alternatives to democracy, he finds 'the sovietic system to be the best' (*ABR* 320). On the whole, Lewis is much less concerned with fascism than in finding out what had gone wrong with Britain's political system.

As stated earlier, Lewis opens the book with a critique of the then-prevalent revolutionary mentality. 'Every one today,' he writes, 'in everything, is committed to revolution' (*ABR* 17). There is a satirical note here, an implicit question as to what might be revolted *against* if revolution is so uniformly endorsed. It seems Lewis is criticizing a general attitude of revolution-for-revolution's-sake, but the critique extends to what he calls 'the *all that is is bad, and to be superseded by a better* attitude'. This attack on the concept of inevitable progress would become the central theme of *Time and Western Man*, and continues the struggle Lewis began in *The Caliph's Design* against change for the mere sake of change. In a significant chapter, 'The Oppressive Respectability of "Revolution"', Lewis reveals his current position:

The 'revolutionary' of yesterday would at present find himself in the tamest situation, surrounded by a benevolent welcome everywhere he went . . . If he were incorrigibly desirous of experiencing the 'revolutionary' thrill and of tasting the rude delights of the outcast, it would be – oh, strangest of paradoxes! – in being *unradical* alone that he could hope to find it. (*ABR* 33)

There is no doubt that Lewis sees himself as the former revolutionary, now forced into the 'unradical' stance of defending some form of authority against a popular cry for change – what he calls the 'official' revolution. This surely develops from the attempt in *The Caliph's Design* to preserve the true artist's authority which Lewis saw slipping against the merely stylistic revolution of the amateur and dilettante.

It is from this position that Lewis's antidemocratic views stem. He sees two alternatives in choosing a type of government: 'Liberalist Democracy' or 'Authority'. He is on the side of authority. When considering the 'dogma of *What the Public Wants*', which Lewis considers 'the capital question of statesmanship . . . it is discovered, at first with a certain surprise, that nothing that can properly be called *will* exists for anything except . . . a simple series of disconnected appetites' (*ABR* 73–4). However, says Lewis, the only difference between democracy and authoritarian rule stems from how the ignorant public is told what to want:

The present rulers of Russia or Italy . . . are intelligent enough to perceive, it seems, that [the human being] is a very helpless child, dependent on others (like a horse or a dog). They realize that he finds his greatest happiness in a state of dependence and subservience when (an important condition) it is named 'freedom.' It matters very little, then, if you outrage often, as you must do to rule successfully, the most elementary principles of 'freedom.' He will be happier with you, dependent, than with other people, *in*dependent. (*ABR* 89)

Democracy, meanwhile, encourages these 'helpless children' to believe, incorrectly, that they rule themselves 'by the operation of this terrible canon of press and publicity technique' (*ABR* 74). To compound the problem for Lewis, the liberal lacks the frankness he sees in 'the sovietist or the fascist, who makes no disguise of his forcible intentions, whose *power* is not wrapped up in parliamentarian humbug, who is not eternally engaged in pretences of benefaction; who does not say at every move in the game that he is making it for somebody else's good, that he is a vicar and a servant when he is a master' (*ABR* 75). It is this view of democracy which Lewis later recants, as well as his views on the beneficence of fascism.

But Lewis, throughout his career, insisted that his main emphasis was always on art, and he dealt with politics only when they encroached on his art. This is an important point to remember when reading the *Man of the World* volumes. That *The Art of Being Ruled*, as well as Lewis's antidemocracy (even profascist) sentiments, is a result of political encroachment into his art is most easily detectable in an untitled chapter which was not included in the final draft.[35] Lewis considered the result of the 'dogma' of democracy as a loss of standards, with 'one person being as good as another. *Life for Life's sake* is the attitude resulting from this – a worthy sister to the theory of *Art for art's sake*' (*ABR* 391). He continues with the comparison, arguing that having a child, though considered 'the supreme creation', is not enough in itself unless the infant goes on to produce something else worth while, preferably something *more* than merely another child. Likewise, Lewis implies, artistic creation is not enough in itself if it only engenders further art. It must somehow transform the world in which it exists. Extending his ongoing antagonism to amateur artists and dilettantes, Lewis here begins to condemn those who merely dabble in life. Just as Lewis, though fighting against the institution of art, recognized the need for authoritarian standards to limit the field, he also seeks to overcome the institution of democracy by the introduction of limits on freedom. Although he is always an advocate of the individualist, those who are '*least* clamped into a system', he suggests that a society of 'free men' would 'immediately collapse'. He continues:

The main thing to remember in such a discussion is that no one wants to be 'free' in that sense. People ask nothing better than to be *types* . . . to be *automata*: they wish to be *conventional*: they hate you teaching them or forcing them into 'freedom': they wish to be obedient, hard-working machines, as near dead as possible – as near dead (feelingless and thoughtless) as they can get, without actually dying. (*ABR* 151)

How far this passage is meant to be ironic remains debatable, exhibiting perhaps the fascist side of Lewis, or merely satirizing the views of contemporary politicians. What is safe to say, I think, is that Lewis saw 'freedom' as having less value than most pretended, especially the more available it was. If this view is applied to the field of art, the increased freedom the public felt for creating their own works of art devalues not only the notion of freedom, but also the concept of 'a work of art'.

That Lewis's worst fear is the loss of the privileges of being an individualist and artist, especially the privilege of having an audience from which he might stand out, is evident in the section entitled 'Sub Persona Infantis'. The millionaire society in wealthy postwar Britain is the cause, says Lewis, of a 'painting, writing, acting, cultural paradise . . . in which everyone is equal (that is, equally "a genius") and every one is free' (*ABR* 155). But Lewis is most concerned about the 'few artists, who are not millionaires'. This democratization of art means that 'those who formerly "patronized" the arts of music, painting, or literature now *do it themselves instead*' – making it nearly impossible for nonmillionaire artists to continue creating at all. Lewis is not speaking here of the commodity value of individual works of art so much as the cultural value of the artist within a specific society – related to what Pierre Bourdieu terms the 'cultural capital' of an artist within 'the Market for Symbolic Goods'.³⁶ Ironically, the devaluing of art by its democratic proliferation stems, according to Lewis, from the recent *recognition* of the artist's value. He laments that the contemporary artist recognizes 'the importance of his function, and its *life* value, vanity value, and social value' since this self-conscious realization leads only to envy on the part of nonartists. Even the simple 'trader', Lewis comments, has come to envy 'the vanity value' that artists command.

Although it was not until 1944 that Theodor Adorno and Max Horkheimer would theorize 'the culture industry', Lewis seems to be writing of art's position within a specific bourgeois-capitalist framework. Norbert Elias's 1935 essay on 'The Kitsch Style and the Age of Kitsch' is perhaps closest to what Lewis is trying to illustrate in *The Art of Being Ruled*. Elias describes the transformation from courtly art to bourgeois art, saying, 'What was lost, above all, was the certainty of taste and of the creative imagination, the solidity of the formal tradition which was discernible earlier in even the clumsiest productions.'³⁷ The certainty of taste, forfeited along with authoritarian standards and tradition, is what Lewis, formerly a revolutionary, now seems to want restored. With every member of society simply producing their own works of art, there is no room for the specialist. Elias continues, 'In this original meaning of the term "kitsch" the whole contempt of the specialist for the uneducated taste of capitalist society is expressed, as well as the tragic aspect of this constellation, in which the specialists, whether artists, dealers or publishers, were obliged for economic reasons to produce and sell products which they themselves despised.'³⁸ That Lewis had tried and failed with his 'pot-boiler' *Mrs. Dukes' Million* early in his career meant that this option was not open to him and there was only hope for him as 'the specialist'.³⁹ But if the 'uncertainty of taste' allowed any potential patron to simply create their own work of art, the specialist would be left with no cultural value at all, and no audience – resulting in what the next chapter of *The Art of Being Ruled* calls 'The Disappearance of the Spectator'.

Lewis begins this chapter by asking, 'Should there be "players" and "livers," art and life, or only one thing?' (*ABR* 157). This leads into a brief description of the work of Vsevelod Meyerhold in Russia, in which, says Lewis, 'the barrier between the audience and the actor' is broken down. The professionals give way to the amateurs, and there is no audience. This represents to Lewis what is happening in all the arts, and is a 'valueless' excuse for any society producing bad art. 'If the *professional* is a bad professional,' writes Lewis, 'that means the society that has produced him is a bad society' (*ABR* 159). If, on the other hand, all art is amateur art, there are no professionals at all through which a sick culture might express itself. The idea of '*every man his own artist*' has just as little chance of succeeding as '*every man his own doctor*', Lewis tells us. But if Lewis is suggesting that artists need some authoritative body to separate the genuine professional from the dilettante, he does not say what it is. On the same page that he denies the validity of '*every man his own artist*', Lewis describes the Royal Academy as 'a perfect justification for social revolution', revealing his distaste for the existing institutions of art which only encourage the work of the 'bad professionals' and the spread of the 'bad society'. One could enquire of Lewis who he thinks should determine what is to be art and who is to be the artist if neither the democratic free market nor the established authority of the academy. But Lewis does not here provide the answer.

There is one other way politics encroaches on art, Lewis tells us, in an argument which leads directly into his first critique of *Ulysses* and the first statement of his preference for the *outside* of things rather than the *inside*. The art which accompanies 'this great movement of corruption and overthrow', which is Lewis's view of contemporary society, is 'actually better' than much previous European art. The problem, though, is that it is simultaneously creating and destroying:

The destroyer cannot be at the same time the creator. The political impulses at work constantly distort the issue. The artist or thinker is apt to find himself making something, but ending it with dynamite, as it were. The political necessities underneath the surface are perpetually interfering, magnetically or otherwise, with artistic creation . . . its detachment, sacrificed. (*ABR* 345)

Even while calling this a problem, he admits that 'it is not easy to see an issue just yet'. Lewis knows that he is the first to recognize an issue which will become apparent only once the age passes more fully into history. He was already aware, though the idea would be developed further in subsequent books, that much modernist art was being sacrificed to historicism at the moment of its creation.

The last two paragraphs of *The Art of Being Ruled* summarize Lewis's position as an antidemocratic, antiromantic and anti-Enlightenment thinker. The only chance for intelligence to regain its former position is 'the passing of democracy and its accompanying vulgarities, owing to which any valuable discovery has to fight its way in the market-place' (*ABR* 375).

But it is more than the vulgarities of the marketplace that hinder the type of artist Lewis wants to be; it is also the vision of society that was put forward two hundred years earlier: 'Our minds are all still haunted by that Abstract Man, that enlightened abstraction of common humanity, which had its greatest advertisement in the eighteenth century. That No Man in a No Man's Land, that phantom of democratic "enlightenment," is what has to be disposed [of] for good in order to make way for higher human classifications' (*ABR* 375). For Lewis, this is the 'art' of being ruled, to remove all notions of mass equality, for each individual to recognize their own place, or type, and allow intelligence to take the appropriate authority. Even if Lewis modified his views in later books, this thesis would remain.

Whether because of the subject matter or the author's long absence from sight, there is little doubt that *The Art of Being Ruled* generated too little notice for Lewis's taste. Even Lewis's former supporters seemed indifferent, as Reed Way Dasenbrock points out. W. B. Yeats was silent, Pound dismissive of 'books all erbout everything in general', and only Eliot, though he never reviewed the book, was supportive, adding the title to the recent works he considered significant in *The Criterion*.[40] This may have been a result of Eliot's loyalty, though, rather than genuine appreciation. Eliot was active in engaging Lewis in an alliance, even when the latter wanted no alliances. In a 1925 letter Eliot reminded Lewis of the 'benefit' of a united front against 'a number of people who would be glad to see and to instrument any possible separation or disagreement between us for their own purposes' (*LWL* 150). He goes on, though, to offer advice on Lewis's devotion to 'eight or ten books at once', an implicit criticism of *The Man of the World* project. Although this letter from Eliot marks a period of uneasiness between the two men, their alliance remained nearly undamaged (with the obvious exception of Lewis's attack on Eliot's criticism in *Men Without Art* (1934)) until Lewis's death.

It is not easy, though, to understand why Eliot was the sole exception in 1927 to Lewis's break with all his former literary associations. It was primarily Eliot's theory – regarding impersonality – which was subjected to implicit criticism in *The Caliph's Design*. Furthermore, Eliot issued comments near the time of *The Man of the World* which seem to contradict the individualist creed Lewis puts forward. For example, the letter quoted above includes a claim by Eliot that 'furthermore I am not an individual but an instrument, and anything I do is in the interest of art and literature and civilisation, and is not a matter for personal compensation' (*LWL* 151). One can hardly think of any phrase which would have provoked Lewis more. But we find Eliot one of the few contributors to the first number of *The Enemy* – the third journal Lewis was to edit – the same issue (January 1927) to which Joyce originally submitted a portion of *Work in Progress*, though the space was devoted instead to Lewis's attack on the Irish novelist. In fact, in Eliot's article in *The Enemy*, he answers a claim made by I. A. Richards that his poetry was separated from all beliefs. Eliot seems intrigued, but never actually refutes Richards. His last sentences concludes:

We await, in fact . . . the great genius who shall triumphantly succeed in believing *something*. For those of us who are higher than the mob, and lower than the man of inspiration, there is always *doubt*; and in doubt we are living parasitically (which is better than not living at all) on the minds of the men of genius of the past who have believed something.[41]

It is difficult to know what to make of this in such a context: how could Lewis, a man of conviction if nothing else, have accepted such a statement from Eliot, unless it was seen as a prophecy of Lewis's own eventual success as 'the great genius who shall triumphantly succeed in believing *something*'?

Even if this is the case, there is little doubt Lewis would have scorned anyone who genuinely considered himself a 'parasite' on the genius of the past. Lewis preferred to ignore the past altogether, which he considers the 'classical' attitude, as we will discuss in *Time and Western Man*. But first more attention must be given to *The Enemy*, which appeared as a sort of preface to Lewis's next book. The 'editorial' appears as a declaration of Lewis's independence – made possible by a new financial patron – announcing that 'there is no movement gathered here (thank heaven!), merely a person; a solitary outlaw and not a gang'.[42] Lewis claims that no 'social impurities' will invade the journal; taking the stance of the enemy, even his social contacts will be limited – he will not even dine with those he discusses, in order to remain free to criticize. The value of his stance is outlined in a quotation from Plutarch, cited as an epigraph. Since no one, it says, listens to the quiet voice of one's friends, 'what remaineth but that we should hear the truth from the mouth of our enemies?'[43] This clearly marks out Lewis's position for the next decade, criticizing modernism from within. The first appearance of 'The Revolutionary Simpleton' followed this preface, in which Lewis made explicit his criticism of many of his former allies.

However, for full impact this essay should be analyzed in the context of the rest of *Time and Western Man*. In the most basic sense, this giant volume is an indictment of what Lewis called the 'time-cult', which stemmed from romanticism, culminated in Bergson and Einstein, and infected all aspects of contemporary society and the arts. Joyce, Pound, Marcel Proust and Gertrude Stein are the most notable literary figures, with Oswald Spengler's *The Decline of the West* (1926–8) providing Lewis with his most consistent illustration of the time-mind. *Time and Western Man* sets up several antitheses, pairing the *Zeitgeist*'s romanticism against Lewis's preferred classicism, history against timelessness, the internal method versus the external, the subjective versus the objective, and most consistently time versus space. Lewis knows this is an over-simplification, but, in finding an orthodoxy of thought on all these levels, wants nothing more, perhaps, than to prove that there is an alternative. Lewis spends much of the preface to Book Two of *Time and Western Man* illustrating why he takes the 'reactionary' stand even when he does not consider himself a reactionary. In a quotation from Edward Caird he defines his own duty as providing 'a disturbing, irritat-ing challenge' to 'awaken thought, and in time produce a modification . . . of prevailing "opinions"' (*TWM* 131).

Lewis then positions himself as the alternative, the enemy of the pre-dominating philosophical dogma, providing the missing half of a dialectic from which he hopes something truly new will emerge. For Lewis *does* believe in progress when it is the product of individual minds, even if he is no Hegelian or Marxist, and even when he disputes the time-cult idea of fatalistic progressivism. Lewis's dialectic works, in *Time and Western Man*, on the cultural topics as well as the socio-political, though each is given its own distinct 'book'. Lewis, in offering himself as an alternative to any prevalent consensus in philosophy or politics, also offers himself as an alternative to the homogenizing influence he sees within the movements of art. Fredric Jameson notes this, suggesting that Lewis engages in a forward-looking attack on the modernism only just emerging, imagining what will happen once it has become established.[44] By recognizing a future coherent 'modernist' ascendancy even before the movement was named or ended, Lewis is ahead of his time, already engaging in an agonistic struggle with his own movement's posterity. Poggioli recognizes the avant-garde tendency towards agonism as a self-sacrifice to 'historicism' and 'a contrast between the work and the atmos-phere in which it is produced'.[45] Similarly, Lewis argues that not all works of art should be mere products of the age in which they are produced, while simultaneously condemning the works of his contemporaries as being nothing more.

There is a paradox here, as in much of Lewis's writings, but not an irreconcilable one. Lewis hopes to prove that one can stand against one's time even when, or especially when, it requires standing against the historicist notion that there is such a determinist thing as 'one's time'. Before the war, he felt himself – and watched his allies – being submerged in history, being carried along by the *Zeitgeist*. In the postwar period he then stood aside while his (former) allies made names for themselves and wrote themselves into literary history by creating postwar masterpieces – exact summaries, as he thought, or products of their age – such as *Ulysses* and *The Waste Land*. After witnessing this process, Lewis became a critic of their success. For instance, his criticism of *Ulysses* might be summed up in Harry Levin's praise for the novel, that 'the very form of Joyce's book is an elusive and eclectic *Summa* of its age: the *montage* of the cinema, impressionism in painting, *leitmotif* in music, the free association of psychoanalysis, and vitalism in philosophy'.[46] Similarly, when speaking of Eliot, Lewis says that *The Waste Land* was written 'to express his feelings about [the postwar period] while it was going on. But that was so successful he got the "waste" into his blood a little' (*BB* 15). For Lewis, art that merely reflects its age is contaminated by it and cannot as a consequence influence it. This is mere dilettantism, an attempt to write a historical document instead of producing something which might, in some future moment, *make* the history of the age in which it was produced. Lewis quickly recognized that his allies in the prewar 'successful revolution' were only forming a new ascendancy, a new orthodoxy, grounded in merely stylistic revolution. He preferred to remain an enemy and wrote *Time and Western Man* to indict the time-cult orthodoxy and provide an antithesis.

Although Lewis, rather confusingly, begins the book with his attack on modern culture in 'The Revolutionary Simpleton', the second, more theoretical section, 'An Analysis of the Philosophy of Time', outlines the foundational ideas more explicitly. In the preface to this section, Lewis illustrates his opposition to those who reduce everything to '*history merely*', changing each individual into a product of what we might call the Hegelian conception of progress. This leads Lewis to suggest, '"Modern" or "modernity" are the words that have come literally to stink . . . but that is not, I argue, because what is peculiar to the modern age, or because the "new" in itself is bad or disgusting, but simply because it is never allowed to reach the public in anything but a ridiculous, distorted, and often very poisonous form' (*TWM* 130). This is the fault, says Lewis, of the 'interpretive performer', whether artist or scientist. It is the idea of progress that Lewis most disdains, the 'myth' of Western Man moving along an inevitable path, without any influence from individual minds – since they are only 'thrown up' by the *Zeitgeist*. The fountainhead of this view of progress, according to Lewis, is 'the perfect priest of the Zeitgeist', Bergson.

The vision of history as a stream in flux, which Bergson advocates, directly opposes Lewis's views. Lewis quotes Bertrand Russell to summarize Bergson's philosophy: 'The beliefs of today may count as true today, if they carry us along the stream; but tomorrow they will be false, and must be replaced by new beliefs to meet the new situation' (*TWM* 190). This is a type of Einsteinian relativism, something like philosophical pragmatism, which Lewis in his classicism and belief in timeless values cannot endorse except as mere reflections of fashion. This is the view of time that Lewis sees stemming from the Enlightenment, a romantic view of history always progressing:

It is a pure dialectical progression, presided over by a time-keeping, chronologically-real, super-historic, Mind, like some immense stunt-figure symbolizing Fashion, ecstatically assuring its customers that although fashions are periodic, as they must and indeed ought to be, nevertheless, by some mysterious rule, each one is *better* than the last, and should (so the advertisement would run) be paid *more* for than the last, in money or in blood. (*TWM* 212)

This view of inevitable progress, Lewis suggests, is actually harmful to real change, though it advocates revolution, because it is ultimately fatalistic. Again, Lewis finds himself in the awkward position of criticizing those promoting revolutionary progressivism (though he believed in progress *and* revolution) because of the manner in which the terms of historical progress were set – that is, in favour of the collective over the individual. 'An historical people is very superior,' says Lewis, 'superior to mere self, and far too respectful towards "destiny" to dream of changing *the Changing*' (*TWM* 216). The humanist position, the evolutionary position, is thus the more passive. The real revolutionary, represented by Lewis, would invest himself in altering the course of deterministic progress – to change the changing. Lewis's satire of the time-cult is biting: 'It is not our place – what next! – *to make History*: it is History that makes us' (*TWM* 216).

Although it is 'The Revolutionary Simpleton' that openly criticizes prominent modernists and their relation to history (as discussed shortly), the second, more theoretical section of *Time and Western Man* engages with them more implicitly. Lewis echoes what he said of modernist stylists in *The Caliph's Design* when speaking of those who subscribe to the historical mind of the time-cult: 'The pretentious omniscience of the "historical" intelligence makes of it an eternal dilettante, or tourist. It does not live in, it is *en touriste* that it tastes this time-district, or time-climate, and that' (*TWM* 217). This is, as we will see, Lewis's main criticism of Pound and Joyce. But even Eliot, who is not mentioned in 'The Revolutionary Simpleton', is entangled in Lewis's critique of the historically minded. This might be expected, since Eliot's early essay 'Tradition and the Individual Talent' takes a view of history which Lewis might find harmful to the production of genuine art. Even if Lewis does not at this point attack Eliot explicitly, his ideas undergo implicit criticism, notably when Lewis condemns Wildon Carr for suggesting that 'not only does every new present action modify the past, it reveals the meaning of the past, and even in that external sense the past is not dead fact to be learnt about, but living development changing continually' (*TWM* 221). Eliot's 1919 essay suggests a similar assertion that 'the past should be altered by the present as much as the present is directed by the past'.[47] Eliot went to some pains to emphasize that he still held these views later in his career.

Lewis's view of history must be placed in this context, remembering that he was first an artist, and only a philosopher or political theorist when required to defend his artistic position. It is important to find out why Lewis felt it essential to oppose the time-cult artists. Firstly, Lewis recognized that the historian cannot be objective, describing a past 'seen through a temperament of a certain complexion, and intended to influence its generation in this sense or that' (*TWM* 247). The historically influenced writer is similar and, for an example, Lewis suggests that 'Proust embalmed himself alive. He died as a sensational creature in order that he should live as an historian of his dead sensational self' (*TWM* 248–9). This forces the reader, according to Lewis, to withdraw from life and from the present, meanwhile engaging with a dead past. 'The historical writer, in every case, is distracting people from a living Present' (*TWM* 249). Proust, Lewis implies, is placing himself among the existing monuments Eliot had spoken of, working his way into a ready-made history rather than making it himself.

Lewis then indulges in what is for him a science-fiction scenario. He presents for us a future couple who project on to a screen a day they spent at Hampton Court many years earlier. The possibility of so easily reliving the past breeds a sense of 'the unreality of time, and yet of its paramount importance', encouraging the substitution of time for space. A type of time-travel is possible, but completely within the mind.

It seems that Lewis envisions a future when life (and artistic creation) will give way to memory (or re-creation). But even more importantly, people who can perpetuate the past 'would have a very different view of their Present from us' (*TWM* 250). This is what horrifies Lewis – not a future where time is easily negotiable, but the changes inevitable to the present if one recognizes this future negotiability with the past. The problem stems from the *self-conscious* act of recording the present with the intention of reproducing it for a future under the label of the Past. In other words, the couple ruin their day at Hampton Court because of their continual awareness that the day should be recorded for posterity. This historicist mindset embalms the living – ironically preserving by means of self-destruction.

This amounts to Lewis's theory of history. With the contemporary emphasis on time-flux and progression, society becomes too obsessed with its place in the stream, and begins to historicize itself. This in itself may not be a problem, but Lewis equates history with death. When history catches up with life, there is only history, and life is over. Lewis again quotes Carr as representative of the time-cult: 'History is what we now are and what we are now doing, it is not a character our actions will assume only when they have receded into the past' (*TWM* 221). But for Lewis, if this were true, there would be no more doing, no further actions, only fulfilling the inevitability of progress. Lewis prefers to see 'the Past as *myth*' containing 'a *dead* people we do not interfere with, but whose integrity we respect' (*TWM* 223). This keeps life in the present, a place where all embalming, if it is done at all, is done to the dead *by* the living. The act of preserving the present moment is the duty of future historians, presumably; the duty of those living in the present is to make it a moment worthy of history.

Although we have already witnessed Lewis acting as literary historian, he continually stressed that there was a line dividing himself from the past he described. Whether this distinction saves Lewis from hypocrisy or not, his criticism of fellow modernists lies in his opinion that they were either, like Pound, never really alive, existing entirely in the past, or, as he says of Proust, in the act of embalming themselves while still alive. In either case, the cause is their preoccupation with history in the present. The fact that an unhealthy interest in the past masquerades as 'the revolutionary' – what we now might term 'modernist' – only compounds Lewis's distaste for his perception of the time-cult. As he says in 'The Revolutionary Simpleton', 'It is clear that we cannot go on forever making revolutions which are returns merely to some former period of history' (*TWM* 34).

Lewis seems to be attacking the modernist precept of engaging with past or primitive traditions – 'monuments' – in the name of being revolutionary or new. He makes this distinction: 'I am not therefore suggesting that where art is concerned other periods, races and countries should be banished. It is the "revolutionary" terminology and propagandist method, alone, that I am criticizing' (*TWM* 36). Lewis wants to call 'a spade a spade' and call 'what the spade digs up old, very old; not new, very new' (*TWM* 35).

We might say then that it is the revolutionary propaganda that launches Lewis on his most significant criticism of modernist artists, with his idea of a separated Present and Past providing the theoretical context. But taking 'The Revolutionary Simpleton' (or any of Lewis's *The Man of the World* essays) in context is difficult because Lewis, incredibly prolific during this period, is constantly inventing new contexts. For example, we must remember that 'The Revolutionary Simpleton' was printed in the first number of *The Enemy*, which provides its first context. But not only does the remainder of *Time and Western Man* form a new setting for the argument, the second number of *The Enemy* came out in the same month as the book. Although the central themes in each case remain the same, each new environment for the criticism in 'The Revolutionary Simpleton' allows a new argument to be made. In his editorial for the second number of *The Enemy*, Lewis restates clearly his ideas on revolution which were simultaneously elaborated in *Time and Western Man*. But here Lewis emphasizes the propagandist power the cult has on society:

There is *one* door through which, in order to be changed at all, everything must pass . . . And they have painted this portentous gateway to look like Destiny: and they abound in bitter arguments to prove to you that there is no alternative to it . . . [They] compel you to patronize it, and the usual advertising devices plaster all roads with a herd-compelling hypnotism.[48]

These are the time-cult 'dogmatists' who insist on writing history as they go. Lewis goes on: '"History" is just what occurs, what gets into Time, as opposed to what does not, or what remains latent, unused or unexplored.'[49] This statement is useful when applied specifically to *literary* history, with the canon represented by the phrase 'what gets into Time'.

That Lewis is speaking in terms of a literary grouping is supported on the next page, where he describes himself as 'against this canon, for what my resistance is worth, and in consequence, no doubt, in the nature of an outlaw'. While the orthodoxy that Lewis opposes includes more than literature, it is fair, I think, to apply these comments specifically to the 'mainstream modernists'. Lewis says that the 'chronological, or "historical," principles are the final object of my critical attack. But I am not the only outlaw this "Wasteland" has made.'[50] The use of the capitalized term 'Wasteland' may allude to Eliot's poem, if we note that Lewis consistently misnamed it 'the Wasteland' instead of 'The Waste Land'. But how Lewis intends this to be read is questionable. It is clear that Eliot was describing in his poem the postwar society of which Lewis makes himself an outlaw. But if we remember that Lewis saw some of the 'waste' infiltrating Eliot himself, and that Lewis would criticize Eliot's ideas on history a few years later, this comment may suggest that it is the poem itself which makes Lewis an outlaw. The 'canon' Lewis claims to be resisting might be represented by Eliot's major poem, which not only reached back into history, employing Eliot's own 'mythic method', but had also already become entrenched in literary history by the time Lewis is writing.

As an outlaw – artistically, socially and philosophically – Lewis evidently feels himself to be the saviour of alterity in a fast-homogenizing world of art and thought. To combat a fixed future history, Lewis finds that he must first combat contemporary fashion, whether in art, thought or politics. As he would write a few years later in his critique of American racial politics, *Paleface* (1929):

Each fresh novelty is accepted with a sort of fatalism as the *only possible* novelty, as an inevitable creation, as though it had dropped from the sky, instead of, as is the case, been invented by a fat little man somewhere in Paris . . . In short, it has *happened*, they feel – the 'new' has happened; not that some other person a little shrewder and more active than themselves has *done it to them* . . . The 'up-to-date' is thus the emanation of some person, or some small inner ring of people. But it is superstitiously regarded as a fatal cosmical event.[51]

The phrase 'up-to-date' shows how far this is a criticism of the problem that artistic and philosophical modernism brings to contemporary society. In modernism whatever is 'new' gains a following simply on the basis of its innovation, regardless of the issue of whether it affects society in positive or negative ways. Even worse, it is accepted as inescapable, unchangeable, already a part of history, despite the fact that the 'new' or the 'revolutionary', if proved worthless, can still be reversed or ignored.

This is what Lewis calls 'single-gauge' change or revolution. That he stands outside of time, outside the dominant mode of thinking, and subsequently history, worries Lewis less than that 'what people call "Progress" today is generally not an advance'.[52] While true progress was achieved in previous centuries, Lewis believes that '*now* there is nothing but a rising and falling of people and cultures, on a dead level as regards value. Change is always merely – change. It is quite evident that if this had been the philosophy of the earliest men no arts, sciences, or anything but wild animal life would have resulted.'[53] This reflects Lewis's argument in *The Caliph's Design*, where each period's offering to the history of art only engages with the shortcomings of the preceding period, with no single period being better (in terms of Lewis's idea of 'value') than another. Lewis's contribution to what we call modernism, then, lies in his recognition that 'modernity' itself is only a correction to Victorian art, and will be surpassed by a following period, a new 'modernity' with its own agenda of correction – that is, unless the stylistic, technical revolution of modernism is accompanied by a revolution of the mind. Art must leave an impression on the age in which it is produced if there is going to be 'progress', rather than merely accepting and reinforcing that which already is. Just as modern society learns to accept whatever happens as inevitable progress, modernist artists grow accustomed to merely reflecting modern society, preferring revolutionary rhetoric and technique to truly revolutionary and progressive thinking.

Lewis opens 'The Revolutionary Simpleton' with an explanation of what makes the literary and artistic revolutionaries – including his contemporaries in the modernist enterprise – an orthodoxy and an institution. He mounts his criticism by labelling these writers and artists products of the advertising age, where success comes to those who cause the most sensation rather than those with the most valuable art. The result, he says, is that 'all idea of a true value – of any scale except the pragmatic scale of hypnotism and hoax – is banished forever' (*TWM* 13). Characteristics of such sensation-seeking are outlined. Lewis mentions first the employment of sex within literature as an advertisement. 'If you are desirous of showing your "revolutionary" propensities, and it is a case of finding some law to break to prove your good-will and spirit, what better law than the dear old moral law . . . So it is that "sex" for the European is the ideal gateway to Revolution' (*TWM* 17). Lewis prefers, of course, the 'will-to-change, or impulse to spiritual advance', which the Greeks, in their classicism, also preferred. Their treatment of sex was 'so much more healthy, it is quite evident, that it is a pity from any point of view that it should not be expected of a "broad-minded" and "modernist" person as a *sine qua non* of modernity' (*TWM* 18).

This is Lewis's first use of the term 'modernist' and there is little doubt he uses it generally to describe an individual who is 'up to date', progressive, or 'of the age'. A few pages later, he uses the term 'advanced' to describe 'the only significant' contemporary literature (*TWM* 22). Yet it is within the 'advanced' that Lewis looks for evidence of the time-cult. He sets himself up in opposition not to the literature of the past, or literature of an inferior sort, but to 'advanced' and 'significant' contemporary writers. He criticizes the new, the 'modernist', simply because it calls itself new while retaining a firm stake in the past. Lewis sees further evidence of the propagandist tone in the existence of literary 'movements' – something Lewis himself had advocated in 1914. 'The effect of that form of organization, to start with, is, inevitably, to advertise the inferior artist at the expense of the better . . . the suggestion being that only a great many cooks can make a really good broth; and the mastery of each individual must be of an unnoticeable, democratic order' (*TWM* 25). The lack of audience for any truly 'advanced' literature means that the proof, which is 'in the eating', is never discovered.

Lewis's first specific target in *Time and Western Man* is Sergei Diaghilev's Ballets Russes. In itself, the critique is less significant than what Lewis will go on to say about Pound, Stein and Joyce. Yet it is a clear illustration of Lewis attacking, along with his former allies, his own former position. In 1919, as Lewis outlined in a letter to John Quinn, he was hoping to design the sets for a Diaghilev ballet, a scheme prompted by the Sitwells, with music by William Walton (*LWL* 111). Although the scheme was abandoned, it shows Lewis, as late as 1919, still hoping to take part in what he labels eight years later 'the most perfect illustration of what I mean in my analysis of the degradation of Revolution . . . and the assimilation of that to the millionaire spirit' (*TWM* 33). Peters Corbett, one of the few critics to mention this change in tack, is right to point out that it is the *success* of Diaghilev's ballets which Lewis attacks. But to claim this is merely 'an elaborate repudiation of the society which has rejected him', as Peters Corbett does, is to take Lewis out of context.[54] *Time and Western Man* runs deeper than a mere reaction to sudden unpopularity. Rather, it is a realization that the former, more popular Lewis was taking part in an institution so narrowly confining in its execution of an inevitable historical narrative that there was no room for the individual.

It is in this context that Lewis criticizes Pound, Stein and Joyce. He begins with Pound, relating their former alliance in *Blast*. But again Lewis puts the period in terms of a revolution that had succeeded, with no need for either one of them to keep up the pretence any longer of being a 'fire-eating propagandist'. Lewis is certain, in Pound's case, that it is mere pretence, since Lewis considers Pound's poetry to be of a 'passéiste flavour'. He satirizes his friend, saying, 'Pound is, I believe, only pretending to be alive for form's sake' (*TWM* 40). Lewis first jumps to attack Pound's willingness to support any 'artist' who claims to be 'advanced', even if the art produced is of an inferior quality. This leads to criticism of a periodical with which Pound was associated, *This Quarter*, which succumbed to the revolutionary propaganda Lewis saw as eroding artistic values. But Lewis's criticism of Pound carries on into another chapter, entitled 'A Man in Love with the Past'. It is here that Lewis places Pound in the time-cult, a reflecter of history rather than a maker. 'It is *we* who produce; we are the creators; Ezra battens upon us' (67). Pound remains only a 'consumer', with 'no originality of any sort'.

Lewis admires Pound's ability, though, to reproduce the past. 'This sort of parasitism is with him phenomenal' (*TWM* 68). It is only because he is so 'worthy' and 'admirable' as 'a living individual', says Lewis, that he is able to 'get into the skin of somebody else'. But the main thrust is that, while Pound exhibits these wonderful tricks, he is not to be trusted as a contemporary mind. 'When he tries to be up to date it is a very uncomfortable business. And because he is conventional, and so accepts counterfeit readily where no standard has been established, he is a danger as far as he exerts any contemporary influence. He should not be taken seriously as a living being at all' (*TWM* 69). This is a serious accusation for someone like Pound, who took his role as the modernist movement's chief publicity agent and organizer very seriously. If modernism can be seen as a coherent literary 'movement' at all, as it often is, this is at least partly due to Pound's organizing influence, an influence here labelled 'a danger' by Lewis. The reason why Pound *can* be trusted with reviewing figures of the past, Lewis seems to say, is that posterity has already established an artistic 'standard' to which Pound must adhere. But Lewis wants to refuse Pound the 'contemporary influence' which might be used to establish what we could call a 'future posterity', a literary history of the present for the coming generations. It is his effectiveness in influencing how writers or artists *will* be viewed that makes him a danger.

This is the point where Pound and *This Quarter* become significant choices for Lewis's attack. That Pound had unselfishly come to Lewis's aid in the past and had been an 'ingenious' publicist for their joint efforts Lewis makes clear in the text itself. But as a letter to Pound in June 1925 reveals, Lewis had by then genuinely turned against all the propaganda and partnerships that had characterized his, and modernism's, career up to this point, even when it was to his benefit. After *This Quarter* had devoted its first issue to Pound, the poet had tried to devote a second number to Lewis. Lewis writes, 'I do not want a "Lewis number" or anything of that sort in This Quarter or *anywhere* else, at this moment . . . Please note the following: because . . . we were associated to some extent in publicity campaigns, that does not give you a mandate to interfere when you think fit, with or without my consent, with my career' (*LWL* 158). Pound had wanted since the early days of 'the movement' to find a single magazine to publish Eliot, Joyce, Lewis and himself for purposes of coherence and publicity. Even though Lewis saw the benefit of such manoeuvres, by the time of his *Man of the World* books he no longer wanted to take part. Lewis was willing for *This Quarter* to publish a portion of his socio-political prose, but they were interested in nothing but fiction, and Pound's only advice was, in Lewis's words, 'that the only sort of writing that should be done is that [which] is likely to get ones friends out of prison, sell their work, etc.' (*LWL* 159). Lewis had by then had enough of such propagandist work.

If, for Lewis, Pound's writing functions only through the past, Stein's exists only within the confines of her 'continuous present'. But although Stein does not emphasize the past or depend upon history, her writing is just as dead as Pound's, reflecting as it does Bergson's ongoing flux. Lewis places her representation of the present in 'the *nature-mortist* school', using the French term rather than the English 'still-life' to emphasize its deadness. The implication is that Stein's work never really comes alive because it is mere reflection and cannot engage with the motion of life. That her texts are the product of 'time-writing' is made clear by Lewis, quoting extensively from *Composition as Explanation* (1926), with its constant beginning again. But he also criticizes Stein for sustaining the child-cult, a refusal to mature which Lewis, despite his stance against the idea of inevitable progress, had denounced already in *The Art of Being Ruled*. The resulting style, Lewis shows, is widely imitated, in both popular and high culture, initiating a *naif*-culture where the child, the primitive or the demented control the *Zeitgeist*.

'An Analysis of the Mind of James Joyce' takes up more pages than the critique of any other individual, most likely because Joyce is placed so 'very high in contemporary letters' (*TWM* 73). Lewis makes clear that he prefers Joyce to Proust or Stein, but he goes to great lengths to confirm Joyce's place in the time-cult. How convincing Lewis is depends on his reader. Most significant, perhaps, is Joyce's own reaction, proclaiming Lewis's attack the best 'by far' of the hostile criticism of his works. But criticism in this vein is limited, as Joyce told Frank Budgeon: 'Allowing that the whole of what Lewis says about my book is true, is it more than ten per cent of the truth?'[55] Even many of Lewis's most loyal defenders think Lewis is correct only 'in a very loose and general way' to bring together those he collects under the banner of the 'time-cult'.[56] Critics of both Joyce and Lewis have outlined the skirmish that followed Lewis's attack, a faintly veiled repartee which infiltrated the literary canon through *The Childermass* (1928) and *Finnegans Wake* (1939). But there are still questions as to what precisely Lewis is attacking in Joyce's time-mind. It is never made clear through all the pages devoted to 'An Analysis', perhaps because there *are* so many pages, jumping from one subject to another. The 'mythic method' which Eliot built as the foundation-stone of his brand of modernism, for example, receives just one throwaway sentence from Lewis: 'As to the homeric framework, that is only an entertaining structural device or conceit' (*TWM* 102).

That this 'conceit' had been at the centre of the campaign to establish *Ulysses* as a modernist masterpiece even before there were any readers makes Lewis's dismissal coherent with his earlier critique of propaganda. It is what lies at the heart of Lewis's argument. He wants to get behind the novel's gimmicks to investigate what *Ulysses* contributes to 'advanced' literature apart from a claim to be 'revolutionary', an exhibition of styles and a representation of the *Zeitgeist*. To get below the surface, though, is hard work because of the 'amount of *stuff* – unorganized brute material – that the more active principle of drama has to wade through' (*TWM* 89). Since any action must take place 'in a circumscribed psychological space into which several encyclopaedias have been emptied', the novel's effect is of an 'immense *nature-morte*'. For Lewis, the piling up of historical detail and period styles only masks the lack of any real substance. Joyce is an executant, like Picasso, a dabbler in style. '*Ulysses*, on the technical side, is an immense exercise in style, an orgy of "apeishness," decidedly "sedulous." It is an encyclopaedia of english [sic] literary technique, as well as a general-knowledge paper' (*TWM* 74). Lewis admires Joyce's craftsmanship, the innovation and 'challenging novelty of the work in question', but insists that the content of *Ulysses* – 'a big variegated heap' – is no more than the combination of Irish 'local colour' and 'the material of the Past . . . with in addition the label of a twenty-year-old vintage, of a "lost time," to recommend it' (*TWM* 81).

The fact that *Ulysses* takes place in 1904 is key for Lewis's attack, since the entire plot unfolds ten years prior to the 'successful revolution' from which all 'advanced' literature stems. Lewis insists that any significant modernist revolution would involve more than mere stylistics. *Ulysses* employs the most innovative styles, and its technique reflects many of the ideas of its age, including, Lewis outlines, the influence of Eliot and Pound's 'scholarly enthusiasms', the 'half-asleep, daydreaming' of Stein, the psychology of Sigmund Freud and even 'the manner here and there' of Lewis's own play, *Enemy of the Stars* (1914), despite the fact that its effectiveness had been 'obliterated by the War' (*TWM* 107). But when the *Zeitgeist* influences have been removed, *Ulysses* is behind the times, stuck in 1904. What Joyce *thinks* is never very advanced, according to Lewis. 'It is the *craftsman* in Joyce that is progressive; but the *man* has not moved since his early days in Dublin. He is on that side a "young man" in some way embalmed' (*TWM* 90). This is similar to Proust, but with the following distinction. 'Proust *returned* to the *temps perdu*. Joyce never left it. He discharged it as freshly as though the time he wrote about were still present, because it was *his* present' (*TWM* 91). This is the reason Lewis places him in the midst of the time-cult: for drawing the past into the present, destroying the only distinguishing line that might render history an escapable nightmare.

Lewis presumably never heard Joyce's comment to Jacques Benoîst-Méchin concerning the insurance of his own immortality, but Lewis must have recognized that *Ulysses* was well positioned in history even before he wrote 'The Revolutionary Simpleton'.[57] He is, then, writing around a monument, even *against* a monument. But Joyce, though already a historical figure, was still alive, as Lewis was well aware, and still capable of change. Lewis makes clear that he is only analyzing Joyce's writings 'up to date', introducing this 'time-clause' in case Joyce will 'be influenced in turn by my criticism' (*TWM* 87). He is at this point acknowledging a future moment which must look back on *his* text with a historian's eye, and judge the success Lewis has achieved. This amounts to a recognition, on Lewis's part, that though Joyce is embalmed in history, that history can still be changed. *Time and Western Man*, as has already been acknowledged, provides its own theory of history just as it attempts to demolish the entire notion. In many ways, this socio-political text is grappling with the question of what can possibly be written *after* the historical and institutional establishment of a modern revolution, once *The Waste Land* and *Ulysses* have summed up the age. Once an age has been summed up, for Lewis, it no longer exists; only the texts carry on, as historical documents.

This is the idea that concludes 'The Revolutionary Simpleton' in its book form, elaborated in an 'Appendix to Book One'. Lewis concerns himself with how a 'great creation or invention of art' must struggle with 'the social organism' to find acceptance (*TWM* 123). This is where advertising comes in for many of his contemporaries. Lewis claims that 'all the up to date, "modernist" afflatus consists of catchwords, and is a system of parrot-cries, in the case of the crowd' (*TWM* 120). This can be applied to those artists who focus only on 'a new and particular form', those who are merely interested in the advertisement connected with the idea of the 'new', and whose works are picked up by their audience who share in the fever of revolution. These works establish, as they infiltrate history, a '*permanent novelty*' (*TWM* 122–3). Although Lewis's phrase is applied to jazz rather than literature, it is particularly relevant to all forms of art, and precedes Pound's famous dictum, 'Literature is news that STAYS news', though here criticizing the same idea Pound champions.[58] The type of literature which attempts to maintain a 'perennial fashion' (to use Adorno's phrase) only mimics the really new.[59] Lewis considers this a 'vulgarization' of the revolutionary ideas, 'a cheap, socially available simulacrum' which 'bears little resemblance to the original' (*TWM* 120). This is a complex idea which needs further attention.

It should be pointed out that Lewis does not consider it the fault of the artist when a work of art is 'robbed of its effect' by society. Even the 'very small number of inventive, creative men [who] are responsible for the entire spectacular ferment of the modern world' produce works that are 'watered down and adapted to herd-consumption' (*TWM* 120). In failing to overcome any work of art, Lewis says, society merely assimilates it. How this occurs has been more fully theorized by such writers as Adorno and Horkheimer in their famous essay on 'The Culture Industry'. They point out that 'the irreconcilable elements of culture, art, and amusement have been subjected equally to the concept of purpose and thus brought under a single false denominator: the totality of the culture industry. Its element is repetition.'[60] Lewis recognized this nearly twenty years earlier, writing about contemporary works of art which were in the process of being assimilated by the 'industry' while he watched. He also recognized that the subordination of the work of art was accomplished by 'a verbal acquiescence and a little crop of coarse imitations'. Each work of art, Lewis suggests, was in peril the moment it attempted to do something new. The peril came in the form of acceptance of the work of art. He concludes, 'Its canonization is the manner of its martyrdom' (*TWM* 123).

There are few phrases which summarize so well Lewis's criticism of contemporary culture. It is at the heart of his attack on amateurs and dilettantes, and provides the grounds for his otherwise inexplicable fear of success. He recognized that canonization meant vulgarization and death, even if a kind of living death – a death embalmed in history through martyrdom. This is a particularly useful term for Lewis since all that is left of the martyr is the name, and perhaps the few scattered relics. To the work of art which has been assimilated by society, Lewis applies the phrase 'a cheap, socially available simulacrum'. He produces no examples, but the idea can be applied to Joyce's *Ulysses*. For one thing, this novel was not, by the time Lewis was writing, merely a text, as it was still hard to find in England or America, and therefore not widely read; society had adopted a simulacrum of that work of art instead, a word flung through the press and uttered in salons with admiration – more an abstract illustration of the *Zeitgeist* than a living text. It did not even require reading, since it had already entered the social consciousness; it required only discussion.[61] One needs simply to look at literary periodicals of the day to see that *Ulysses* was widely discussed even without the novel being readily available. For example, the March 1934 issue of *Vanity Fair* reports of the first American edition of the novel that 'two printings were exhausted in advance of publication', so eager was the public to finally read the work they had heard so much about. The novel had become not only a commodity but a symbol of high modernist success, as Joyce is credited with being the figure 'to whom a whole school of modern writing owes its existence'.[62] The announcement is accompanied by a caricature of Joyce clutching his novel protectively, accompanied by the caption 'Portrait of the Artist as a Best-Seller'. High modernism had by this point taken a stride nearer to the establishment.

If canonization results in death, as Lewis implies, it is at least the death of a martyr. Although Lewis considers all his fellow modernists to be 'dead', counted out by history, at least they will be remembered in recompense. But this type of martyrdom is worth little to Lewis. Although *Time and Western Man* is perhaps Lewis's clearest illustration of his position in respect to his fellow modernists, it leaves him in a difficult position with few ways out. While Lewis seems to imply that a work of art can enter history only by giving up its life and becoming a token of itself, he does not present any alternatives. Presumably, the only way a work of art can escape with its 'life' is to avoid canonization and history altogether, perhaps by nurturing unpopularity as Lewis was successful in doing. But the problem Lewis could not solve in *Time and Western Man* was, in criticizing those that are self-conscious of a future posterity, how to avoid one's own self-consciousness towards that future moment. Lewis could not condemn historicist efforts while remaining ahistoricist himself. Like-wise, it was futile to condemn the popularity of his contemporaries without some form of audience – without catering to some kind of popularity himself. Arguably, these problems would not be resolved until the publication of *The Apes of God*.

Lewis must have been aware by 1930 that his *Man of the World* books were not making much impression. According to Paul O'Keeffe, *The Art of Being Ruled* sold only about a hundred copies per month for the first six months, and *Time and Western Man* sold only marginally better.[63] Of course, Lewis never intended to be a bestseller, or even to 'make history' within his own age. As early as *The Art of Being Ruled*, he had announced his intention of finding only a 'few dozen readers . . . from whom eventually all authority comes' (*ABR* 13). Lewis counted on posterity to make history of his age, opposing any attempts by his contemporaries to steal their way immediately into the 'general consciousness' by more populist means. But by 1930, this process may have seemed too slow, if for no other reason than that Lewis could not subsist without some immediate success. *The Apes of God*, a novel he had begun in 1923, with two chapters published in *The Criterion* in 1924, finally emerged in 1930, marking the furthest he would plunge into the self-marketing world he criticized so openly. More than any other work by Lewis, this novel is a self-conscious monument to, and a simultaneous criticism of, the history of his own age.

The Apes of God is the most intense example of Lewis's inconsistency between what he says and what he does, as I hope to show. In this novel Lewis engages in the very tactics that are criticized within it; yet this, I would argue, is merely part of the satire Lewis makes central to the book. Lewis suggests as much with the introduction of Pierpoint's encyclical. Pierpoint is, of course, the character that comes closest to Lewis's own position. But Pierpoint is far from ideal. He, too, is implicated in the games and crimes of the other 'apes'. Pierpoint recognizes this, and insists that he is 'a party' to the society he criticizes. He claims, 'What we call a judge is a successful partizan' (*AG* 118). Pierpoint then condemns, broadcasting Lewis's own beliefs, what he calls the '*societification* of art' and the emergence of dilettantes and '*amateurism*' within the bohemian world which causes real damage to the success of genuine artists. These amateurs are the '*apes of god*' of the title. Pierpoint concludes the encyclical by returning to the topic of his partisanship, insisting that 'the secret of *artistic* success' does not lie in the concept of 'impersonality'. 'The flourishing and bombastic role that you may sometimes see me in . . . is a caricature of some constant figure in the audience, rather than what I am (in any sense) myself. Or, to make myself clearer, it is my opposite' (*AG* 125). Pierpoint plays the role of the enemy, like Lewis. The enemy never pretends to be objective and is nothing like an 'impartial and omniscient' judge. Rather, he is a satirist, taking up the role of his opponent in the game he is criticizing.[64]

Lewis's theories of satire are outlined explicitly in *Satire & Fiction* and *Men Without Art*, but they also infiltrate the *Apes of God* satire itself. In the novel Zagreus, 'broadcasting' the ideas of Pierpoint, illustrates these ideas most clearly in the chapter 'Chez Lionel Kein Esq.', using Proust as an example of writers who take real personages for their characters. Lewis was, of course, self-consciously doing a very similar thing with his characters, since this entire conversation takes place with 'Lionel Kein', a caricature of Sidney Schiff, translator of Proust and one-time patron of Lewis.[65] Zagreus labels Kein '*a perfect Proust character*', which Kein accepts as flattery (*AG* 246). He points out that Kein 'would be one of the first notorious Proust-characters to appreciate the honour'. Kein responds, 'I believe I regard myself just as objectively as Proust could' (*AG* 255). But Pierpoint (through Zagreus) dismisses the idea of objectivity in literature. He says:

> The Fiction we are discussing pretends to approach its material with the detachment of the chemist or of the surgeon. But in fact what happens is that, as it is *Fiction*, not *truth* . . . the paraphernalia of 'detachment,' used by the average literary workman, result[s] in something the opposite of what you are led to anticipate. The Fiction produced in this manner becomes more *personal* than ever before. (*AG* 259)

Pierpoint, like Lewis, prefers literature which shapes reality rather than merely reflecting it. Literature that pretends to represent life objectively and *as it is* does not generate change, as Zagreus notes of Kein's failure to change, despite his objective 'regard' for himself. Zagreus is led to say, 'So, then, what is called "Fiction" is in large part the private publicity-machinery of the ruling Society' (*AG* 264). And later, 'Those works will be contrivances only, and too simply, for the securing of "power" (in the ordinary, vulgar, nietzschean sense) – not instruments of truth' (266). Lewis recognizes that any claim to 'objective reality' merely seeks to hide the subjective stance, though without the commitment required of the satirist. This 'impersonal' literature, Lewis says, merely enforces the subjectivity of what already is, instead of provoking change.

Zagreus's sermon is applauded by the ones it condemns, for he is only an actor, an ape, and Pierpoint's message is diluted to ineffectiveness. There is no possibility of convicting the apes – the dilettantes and amateurs – because they always believe themselves a step beyond the rebuke. As the novel progresses, the breakdown of authority is made clear, as principal characters, once trusted, prove themselves untrustworthy. This comes to a climax in the ultimate chapter, where Dan is betrayed by Zagreus, having been replaced. A sobbing naïf, Dan collects all his letters and his journal describing the apes, which together represent the history of the progress of the world, as well as the novel, which has come to an end. 'But he could read no more in that sad historic log. For him the last Ape he was ever to meet had been met with – his log was at last a museum of natural history – there was every variety of ape-like creature, to show like Darwin out of what men came – submen and supermen' (*AG* 607). Dan tears this history to pieces, in a symbolic act, during the height of the General Strike. His fingers 'divided everything – everything in the world – into smaller and smaller pieces – till no sentence at all was intact in all that mass of flattering precept and objurgation.' This is the end of Lewis's postwar period – in the quiet of the General Strike, an ineffectual revolution – and also the end of literary history. All genuine advance defers to the counterfeit change stimulated by the aping of the gods.

Lewis does not implicate only the wealthy play-actors in *The Apes of God*. Pierpoint's encyclical makes clear that there are two types of ape, those who are merely 'friends of art', but also the '*productive*' apes. One of these is the 'split man', Julius Ratner. While Paul Edwards identifies this character with John Rodker, there are also many clues, as Geoffrey Wagner pointed out while Lewis was still alive, that 'Jimmie' Ratner can also be linked to Joyce.[66] Lewis uses Ratner to caricature particularly Joyce's production of *Ulysses*, the split man signifying the apparently separate agents active in making that book a success. Lewis says:

since Mr. Julius Ratner kept a highbrow bookshop, a certain Mr. R. was able to sell his friend Joo's books – and because as well Jimjulius was a publisher, Joo was luckily in a position to publish his particular pal Ratner's novels and his poems – and on account of the fortunate fact that J. Ratner & Co. were the Publishers and distributors of a small high-brow review called simply *Man X* it was possible for Juliusjimmie to puff and fan that wan perishable flame of the occasional works of his old friend Jimjulius. (*AG* 150–1)

This, as Wagner recognized, can be seen as Joyce working within the publicity world of Shakespeare & Co. and *transition* (called in the novel *Man X*, says Wagner, after Man Ray/x-ray). Whether or not Ratner is modelled on Joyce, it should be noted that Joyce visited Lewis immediately after *The Apes of God* was published, an event Lewis groups with the death threat from an airman as evidence of the 'good deal of disturbance' caused by the novel's publication (*LWL* 190).

But it would be reductionist to pin all of Ratner on Joyce, since Lewis goes on to describe what might be as easily applied to anyone involved in the production of the modernist literature industry. Ratner, for example, makes his living by publishing limited-edition books, not only contemporary volumes but also those from 'the golden days of Europe, pre-Marx and pre-Bonaparte', so that when a book is produced 'to appease Mr. J. R.'s personal vanity' it is immediately positioned among these classics of literary history, instantly valuable in its limited state. This is reminiscent of Eliot's linking modern works of art with past 'monuments'. 'Such was the involved interplay of business and the mildest of literary power-complexes indulged invariably in a *gentlemanly* manner' (*AG* 151). Lewis is here caricaturing his contemporaries' successful production of cultural value. Ratner, the split man, engages in all the self-publishing and history-making tactics Lewis saw in his fellow modernists. This leads Mark Perrino to see *The Apes of God* as both a first-hand observation of the construction of modernism and an illustration of its relationship to mass culture at the same time.[67] Lewis's proximity to the movement he is satirizing encourages many readers to misunderstand his target. But Lewis repeatedly emphasizes that he is a partisan as well as a critic.

This partisanship is most clearly illustrated by Lewis's self-publication of *The Apes of God*. Lewis had always given this novel primary position among his own works, and when Chatto & Windus offered an advance for the book, Lewis declined, suggesting it was too slight. The result was an end to Lewis's relationship with Charles Prentice, one of his most important allies; but this gave him the opportunity to publish the book under his own Arthur Press imprint, which had brought out *The Enemy*. There is evidence that this was Lewis's plan all along. He told the London *Star* in 1930, 'People might think I started to publish my own work because I was dissatisfied with my publishers. This is not so . . . This new book, however, was of the class that always does best when published by a private press.'[68] The result was a massive book, perhaps intentionally larger and heavier than *Ulysses*, limited to 750 copies (more limited than the first printing of Joyce's novel), signed, numbered and valued at three guineas each (equal to a limited-edition *Ulysses*). We might apply the famous phrase of a Lewis disciple already mentioned – Marshall McLuhan – a cultural commentator in the Lewis mould, who claims, 'The medium is the message.'[69] Lewis, clearly aware of commodity values in the cultural milieu, was entering the political and cultural battlefields he had been describing. Perrino points out that only the subjects of the book, the apes themselves, could afford to buy the novel.[70] This was, no doubt, the point. Lewis was in many ways producing his own monument, a parody – both in the text and in the production of that text – of Joyce's *Ulysses*. In playing the role of self-publisher, a fact Lewis kept hidden from many of his contemporaries, he was providing one more (though postpublication) model for his caricature, Julius Ratner.

We see here Lewis entering the arena he condemned as a staged manipulation of cultural power and history. After condemning modernist propagandist tactics and sensationalism several years before, Lewis began to stir the controversies surrounding his own *The Apes of God* until scandal attracted a significant readership. A pamphlet, *Satire & Fiction*, followed the novel to intensify the debate and publicize the critical 'boycott' of the press. Lewis was once more in all the papers and journals, favourably or unfavourably. Reviewers urged Lewis to produce a popular edition, a cheaper alternative to the limited run. Lewis began to make plans for this 'popular edition' in late 1930, announcing in a circular letter the initiation of '*a unique event in the publishing world*' (*LWL* 196). It was not enough for Lewis to lament the vulgarization and 'societification of art' *within* the book – the cheap edition was to be published '*with advertise-ments*'. He continues, 'The adverts. will not be confined to those of publishers and bookshops. We are including adverts. of Steamship Lines, tooth-pastes, and lawn-mowers' (*LWL* 196). This edition never appeared, and it is possible it would not have appeared even had Lewis received the necessary advertisements. The letter was perhaps enough by itself, with its satiric emphasis on the 'permanence' and large readership of books as compared to magazines. Such an edition, had it come out in this form, would have heaped satire on satire, funding Lewis's condemnation of the commodification of art with material illustrations that it was itself a pure commodity. It was no longer possible, Lewis seemed to say, *not* to sell out.

This marks a significant point in Lewis's career. *The Apes of God* did eventually come out in a cheap edition, published by Grayson instead of Lewis himself or Chatto. It earned him, uncharacteristically for a Lewis book, more than his advance. But although this was a turning point, it was not towards financial success. Lewis's works of the 1930s made him almost no money – either because they were seen to support fascism or because they took a form of satire particularly susceptible to accusations of libel. For Lewis, art was over. This is not to say his career was over, or that he would stop producing. The novels of the 1930s are some of his most highly rated, and *Men Without Art* continued Lewis's stance as the enemy, with intensive criticism of his fellow modernists. These included Ernest Hemingway, William Faulkner, Woolf and Eliot. Lewis attacked Eliot openly for all the reasons he had previously hinted at: his 'scientific' emphasis on impersonality; his partnership with the critics; his lack of conviction, which renders him a *pseudo-believer*; and for engaging in what Lewis called '*the manufacture of poets and poetry*'.[71] Although Lewis never criticizes Eliot's poetry, he holds his friend up as an example of all that is wrong with literature and art in this period.

Lewis would not abandon his stance, but by the 1930s he was increasingly aware that the new beginning he had continually celebrated since 1914 was also the beginning of the end. In discussing the uselessness of the terms 'classical' and 'romantic' because they 'are terms applicable only to an historical see-saw of influences', Lewis is led to proclaim in *Men Without Art* that 'it is the end of history, and the beginning of historical pageant and play'.[72] Cultural and historic events, Lewis suggests, are giving way to mere pretence: revolution of thought yields to revolution of form and fashion. Commodity culture is where Lewis, in *Blasting and Bombardiering*, lays the blame for the emerging 'Art-less Society':

> Organization . . . in the business of the publishing and selling of books, imposes every day a greater handicap upon the book that is a work of art rather than a business commodity . . . It will shortly be quite impossible to imagine a book of a very high order of excellence being written any more . . . We are already prepared to feel that maybe great literature is a thing of the past, just as we have grown accustomed for a long time now to think of great music as a thing of the past. I doubt if the toughest master of words can really stand up against the massed attack of the syndicated 'Book world'. (*BB* 260–1)

Lewis carries on for pages, seeming to enjoy his role as the prophet of doom, taking issue with the medium of modern literature rather than its message. Yet the future, for the benefit of which he writes, is not altogether hopeless. For later readers and writers will have monumental names as their forebears. 'So heroically these "pioneers" will stand out like monosyllabic monoliths – Pound, Joyce, Lewis. They will acquire the strange aspects of "empire-builders"' (*BB* 254). If art is already a thing of the past, Lewis hints, at least the future will have the consolations of a *history* of art.

There is irony here, not lost on Lewis, that the empire built by the modernist artists will be an 'art-less society'. Lewis, who is hoping by writing *Blasting and Bombardiering* to 'fix for an alien posterity some of the main features of this movement', is engaged in his best satire yet, masked thoroughly within the 'memoirist' discourse. Lewis's book is for tourists, a guide for future historians to see the monuments so completely established within their own time that art could never again be produced. He predicts that 'by the end of this century the movement to which, historically, I belong will be as remote as predynastic Egyptian statuary' (*BB* 254). Lewis, by 1937, may have given up hope of ever convicting or converting his contemporaries so intent on entombing themselves. He decides instead to help them. He takes part in the embalming process, making it his 'business to preserve' even irrelevant details for 'the Ludwigs and Stracheys of a future time', including 'Joyce's little beard, and Eliot's great toe', making a mockery of these future tourist sights. But Lewis is also returning to an old theme, and remembers to take caution in historicizing. 'However,' he says, 'I may sweep on too fast and far, and to speak as if Mr. Eliot were not there, alive although no longer kicking, to write a morality next year' (*BB* 255). No one, Lewis hints, even those buried alive in history, should be written off.

This is the context for an often-quoted, though rarely understood passage from *Blasting and Bombardiering*, a context which reminds us Lewis is still a satirist, and still intent, though he takes up the role himself, on blasting historians. 'We are not "the last men of an epoch" (as Mr. Edmund Wilson and others have said): we are more than that, or we are that in a different way to what is most often asserted. *We are the first men of a Future that has not materialized.* We belong to a "great age" that has not "come off"' (*BB* 256). To be the first men of a future that does not exist is also certainly to be the last men of a very short epoch. The only thing to which these four men can cling is the year 1914. It is the beginning and the end, the shortest epoch ever proclaimed. For if every-thing before was leading its protagonists towards it, all things after that date move backwards. Lewis says of his own time, 'The rear-guard presses forward, it is true . . . advances towards 1914, for all that is "advanced" moves backwards, now, towards that impossible goal, of the pre-war dawn' (*BB* 256). The avant-garde, Lewis hints, no longer leads, but is led. Art is dominated by society, contaminated by commercialism, fin-ished. The artist has not created the *Zeitgeist*, but followed it. The contemporary artist, says Lewis, has 'not the chance of the proverbial Chinaman in the "new" age of which they were so naïf as to allow themselves to appear the clamorous harbingers' (*BB* 256). Lewis includes himself in the accusation of naïvety, for he was one of the loudest. But he is one of the first to recognize the effects of such clamour.

Lewis begins *Blasting and Bombardiering* with the statement, 'This book is about myself' (*BB* 1). He ends with the realization, 'Yet one can't epitomize *oneself.* An attempt to do so would only lead to one's appearing either too pleased with oneself or not pleased enough' (*BB* 343; Lewis's emphasis). Similarly, one cannot epitomize an age or an epoch without becoming entangled in it. If Lewis is ahistoric, this is the reason. He plays at history in *Blasting and Bombardiering* as a satirist, perhaps unsuccessfully, mocking his contemporaries and friends who continued to write their own posterities. But it is difficult to gauge Lewis's success on any level. It is true that he never sold well and is still read far less than most major modernists. But what is impossible to estimate is what modernism would have been without him. He was the lone 'member' to consistently dissent. 'Unanimity is suspect,' Lewis wrote to Augustus John in 1930 (*LWL* 195). Is it possible that a modernism with Lewis near but not at its centre encourages us to be less suspicious of those who are positioned at its heart? This is the reason it is essential not to dismiss Lewis entirely, as some do, for being 'wrong' on so many topics. Lewis was the enemy, choosing, in some cases, to *be* wrong, hoping in this way to avoid a self-destructive closure. Although the label 'modernism' was not widely in use yet, Lewis was one of the first to ask the question what can possibly come next, once this age's concept of 'the new' or 'the modern' is made historically permanent? What can succeed a 'permanent novelty'? Lewis could see only an end, a termination. The tendency of evolution led towards an 'art-less society'. For this reason, in an age when he saw few alternatives, Wyndham Lewis stepped out of fashion, out of the historically ordained modern, to play the 'enemy' against his own movement.

CHAPTER 2

Laura Riding, modernist fashion and the individual talent

'Whole is by breaking and by mending.'
Laura (Riding) Jackson, 'Autobiography of the Present'[1]

Like Wyndham Lewis, Laura Riding saw problems inherent in the very existence of an institutionalized modernist revolution, leading to an artless society. There are astonishing similarities between the kind of criticism produced by both writers between 1927 and 1934, with both of them aware the modernist project had succeeded but also intent on identifying where it had gone too far, or not far enough – sometimes in very similar terms. Still, there are differences between them as well, not the least of which was Lewis being two decades older than Riding. While there is evidence that Riding, early in her career, might have envisioned her seamless entry into the modernist ascendancy – with acclaim coming her way from poetic circles orbiting the cultural centre of T. S. Eliot in the early 1920s – she was never as near the centre of high modernism as Lewis, even in the latecomer phase of his career. And although they share a distaste for official literary history, for the group mentality, for the officially sanctioned version of change or revolution, Riding considered Lewis too much of a high modernist himself to see him as a potential ally.

Riding's opposition to the high modernist institution would stem much more from a disapproval of systems and institutions in general than Lewis's disapproval of the single system, the time-mind, instituted by his contemporaries. A year after Lewis published *Time and Western Man* (1927), Riding would devote a major critical essay in her own *Anarchism is Not Enough* to her assessment of his success. Although Lewis is considered 'right' and Oswald Spengler (and others Lewis attacks) 'wrong', Riding asserts that Lewis enters too much into the system he criticizes and is therefore complicit. Lewis opposes the fluid view of history with a spatial view; but Riding suggests, 'He thus reduces the difference between himself and Herr Spengler to a difference in taste rather than in principle.'[2] While

77

Riding supports Lewis in opposing the high modernist system, she does not support him in proposing an alternative, since Riding's main criticism of high modernism, as we shall see, is its 'classicism', its 'scientific' qualities and its 'systems' – all enemies, for Riding, of poetry. Riding goes on to claim:

> The opposition then of *intellectual* to *physical* (of Herr Spengler, say, to Mr. Lewis) or of intuition to intelligence (of John Middleton Murry, say, to T. S. Eliot) is a restatement of the more hackneyed opposition of *emotional* to *intellectual*; which in turn proves itself to be not an opposition at all but an expression of degrees of historical advancement.[3]

This represents her criticism of the other significant critics of high modernism, but also hints at the thrust of her opposition to high modernism itself. Lewis is 'right', but embraces too much the institution he fights – ultimately, an institution of 'historical advancement'. In the late 1920s Riding had found herself incapable of embracing either side of the modernist dialectic – neither tradition nor advancement, neither emotion nor intellect – because high modernism had already built its revolution upon the interplay of these opposite poles. There was only one kind of new, Riding would find, and it had been built on a view of progress as systematized, institutionalized and traditional.

Born too late for the initial phase of modernism, Riding was thirteen years old, attending school in Brooklyn, when the First World War began to unravel the London vortex. By the time her poetry was noticed by anyone at all, *The Waste Land* and *Ulysses* (both 1922) had already been proclaimed the models for the modernist poem and novel respectively. While Riding's poetry is decidedly modernist, by the late 1920s there were reputations already so settled that the high modernists themselves already seemed her predecessors. Her late arrival on the literary modernist scene had its effect on her poetic and critical project, since many of her 'contemporaries' had, in her view, already written themselves into history. Although many see Riding and her collaborator, Robert Graves, as among modernism's first historians, the authors of *A Survey of Modernist Poetry* in 1927 would have considered themselves in fact attempting to break open a history which had already been written prematurely. Finding themselves modernist latecomers, the only way forward in making whole the poetic tradition of the 1920s seemed, as Riding would write in a poem, to be through breaking and then mending.

While the words come from the poem 'Autobiography of the Present', it is Riding's prose criticism which systematically went about breaking the emerging monolith of modernism, then mending it in places. There is no doubt that Riding, along with Graves, was one of modernism's earliest commentators and critics, devoting much of her prose nonfiction of the 1920s to determining what modernist poetry was and how much of it had, in her view, gone wrong. Yet, as we shall see, much of the criticism of how poetry had gone wrong involved precisely the things the high modernist poets had done right to secure their places in the modernist canon. Opposed to everything that had made her predecessors successful, Riding had the unenviable habit of doing everything that might make a poet *un*successful. In the period where poets were busy finding a place for their poetry to belong, whether in history, tradition or a literary group, Riding was convinced that the key to modernist poetry was in 'a declaration of the independence of the poem' – that is, in not belonging anywhere (*SMP* 124).

Just as early modernists had first found their audience by labelling the existing literary establishment passé, so Riding and Graves found themselves criticizing the high modernists for becoming the new establishment. The move was in some ways premature, though, since the high modernists had gathered a reputation based on their innovation, and could not yet be dismissed as passé. As if the act of criticizing such an influential circle was not limiting enough to a young poet's chances, Riding then compounded her relative literary obscurity by criticizing some of the more useful literary institutions, such as major literary journals and anthologies, refusing, with some puzzling exceptions, the appearance of her poems in any. These tactics hurt her chances of success, but Riding's poetic career was even further devastated in the 1940s and 1950s. She summarized the reasons herself in 1974: 'Many years ago I renounced poetry. Then, for a long time afterwards, I prevented, as I could, the reproduction of my poems.'[4] After three decades of poetic silence, the printing of her poems was once again allowed, as long as a preface of Riding's renunciation of poetry was included, but the damage to her career was largely done. Any audience she ever hoped for had largely disappeared.

Riding's career-crippling moves have generated some attention, notably from Hugh Kenner in the introduction to a book-length study of her poetry, but more fully developed in articles such as K. K. Ruthven's 'How to Avoid Being Canonized'.[5] The focal point of most of these has been the effect her silence has had on her canonicity and our reading (or nonreading) of her poems. But the careful reasoning behind Riding's actions is sometimes neglected, and it seems no one has paid very serious attention to the stance she develops in her prose criticism or to the unique literary field in which she wrote, which seems to have led her to it. While Riding's poetry is clearly deserving of more attention, her consistently critical response to ascendant modernist poetry is also too easily neglected, yet is essential to understanding not only her poetry, but the position of the second-generation modernist in general and why she mistreated her chances of a real audience.

It took nearly two years of writing poetry before Riding was noticed by the Nashville group of poets including John Crowe Ransom, Donald Davidson and Allen Tate who called themselves the Fugitives. Four days after hearing she had won the Nashville Poetry Prize in 1924, she sent a message to the Fugitives announcing her arrival in Nashville the following weekend.[6] Her subsequent attempt to join the group officially, however, came to nothing, which may help account for her later hostility to literary circles and the group mentality. What made the situation painful was that the Fugitives praised her poetry, but were unwilling to accept her into their social circle. Ransom later admitted that he did not understand her visit, saying, 'We quite missed the point. She on her side did not realize that . . . we were open to literary relationships but not to personal.'[7] The problem went deeper than misunderstanding, though. One of the Fugitives' members, William Elliott, feeling out of touch with the 'Group Mind' himself, wrote to Fugitive Davidson, 'Your poetry is too *social.* It is done for approval . . . When a stranger comes among you, he is a marked man.'[8] This illustrates quite clearly the problem Riding shares with many modernist latecomers, where the established group is willing to bestow their blessings upon the new poets, but less willing to welcome them into their ranks. Whether Riding would have made a good Fugitive or not, and what effect such an inclusion might have had on any of these poets' work, is unknowable. There is not much evidence, as Louise Cowan notes, that Riding was significantly influenced by the Fugitives' poetry.[9] But there is no doubt that the effect on Riding of being the 'marked man' was profound. Her self-confidence was undermined by their rejection of her person just as it found footing on their acceptance of her work.

Yet the rejection by the Fugitives was neither total nor final. Tate was the first Fugitive Riding had met and she formed a more intimate relationship – including a romantic connection – with him than with the others in the group. When she left both Nashville and the Fugitives behind her, settling in New York to start her career afresh, Tate's role in her life continued. Even while she established new friendships with other poets, including Hart Crane and e. e. cummings, most of these acquaintances resulted from introductions arranged by Tate. Riding retained a certain gratitude towards him, since he had been the first poet and critic to give her the appreciation she considered essential for becoming a poet.[10] But the gratitude she felt for Tate, the first 'professional' poet to support her aspiration, was diminished by her criticism of his attempts to further professionalize poetry. Years later, just after Tate died, Riding would claim, 'Ambition of a respected reputation was Allen Tate's guiding star . . . There is an effect of triumph of discretion over passion of conviction.'[11] While illustrating Riding's views of Tate, this statement is perhaps a better illustration of her own poetic priorities. There is no doubt Riding possessed the passion of conviction, but often lacked the necessary discretion to find an audience for herself.

This is evident not only in her later reflections, but also in her earliest criticism. Her first published article, 'A Prophecy or a Plea' (1925), written while she was still struggling to find her relation to the Fugitives, reveals her strong convictions about what poetry was and was not. The article's plea is for a poetry set free of the conventions, traditions and rules she sees encroaching on even the more modern poetry. She suggests in response, 'The quality of beauty is rather an accidental, a peculiar flavor of the poet's own soul . . . The taste may be whatever pleases the whim of the moment. There is no eternal form, no ideal.'[12] This view is not merely an answer to Ransom's traditional view on poetic form, but also a rejoinder, it seems, to Eliot's influential essay 'Tradition and the Individual Talent' (1919). Riding does not see the modern poet extinguishing her personality in favour of the 'eternal ideal' of tradition, taking issue with Eliot's line, 'What happens is a continual surrender of himself [the poet] as he is at the moment to something which is more valuable.'[13] Riding's insistence on poetry coming from 'the whim of the moment' and from 'the poet's own soul' confronts Eliot's beliefs in 'existing monuments' and the 'extinction of personality'. Riding goes on to say, 'Even so radical a poet as T. S. Eliot becomes, as a critic, thoughtfully traditional . . . Mechanics outrun metaphysics. Do not Philistines lead the race?' In this early article can be seen the seeds of Riding's many books of criticism, her desire to free poetry of any form or system other than its dedication to 'truth' – an absolute she never defines. It also initiates a decade of struggling with Eliot's reputation.

Although Riding believed poetry to be the expression of individual personalities, there are also instances when she seems to share Eliot's theories on the exclusion of personality from poetry. For example, she and Graves suggest in *A Survey* that 'the important part of poetry is now not the personality of the poet . . . but the personality of the poem itself' (*SMP* 124). This has led certain critics to conclude that Riding and Eliot were in agreement, but certain distinctions must be made.[14] Where Eliot wanted to keep personality out of poetry, to free it of romantic sentimentality in favour of classicism, to free it of the individual in favour of tradition, Riding preferred to leave personality in the poem, but distance the existence of the poet and his or her reputation – something she considered a key element of Eliot's verse. In fact, in 1936, Riding would write, mentioning Eliot by name, of poets intent on keeping the fact of their authorship in the reader's minds, being 'more wedded to the public mind than to literature, which they officially serve'.[15] Riding was, in word if not in deed, always opposed to providing biographical or other contextual accompaniments to her poetry. In this way, her beliefs were congruent with I. A. Richards's experiments of this time, published as *Practical Criticism* in 1929.[16] Riding's stance is most evident in her 1930 poem 'As to a Frontispiece', which addresses the audience directly. The first two stanzas suggest that her readers choose for her an identity for which she will write a poem. The third stanza adds,

> But if you can't make up your mind
> What poetry should look like,
> What name to call for,
> I think I have the very thing
> If you can read without a picture
> And postpone the frontispiece till later.[17]

Riding's position throughout her writing is characterized by the notion that poetry should be a simple dialogue between poet and reader with no inhibiting interference of poetic personality, criticism, tradition or politics.

From the beginning of Riding's association with the Fugitives, she had had to deal with Eliot's influence. Not only was Tate's poetry and criticism largely governed by Eliot's work, but the other group members, if less easily influenced, spent much of their time discussing what Ransom called the 'Waste Land question'. Even Ransom, who took the most oppositional stance to Eliot's poetry, saw 'so much wisdom in his prose'.[18] There was a general feeling, put into words by Tate, but shared among the group members, that 'Eliot in England is with us'.[19] In June 1925 Davidson, reviewing Eliot's essays in *Homage to John Dryden*, announced, 'A better apologia for a great part of modern poetry, especially a character of poetry in which *The Fugitive* has been interested, could hardly be devised.'[20] These attitudes shared by the literary group which simultaneously incorporated and isolated Riding must have had their effect. Ruthven points out that the very terms by which the Fugitives were to read Riding's work were framed by Eliot's 1921 essay 'The Metaphysical Poets'.[21] It seems likely that Riding, finding herself encouraged by the Fugitives, may have felt pressure to follow Eliot's example. Even after Riding's break from the Fugitives, she would still feel Eliot's reputation haunting her for several years.

As the distance between Riding and the Fugitives grew, she looked more eagerly for support from other sources. In 1925 she still felt such want of appreciation that when a letter of praise for one of her poems came from Graves in England, she boarded a ship to see him, following him and his wife, a matter of days later, to Egypt. But if Riding, in leaving New York to join Graves, was distancing herself from the Fugitives' influence, she was coming closer to Eliot's. Just as Tate had first promoted her as being in the Eliot mould, so Graves, who actually knew Eliot, began to compare the two. Just before Riding's entry into his life, Graves had agreed to collaborate with Eliot on a projected volume of criticism, entitled *Untraditional Elements in Poetry* – a work which, had it been completed, might have shown a new side to Eliot's criticism. In the same letter in which Graves promised to get on with his share of the work, he also sent Eliot some of Riding's criticism for the *Criterion*.[22] From Cairo, Graves wrote again, having heard that Eliot was too busy to get any work done for several months, saying,

I am going on with the proposed *Untraditional Elements in Poetry*. Have you any objection to her [Riding] collaborating in this business after what you have seen of her work? She is far more in touch with the American side than I am and is anxious to get ahead with it. She suggests that at the end of the year – until which time you could promise nothing – you might come in as arbiter between our contributions. Please tell me how you feel about this. Her list of poets corresponded exactly with yours: and her critical detachment is certainly greater than mine.[23]

This proposal seems to have met with Eliot's approval, as it put him in the safer position of arbitration, a role he was finding more comfortable with his newfound cultural authority.

As Riding's influence over Graves intensified, Graves's relations with Eliot suffered. Seven months later, Graves was apologizing to Faber, and separately to Eliot, that the finished work was going for publication instead to Heinemann, since he and Riding had found too much overlap in two distinct projected collaborations, the proposed *Untraditional Elements* and the work eventually titled *A Survey of Modernist Poetry*. Graves justifies the move with flattery, telling Eliot that at least now the authors can discuss Eliot's poetry openly and objectively, without which a book on modernist poetry would be *Hamlet* without the Prince of Denmark.[24] Yet the change in contributing authors undoubtedly resulted in a volume of criticism fundamentally different from that originally proposed.

Riding and Graves's *A Survey of Modernist Poetry* begins, perhaps, as it was originally intended to continue, as a defence of modern poetry addressed to the hypothetically unappreciative ordinary reader. The opening lines discuss the common complaint against modernist poetry – its differences from traditional poetry. The purpose of the book then is to 'justify [these differences] if their effect was to bring poetry any nearer the plain reader' (*SMP* 9). The early chapters not only explore what makes modernist poetry difficult and unpopular, but begins in the third chapter a pedagogic campaign to instruct their readers in how poems should be read. The now-famous reading of Shakespeare's sonnet 129 was acknow-ledged by William Empson as a prime influence on his *Seven Types of Ambiguity* (1930), establishing Riding and Graves in many critics' minds as forerunners of the New Criticism. The pedagogic tone persists in later parts of the book.

It is impossible to detect with any certainty how far Riding and Graves were consciously trying to institute their own beliefs and establish a better readership for their own poetry, but it is at least a subconscious intent. Any criticism of poetry by poets naturally incorporates in some way a defence of the poet's own work. The sixth chapter, 'The Making of a Poem', is a pivotal one in this sense. In it, Riding's poem 'The Rugged Black of Anger', without ever being attributed to her, provides an example, they claim, of how an essentially unambiguous and clear poem might be considered obscure, and therefore dismissed by critics and plain readers alike. Although this chapter owes much to Graves's earlier volume *On English Poetry* (1922), revisiting his technique of observing a poet at work, it is Riding's own defence of her poem and earnestness in making clear what meaning lies inherent and unadulterated in a poem, regardless of style, history or poetic reputation, that shows the real purpose of *A Survey*. In this way, it returns to the theme begun in 'A Prophecy or a Plea'. Without any sense of irony, Riding is producing what we would call a 'new critical' reading of her poem, ignoring all factors of biography, fashion or literary history, focusing instead on its expression of something more 'true' – despite the 'insider' knowledge any poet would have in dealing with their own poem.

While the authors of *A Survey* position themselves as the defenders of modernist poetry, as the book progresses there are increasing instances of attacks on the modernists themselves. Although almost all the poets mentioned are producing the type of modernist poetry the authors are defending, few, if any, are mentioned in purely positive terms; those coming out best include Eliot, cummings and Edith Sitwell. What is significant in the choice of poets, however, is the criticism levelled at those already credited with modernizing poetry. Despite early modernists, especially Ezra Pound and those in his circle, having already emphasized the revolutionary attitude and the making of the new, Riding and Graves, as late modernists, were sometimes critics of the newness of the new. As their critical stance might suggest, they were suspicious of poetry written under any social, political or stylistic programme. It is notable that the foil against which Riding's poem, mentioned above, is praised is an early poem by Pound. 'The Ballad of the Goodly Fere', a poem far inferior to others Pound had produced by 1927, is criticized by Riding and Graves for its prosy style. Clearly, it is the early Pound that is being criticized, the poet who issued manifestos and propagandist rules for poetic modernism, and *A Survey* seems aimed at establishing a readership somewhere between those who solely enjoy traditional poetry and those who appreciate the new poetry simply because it is untraditional – tying Riding and Graves in some respect to Lewis's position as outlined in the previous chapter.

The first really significant claim the authors make that concerns the survey's examination of modernism as a movement comes in the fourth chapter: 'Poetry, like fashions in clothes, has to be "accepted" before the man in the street will patronize it' (*SMP* 102). The word 'fashion' is important for poets coming late to a well-established movement – especially one even now labelled 'modernist'. There is no doubt that Riding and Graves were aware of early modernism's assault on Victorian tastes by experimenting with new fashions which were considered radical. This leads Riding and Graves, a few sentences later, into their first definition of the term 'modernist', making a distinction between it and the term 'modern' – perhaps the first time such a distinction was made. '"Modern" poetry means to [the plain reader] poetry that will pass; he has a good-humoured tolerance of it because he does not have to take it seriously. "Modernist" poetry is his way of describing the contemporary poetry that perplexes him and that he is obliged to take seriously without knowing whether it is to be accepted or not' (*SMP* 102). In essence, the added suffix 'ist' indicates, in Riding and Graves's view, poetry that is not merely new (or simply modern), but which might also extend *beyond* the contemporary moment and become classic. This is an extraordinary recognition considering the date, prefiguring theoretical notions of 'the modern' as a historical marker which would be detailed much later, as 'the postmodern' came into existence.[25] Modernist poetry must be taken seriously because it may prove to endure beyond the merely modern fashion.

This definition of modernism seems similar to what Paul De Man considers to be 'the radical impulse that stands behind all genuine modernity when it is not merely a descriptive synonym for the contemporaneous or for a passing fashion'.[26] The latter category Riding and Graves label modern, as distinct from modernist, since it will inevitably pass with the introduction of a new 'mode'. And though De Man recognizes that there is an opposition between notions of modernity and history, he also concludes that modernity, despite its apparent break with the past, 'also acts as the principle that gives literature duration and historical existence'.[27] Literary duration and historical existence are key phrases when discussing Riding's later criticism, since she dismisses what she calls the fashions of poetry as distinct from those innovations which will, paradoxically, become lasting – just as Lewis had before her. As we will see, Riding and Graves go on to recognize (with some envy) certain modernist poets who had already marked themselves out for this 'historical existence'. Once a modern work achieves duration, there is little that can prevent its endurance.[28]

Modernism gets many definitions in *A Survey*, the authors counting themselves as taking part in some ways and remaining distinct from others. In the chapter under discussion, they suggest that 'modernist poetry, if it is nothing else, is an ironic criticism of false literary survivals' (*SMP* 110–11), the very task Riding and Graves set themselves in the remainder of *A Survey*. Thus the fifth chapter is titled 'Modernist Poetry and Dead Movements', separating the aforementioned more durable modernist innovations from the merely transient (the merely modern) programmes. The authors suggest, 'A dead movement is one which never had or can have a real place in the history of poets and poems' (*SMP* 115). Riding and Graves suggest the primary difference is between those poets whose peculiarities 'resulted from a concentration on the poetic process itself' and those poets 'intent on advertising poetry for its own sake rather than for the reader's', most notably by 'jazzing up its programme'

(*SMP* 114–15).[29] These groups are considered 'dead' because they pass like a temporary fashion, while 'they never had any real poetic excuse for being' (*SMP* 116). Like many late modernists, including Lewis in the previous chapter and Henry Miller in the following, Riding and Graves are quick to acknowledge certain high modernist institutions and authors as 'dead' because of the finality with which they created the literary fashions of the period.

The most notable examples Riding and Graves give are imagism and Georgianism, the former – if not as active by that time as it once had been – still very much a part of the modernist legacy and the latter being Graves's own former literary affiliation. The authors remark, 'Imagism is one of the earliest and the most typical of these twentieth-century dead movements' (*SMP* 116). It should be observed that the phrase 'twentieth-century' is used instead of modern or modernist, a choice rarely made throughout the rest of the book, placing it in a distinctly historical frame while dislodging it from its place among the enduring works of the 'modernist' period. According to Riding and Graves, though, the necessary exclusion of imagism from authentic modernist poetry is due to its foundation on a 'public manifesto'. For though imagism 'had the look of a movement of pure experimentalism and reformation in poetry,' in fact a number of things, including

> its massed organization as a literary party with a defined political programme, the war it carried on with reviewers, the annual appearance of an Imagist anthology – all this revealed it as a stunt of commercial advertisers of poetry to whom poetic results meant a popular demand for their work, not the discovery of new values in poetry with an indifference to the recognition they received. (*SMP* 116–17)

This idea that modernist poets were actively engaged in advertising and self-publicizing their own movement has characterized recent criticism, attempting to define canonical modernism in Bourdieuan terms of cultural capital. Riding and Graves, writing in 1927, recognized and rejected the marketing of brand-name poetry, believing rather that poetry should be concerned with nothing but 'truth'. The ironic fact remains that the vessel of their criticism, *A Survey*, was itself a kind of poetic programme.

But it is not only the commercial venture of imagism which the authors criticize. To Riding and Graves, imagism, like Georgianism, was too concerned with an exclusive *style* of poetry, rather than focusing on the idea. They say, 'Authentic "advanced" poetry of the present day differs from such programmes for poetry in this important respect: that it is concerned with a reorganization of the matter . . . rather than the manner of poetry' (*SMP* 117–18). The authors' criticisms of imagism recall Lewis's criticisms of Pablo Picasso as early as 1919 – that instituting a new fashion in art is not enough to ensure a work is lasting. Even worse for Riding and Graves, the imagist programme was more than self-advertising, it was a set of rules for how poetry should be written, rules which the authors of *A Survey* rejected, not because they disagreed with them but because they did not want rules to interfere with true innovation. 'They [the imagists] *believed* in free verse; and to believe in one way of writing poetry as against another is . . . to be in a position of selling one's ideas rather than of constantly submitting them to new tests. That is, they wanted to be *new* rather than to be poets' (*SMP* 117). This is an important criticism, since it distinguishes the desire to 'make it new' stylistically simply for the sake of the commerciability of innovation from the desire to revolutionize thought itself.

Riding and Graves turn from the perceived weaknesses of imagism as a movement to those of H. D. in particular, presumably building on Riding's article rejected by Eliot for the *Criterion*. Their criticism is meant to be damning:

> her work was so thin, so poor, that its emptiness seemed 'perfection', its insipidity to be concealing a 'secret', its superficiality so 'glacial' that it created a false 'classical' atmosphere. She was never able, in her temporary immortality, to reach a real climax in any of her poems . . . All that they told was a story of a feeble personal indecision; and her immortality came to an end so soon that her bluff was never called. (*SMP* 122–3)

The first thing we notice about these statements, from our twenty-first-century perspective, is their past-tense description, certainly premature in 1927 since H. D. was still alive and writing. Any efforts by Riding and Graves to push H. D. into a fading past were met by arguably her best poetry nearly two decades later. The use of the phrase 'temporary immortality' is meant ironically, of course, effectively reversing the paradox of 'modernist classic' and intimating that her reputation as a poet of lasting value was itself a passing fashion. Clearly, as historians, Riding and Graves are working too close to the period in question and, significantly, both survived long enough to see the marked revival of H. D.'s poetic reputation in the latter decades of the twentieth century.

More important, though, than that Riding and Graves were proved wrong in dismissing H. D. and imagism from literary history is their concern over which poets and what type of poetry will last. Simply by labelling certain movements 'dead', Riding and Graves hoped to reveal the emptiness of poetry written according to rules or programmatic publicity. That a poem might be lasting and true *and* publicized according to a certain programme seems not to have occurred to the authors of *A Survey*, but what matters here is that Riding and Graves felt the literary field of their day to be contaminated by the self-advertising and the 'selling one's ideas' which they witnessed in their contemporaries. To make matters worse, the commercialism and market intrusions had an influence over the creation of literary history, so that those who were successful in 'selling' their ideas on what defined good poetry according to the movement could exclude those who wrote in some wholly different style – could, in effect, make their work 'good' in a lasting context.

The unifying theme in *A Survey*, whether in catering to timid plain readers or introducing new-critical explication or condemning dead movements and poetic programmes, seems to lie in finding (or making) an audience which reads poetry as nothing more than the words on the page. Riding and Graves's objective, if nothing else, seems to be the liberation of poetry from undue difficulty and obscurity, from programmatic movements or group mentality and from tradition or history. This last issue is perhaps the most significant in terms of Riding's later criticism, and is evident throughout the book in the phrases used, such as 'authentic "advanced" poetry'. That Riding and Graves were trying to free poetry from imposed structures is often obscured, it seems, by their own occasional indulgence in forming their own structure. The very fact that *A Survey* is in many ways a historicizing work, one of the first to use the word 'modernist', at least in its title, reveals how inconsistently they managed to stay clear of fitting modern poetry into the tradition of periods and movements.

In *A Survey*, however, that this is their aim is nowhere clearer than in the chapter entitled 'Modernist Poetry and Civilization'. It begins, 'The vulgar meaning of modernism . . . is modern-ness, a keeping-up in poetry with the pace of civilization and intellectual history . . . It is deliberately adopted by individual poets and movements as a contemporary programme' (*SMP* 155). This may seem plain enough to us now, but it is a vitally significant recognition within the period itself. It leads Riding and Graves to what they consider the 'main issue', presumably the question which worried them most as critics and poets: 'may a poet write as a poet or must he write as a period?' (*SMP* 155). It is an odd question, asked by poets who were markedly modern, who had, if briefly, already belonged to small movements within the period they discussed. But there is also a certain fear of belonging evident in the phrasing, a latent criticism of period poetry and trying to keep up to date. So far as modernism is defined as a 'contemporary programme' which is trying to find its way into 'intellectual history', Riding and Graves do not want to belong.

But Riding and Graves are setting their own definitions in *A Survey* and they then proceed to suggest that modernism is not always a vulgar 'keeping up'. Their preference for modernism free of 'the movement' shows in their language. 'There is, indeed, a genuine modernism, which is not a part of a "modernist" programme but a natural personal manner and attitude in the poet to his work, and which accepts the denomination "modernist" because it prefers this to other denominations' (*SMP* 156). There is a certain admission here that it is impossible for a poet to completely avoid writing poetry which is part of a larger whole – that there must be some 'denomination', if not a programme. But it is not enough merely to avoid the programmatic, either: 'Of some contemporary poets "modernist" is used merely to describe a certain independence in them, without definitely associating them with modernism as a literary cause: though content to stay in the main stream of poetry, they make judicious splashes to show that they are aware of the date' (*SMP* 176). Among these are counted Robert Frost and Siegfried Sassoon, whose 'tactical position . . . consists in an aloof moderateness and sensibleness in all directions', and W. B. Yeats, who has 'neither the courage nor the capacity to go the whole way with modernism and yet [has] not wished to be left behind' (*SMP* 176). That Yeats, in his decades-long career, had developed a more modern style seems, to Riding and Graves, to be untrue to his 'natural personal manner', their translation for 'genuine modernism' rather than the vulgarity of showing awareness of the date.

But after these attempts at breaking open the system, the authors set about mending, as the next few pages begin again to construct what modernism should be from what it should not. Although Riding and Graves see modernist poetry as being weakened by its race to keep up with the date, they admit that 'the best poets happen to be modernists' (*SMP* 178). They go on to add that 'they can be called modernist if only because they are good, and because what is good always seems advanced'. There is a certain circularity here: modernism generates good poetry because good poetry is often modernist. The association of the value judgement 'good' alongside the time-word 'modernist' and the progressive word 'advanced' is at the same time a dissociation, the authors suggesting that good poetry is good whether it is advanced or not, and it is 'modernist' – that is, of its age – only by fitting into what has become characterized as advanced. While this is highly convoluted, things are made clearer in the following sentence: '*Modernist*, indeed, should describe a quality in poetry which has nothing to do with the date or with responding to civilization' (*SMP* 178). What qualities the term *should* describe are unspecified, mainly because the authors are against establishing their own programme, but the problem they encounter is made clear. The contemporary conception of 'modernist' poetry was too closely linked to the period and its progressive fashions, rather than the more substantial qualities an advanced poet produces – thus marginalizing even some of 'the best poets'.

Still, for Riding and Graves the adjective modernist is a 'quality', at least when not tied to a political programme or limited period. What makes modernist poetry good is that 'its modernism would lie in its independence, in its relying on none of the traditional devices of poetry-making in the past nor on any of the artificial effects to be got by using the atmosphere of contemporary life to startle or to give reality' (*SMP* 179). Thus modernism seems to be a positive characteristic of good poetry so long as what is modernist does not itself become fully consolidated or insitutionalized – ironically, exactly what *A Survey* has been credited with doing in naming the period. Inherent in this construction of what is 'good' in modernist poetry is a criticism of the established 'modernist' poets. Perhaps aware of Pound's and Eliot's frequent glances towards the calendar, the authors suggest that 'the most intelligent attitude toward history is not to take one's own date too seriously' (*SMP* 179). Seeking the independence of the poem, Riding and Graves consider their contemporaries too consumed with the past and its appropriation of the present, too aware of their place in history, which results in a contrived and uneasy poetic position. They say, 'Most of all, such [truly modernist poetry] would be characterized by a lack of strain, by an intelligent ease' (*SMP* 179). Yet the paradox remains that an 'attitude toward history' is still required, even if that attitude is to write *without* historical constraint.

At the end of the chapter, the authors begin to feel the need to justify their attack on modernism in a book intending to find new readers *for* it. But the problem for Riding and Graves is that, instead of finding readers who appreciate modernist poetry for being inspired by 'necessity, sincerity or truthfulness', they see

the danger, in fact, that the plain reader may fall in love with the up-to-dateness of this poetry. In this case, with modernist poetry seen and applauded as a part of the movement of civilization, the demands made upon it as such would become intensified. A world of plain readers hungering for up to date poetry would turn poetry into one of the gross industries. (*SMP* 188)

Riding and Graves seem to fear a public which gets a taste for the 'modernity' of modernist poetry, forcing writers into a market demanding only the most innovative verse rather than the 'best' verse. Yet it is a warning to *readers*, rather than to writers, and as such seems to suggest that modernist poets are to be watched suspiciously lest they are allowed to reduce poetry to mere commodity. If Riding and Graves had been primarily concerned with the market for up-to-date poetry, the criticism would be more properly levelled at the consumers of poetry and not the producers, whom they consider responsible for the way poetry is treated. But if the poetry industry (they might have called it the 'modernist industry') was a concern for Riding and Graves, even more worrying was the monolithic form or the homogenizing effects that certain poets had brought into that industry.

Even if Riding and Graves believed themselves capable of writing as independent poets and not as a larger period group, they saw most of their contemporaries as conforming to the agreed stylistics of the modernist age; the only variation between these poets, according to them, stemmed from a competition to become the exemplar of modernist poetry for the period. 'Once there is a tacit or written critical agreement as to the historical form proper to the poetry of any period, all the poets of fashion or "taste" vie with each other in approximating to the perfect period manner' (*SMP* 196). This leads to the creation of groups within modernism, each with their own 'group originality', a paradoxical phrase to describe those who came together in numbers for the express purpose of being unlike everyone else. The formation of groups, however, revealed even more the lack of variation, establishing a *cher maître*, what Riding and Graves call 'the Queen Bee' from whom 'the drones' take their cue. The fact that imitation was taking place was another indication of a poetic dependence on style, about which Riding and Graves say, 'if it can be easily imitated or defined as a formula it should be immediately suspect to the poets themselves' (*SMP* 205). Imitation, they say, leads to much poor poetry following the lead of that considered 'good', if only because it seems 'new'.

But imitation was more than the cause of poor poetry; it was also a threat to what they consider good poetry, since it caused a mainstream effect, excluding those who were outside it. Riding and Graves claim that the group mentality led to a certain lack of variation in modernist poetry. Specific examples are provided, showing similarities of style between Eliot, Osbert Sitwell and Tate, then between four short poems by Richard Aldington, William Carlos Williams, Pound and Wallace Stevens. Riding and Graves blame the replication they see in modernist poetry on the cohering effect and 'bigoted inefficiency' of criticism, calling for it to be 'replaced by an intelligent policy of laissez-faire; which would allow that a variety of modes may exist side by side' (*SMP* 214–15).[30] This brief reproach to modernist criticism would be expanded by Riding in later texts; here it can be seen as a passing shot at Eliot's 'The Function of Criticism' (1923), which had demanded from criticism 'the correction of taste'.[31] The call for laissez-faire criticism is significant in this context, since, as we have seen, there was no room for Riding's poetry under Eliot's pervasive influence. Poets outside the dominant tradition, style or group deserved to be left alone by contemporary critics – an ideal often fought for by modernist latecomers.

But there was a further problem caused by the coherence of many modernist writers: it led to insecurity on the part of the plain reader, who no longer trusted himself or herself to judge contemporary poets appropriately so long as literary tastes were decided according to group membership or critical affiliation. 'Better, he thinks, presumably, that ten authentic poets should be left for posterity to discover than that one charlatan should be allowed to steal into the Temple of Fame' (*SMP* 219). This leads to the suspension of recognition for truly gifted poets, who might be appreciated if only the readers were left to form their own tastes. Riding and Graves name Isaac Rosenberg as an example of a poet left out because of his nonconformity, going on to outline the various options open to contemporary poets:

For an individual poet to achieve the smallest popular reputation to-day he must, indeed, have a certain 'groupish' quality, or, to put it differently, he must suggest a style capable of being imitated; or he must be a brilliant group-member or imitator. Otherwise he is likely, as one of the consequences of the diversification of poetic activity, to be lost to the literary news-sheets of every critical colour and not even to occur as a subject of the plain reader's suspicion or of the critic's caution: to exist, in fact, only unto himself. Which is not, if the poet appreciates the privilege of privacy, so bad a fate as it sounds. Never, indeed, has it been possible for a poet to remain unknown with so little discredit and dishonour as at the present time. (*SMP* 222)

Coming from the still relatively unknown Riding and the former group-poet Graves, these are self-encouraging words for poets who exist only unto themselves. But the dilemma outlined here is that avoiding discredit and dishonour does not automatically result in credit and honour. Poets existing only unto themselves have no audience which might honour them, and only manage to avoid dishonour, presumably, for the same reason. Yet there are only two other options: to join an existing group and conform, or design some new easily imitable form of verse to attract one's own followers. This situation, as we have seen, is typical of the late modernist position, to have to choose between being ignored, or to play one of two roles in the modernist system, either as a member of the established group or as a revolutionary upstart. Riding and Graves suggest that there is more honour in being ignored, but as we have seen, this has its own influence on the formation of literary history, to the detriment of those ignored.

The conclusion to *A Survey* begins a new tack in the authors' criticism deviating for the first time, as they admit, from word-by-word collaboration. The chapter takes parts from a long essay of Riding's, another section of which had already been published in *transition* 3, and the rest of which would be published in Riding's *Contemporaries and Snobs* (1928) as 'T. E. Hulme, the New Barbarism, and Gertrude Stein'. The shift in attitude is spelled out clearly by the authors:

So far our sympathy with modernist poetry has been contemporary sympathy. We have been writing as it were from the middle of the modernist movement in order to justify it if possible against criticism . . . It is now possible to reach a position where the modernist movement itself can be looked at with historical (as opposed to contemporary) sympathy as a stage in poetry that is to pass in turn, or may have already passed. (*SMP* 258)

There is no doubt that the shift in stance from defence of modernist poetry to implicit criticism was gradually taking shape throughout *A Survey*, but here the authors are making clear their desire to step outside modernism as a period, viewing it from a point beyond its end. The desire to end modernism, as we will see, seems to be a recurring aim for modernist latecomers, and Riding and Graves here show themselves attempting to separate the contemporary from the modernist, repositioning themselves in relation by pushing that which is modernist into the past.

But Riding and Graves seem to feel compelled towards this historical categorization, making it not merely for their own benefit but in order to recognize the newly historical literary field that the high modernists themselves had established. Again, the authors' emphasis is on poetry which does not cohere to any period, suggesting, 'As the poet, if a true poet, is one by nature and not by effort, he must be seen writing as unconsciously as regards time as his ordinary reader lives. For one remembers the date only by compulsion' (*SMP* 259). This 'compulsion', which Riding and Graves take to be a characteristic of modernist poetry, they call the 'historical effect', certainly a paraphrase of Eliot's 'historical sense' in 'Tradition and the Individual Talent', which they describe as the 'relation of a poet's poetry to Poetry as a whole and to the time in which it was written' (*SMP* 259). The historical effect immediately puts poets on the defensive, finding a need to professionalize poetry and justify its existence while writing it, categorizing themselves within a period and a system.

Examples of those guilty of this categorization are not just implied, but named outright. The self-conscious compulsion to write poetry according to the period becomes in Riding and Graves's view a self-defeating practice, even if it effectively fits a poet neatly into 'the tradition':

It [self-consciousness] invents a communal poetic mind which sits over the individual poet whenever he writes; it binds him with the necessity of writing correctly in extension of the tradition, the world-tradition of poetry; and so makes poetry internally an even narrower period activity than it is forced to be by outside influences. In consequence the modernist generation is already over before its time, having counted itself out and swallowed itself up by its very efficiency – a true 'lost generation'. Already, its most 'correct' writers, such as T. S. Eliot, have become classics over the heads of the plain readers, having solved the problem of taste, or period-fashion, so strictly and accurately by themselves and having been so critically severe with themselves beforehand, that their 'acceptance' by contemporary or future plain readers has been made superfluous. Creation and critical judgment being made one act, a work has no future history with readers; it is ended when it is ended. (*SMP* 264)

This is quite probably the most significant passage in the book, and raises more than one relevant issue. The idea that writing in 'the tradition' harms poetry is one thing, but that it binds itself to such a narrow field that it cancels itself out altogether is another. Yet it sets a precedent for recent criticism, which has begun to suggest that modernism under Eliot and Pound tended to historicize itself even while it was being constructed.[32] Even their contemporaries could see how far the movement positioned itself in history, polishing its own image (for posterity) even when beginning its self-conscious career.

That Riding and Graves should note this in 1927 might tell us something of the power of Eliot. Although Pound is among the contemporaries criticized most strongly, Eliot often serves throughout *A Survey* as one of the favoured modernist poets, alongside cummings and Edith Sitwell. Yet, the criticism of Eliot is always implicit, as above, where he is named a 'correct' writer, a 'classic' poet, even 'critically severe', all terms which feel strangely hollow, carrying no sense of admiration, though perhaps of awe.

For it is his critical severity and correct form which has immediately placed his poetry among the 'monuments', and has made it an instant classic. There is an element of resentment in the description of modernist poets who 'solve the problem of taste, or period-fashion', given that Riding and Graves had earlier made clear their belief that fashion or 'style' in poetry was a problem which could not be solved except by active manipulation or simple neglect. The most central problem for the authors of *A Survey* seems to involve the narrowness of vision in modernist poetry, where a few poets manage to gain the cultural power to establish the 'period fashion' and thereby preordain their own classical status as the poets of the age.

These two 'late modernists' find themselves in the conclusion of their 'survey' criticizing the main protagonists of the movement they are naming and helping historicize, criticizing them mainly for having so successfully packaged themselves within the poetic tradition. If, as they say, the problem of taste had been solved by the acceptance of Eliot as the archetypal modernist poet, the only options for Riding and Graves in 1927 seemed to be to imitate, or to be 'lost', existing only unto themselves. Of these two, it is clear that they chose the latter, immersing themselves in exile and self-publishing, earning money (or recognition) only through Graves's more popular prose. But Riding and Graves always maintained the belief that poetry was 'good' poetry not necessarily for being 'modernist' in style but for being simply poetry written well, regardless of the period fashions or the contemporary sense of tradition.

Despite the fact that Riding's *Contemporaries and Snobs* was less well reviewed on publication than *A Survey* and plays a less significant role in our own construction of literary modernism, Graves considered it the more important work. Writing to Sassoon, he calls *A Survey* 'more courteous', but *Contemporaries* is 'the better book', one which he characterized in an earlier letter as 'a bombshell for the *Criterion, Dial, Calendar* and similar coteries'.[33] That it is a book against coteries in general is only vaguely clear, as Riding's prose suffers from the lack of Graves's steadying influence. The reviewer in the *Times Literary Supplement*, without taking much of a stand, admits to not always understanding the criticism, suggesting, 'A philosophy of time seems to be involved in the matter', though in the end he cannot make it out.[34] Arguably, *Contemporaries and Snobs* suffered a poor readership because it is, in some places, unreadable. However, despite the abstractions and breathless flights of ideas in certain passages, a structure and argument can be discerned. Indeed, there is more likelihood that the text was largely ignored because the problem it addressed has only recently been fully recognized as a complication within literary history.

The 'problem' Riding focuses on is the same one she had addressed since 1925, specifically, how poetry had become subjected to history, tradition, criticism, politics and group mentality. There are no more declarations of independence for poems, only protests against those whom she considers to be making poetry dependent on criticism. The book is a compound of three separate sections, the first then subdivided into six shorter segments, addressing criticism and snobbism. The latter two sections are 'T. E. Hulme, the New Barbarism, and Gertrude Stein', a part of which has already been discussed, and 'The Case of Monsieur Poe', which comments on Edgar Allen Poe's renewed popularity with contemporary poets and critics. It is the first part, though, that gives the book its title.

Riding returns to the discussion of poetic personality in the first chapter, entitled 'Shame of the Person'. Once more taking issue with Eliot's premise in 'Tradition and the Individual Talent', Riding says that 'professional literature develops a shame of the person, a snobbism against the personal self-reliance which is the nature of genius' (*CS* 10). This is the core of *Contemporaries and Snobs*, and several phrases in it are defined or expounded later. 'Professional' or 'official literature' is that which is 'born of a critical rather than of a literary sense; it is a social institution which the poet is hired to serve' (*CS* 15). That Riding favours poetry born of the 'literary sense', which she seems to identify with the personal in poetry, rather than the critical, is clear enough, but living in the age of Eliot's critical dominance, she is forced to lament that such poetry is 'made to apologize for itself because, being a personal attribute, it seems irregular and behind the times' (*CS* 84). Riding disagrees with Eliot that the creation of poetry needs to be closely tied to criticism, even quoting his now mostly forgotten essay of 1919, 'A Brief Treatise on the Criticism of Poetry', published alongside essays by F. S. Flint and Aldous Huxley, as *Three Critical Essays on Modern English Poetry* in *Chapbook* 9 (March 1920). Riding quotes him here: 'Every form of genuine criticism is directed toward creation. The historical or the philosophical critic of poetry is criticizing poetry in order to create a history or a philosophy; the poetic critic is criticizing poetry in order to create poetry' (*CS* 65).[35] She counters with the claim, 'The presence of excessive criticism in a time is a sign that it fears its own literature; and over-zealous critics are the agents of a compromise between poetry and society' (*CS* 16). Riding seems to predict the loss of the writer's authority at the hands of critical theory, observing the modernist critics attempting to position themselves as mediators between text and reader. She seems to suggest that the role of the critic is to provide a buffer between the two, thereby reducing the effects of literature in order to reduce the reader's fear, though, in Riding's opinion, simultaneously rendering literature subservient to criticism.[36]

Poetic snobbism, in Riding's vocabulary, is the result of a poet who is afraid to invest himself or herself fully in poetry, but makes excuses and compromises with society through criticism. Riding outlines her view that the poet, who had once been 'tribally useful', had more recently become ostracized from society, even made a joke. 'The poet who did not wish to come to blows with the *Zeitgeist* had no other alternative than to become a snob. The snob is one who defeats circumstances which are against him by not committing himself' (*CS* 107–8). That she is targeting, above anyone else, Eliot and the high modernists becomes evident when she addresses specific works. 'The most notable exponent of this non-committal epic was T. S. Eliot. His period poem fulfilled the time-sense requirements even to the point of self-extinction. It was indeed everything and nothing. It composed and decomposed' (*CS* 26). *Ulysses*, too, is labelled an 'epic of cancellation' (*CS* 35). Later in the book, she would say, 'These arrivistes, by regarding the universe as completed in effect and by covering it with a thin coat of historicity, have achieved an immediate aesthetic absolute. If the end has been reached, then every act is posthumous and has a posthumous finality' (*CS* 111). That Riding chose these two modernist monuments as targets reveals a poet who regretted that her period had been summed up and placed in history even before she had written a poem. Like many other modernist latecomers, Riding seems to suggest that there is nothing left to write after *The Waste Land* and *Ulysses*, not simply because they are such immense or successful works, but because they ultimately place historical duration and finality upon the modernist effort.[37]

Riding's choice of language in *Contemporaries and Snobs* reflects, at times, a reading of Matthew Arnold, though she never mentions him by name. The term snob, never used by Arnold, is employed by Riding in such a way as to suggest his remarks in *Culture and Anarchy* (1869) on 'our aristocratic class' which was in need of, 'for ideal perfection, a shade more *soul*'.[38] That this is the case for Riding's snobs can be seen in her language, mentioning the 'flippancy' of the snobs, and her belief that 'the snobbism of progress, disguised as literary modernism, obscures the anarchic nature of creative activity' (*CS* 90). For Arnold, it is immediately after criticizing the aristocracy for having too little soul that he labels them '*the Barbarians*', to keep them distinct from 'the Philistines proper, or middle class'.[39] If we remember that the term 'Philistines' had been in Riding's vocabulary since her first published criticism, it is no surprise that the second section of *Contemporaries* should carry the term 'the New Barbarism' in its title.

Riding's view of barbarism, however, is not quite Arnoldian, for she uses the term in a more conventional way than Arnold, as an opposite for civilization. That Eliot had labelled Stein (who was one of Riding's few literary allies) part of a barbarian future Riding is quick to point out, quoting Eliot on Stein's work: 'If this is the future, then the future is, as it very likely is, of the barbarians. But this is the future in which we ought not to be interested' (*CS* 156). Riding agrees that Stein's use of language reveals words which have no experience or history before her use of them (*CS* 188). But the snobs, too, have embraced barbarism, says Riding, in the form of Hulme's philosophies. This is the *new* barbarism, a distinction she makes without satisfactory definitions, which is a response to the demands placed on poetry to professionalize itself in the context of philosophy, religion and science. Riding summarizes the view:

Poetry cannot be left to its fate with the poet . . . The only way to give poetry formal authority is through some philosophical system like the one that Hulme roughly suggested.
    Hulme's ideas have by now been absorbed by sensitive contemporary criticism and indeed inspire, however remotely, most contemporary poetry consciously written as part of a co-ordinated period-production: 'he appears as the forerunner of a new attitude of mind, which should be the twentieth-century mind', was the *New Criterion*'s summary of his significance. (*CS* 153)

Riding's concept of the 'new barbarism' seems to be a sort of civilization itself, though attempting to compartmentalize itself and stand aloof from individual poets.

Riding herself seems mystified by the popularity of the coordinated group and tradition. She says, 'No one seems to realize that the destruction of poetry as a tradition would not destroy poetry itself' (*CS* 141–2). But, she suggests, poets have been content to ignore the fact, replacing poetry with a 'group dignity'. Calling the notion that poetry must be written coherently within a period 'fundamentally Bergsonian', she observes:

It is as if all individual consciousnesses were expected to be able at will to submerge themselves completely in a single race-consciousness and for a protracted period evolve with great intensity and at great strides, without variation, digression or error. All separate poetic faculties, that is, are supposed to merge into a single professional group-faculty of which each poet is separately possessed. The poetic production as a whole, where such an effort is made, would have great theoretical simplicity because criticism had conceived and directed it as a whole. (*CS* 145)

This passage carries more significance for Riding than a simple declaration of independence from the 'professional group-faculty' spearheaded by the high modernists. She had done that before. Specifically, it struggles with a passage in Eliot's essay 'The Function of Criticism', a passage which must have been particularly galling to someone of Riding's convictions. Eliot declares, 'Between the true artists of any time there is, I believe, an unconscious community . . . The second-rate artist, of course, cannot afford to surrender himself to any common action; for his chief task is the assertion of all the trifling differences which are his distinction.'[40] This was too much.

Riding knew from her time with Tate and the Fugitives the sway Eliot held over literary circles, but she resented the critical corral he had established into which all 'true' artists must go. That she recognized Eliot's establishment of his own place in literary history is significant; but what mattered to Riding was that she be allowed to write her poems as an individual rather than as a 'second-rate artist' – to write poetry without needing to fold herself into the flock. There is a feeling of helplessness in Riding's prose, especially when she speaks of the period's most 'correct' writers, the 'official literature' which had the sanction of those with cultural authority, progressing 'without variation, digression or error'. If variation was a synonym for error or the second rate in art, Riding saw herself already counted out as a poet.

There is hope in the essay, though, as Riding finds a positive side to the 'historical effort' encroaching on modernist poetry. It is tied to the new barbarism, now once more a positive value dissociated from Arnold's use of the term, or Hulme's coordination; the new barbarism is what comes after the complete infiltration of civilization into literature. She notes, 'It looks indeed as if the poetry of the period could be written by historical effort alone; as if poetry has become so civilised, so all-aware, that in its most advanced stage it is on the brink of a new primitive stage. It seems about to begin again as from the beginning but drawing on the experience of its tradition' (*CS* 129). There is, here, a brief acknowledgement of the value of the tradition, if only because it has proved the need for a new beginning for poetry. Riding admits the next stage has not begun, and has only been implied:

It is almost just to say that at the present moment there is no poetry but rather an embarrassing pause after an arduous and erudite stock-taking. The next stage is not clear. But it is not impossible that when the embarrassment has passed there will be a resumption of less foppish, less strained, more critically unconscious poetic methods of writing, purified, however, by the period of historical effort behind it. (*CS* 129)

This is Riding's one hope, that the high modernists' historical efforts will so perfectly polish off the period that she may begin again as a new barbarian.

Riding's second word-by-word collaboration with Graves, titled *A Pamphlet Against Anthologies* came in the same year as *Contemporaries and Snobs*. While the volume fits neatly with the critical and theoretical works they produced during this period, it is exceptional in subject matter, taking a remarkably self-conscious look at the contexts and factors affecting poetry in terms of commercialism, institutions and social emphases. The title is somewhat misleading since the authors distinguish between genuine anthologies, which fulfil a necessary function to resurrect neglected or otherwise misplaced pieces of poetry, and the false constructions produced solely with the literary market or poetic politics in mind. Although the latter more marketable types of anthologies are discussed more widely, it is worth noting, especially given Riding's choice to appear in select anthologies herself, that the anthology is not dismissed without exception. The volume which brings together 'loose poems or fragments of poems . . . that cannot be formally classified among the collected works of any known author' are necessary to complete a broader notion of literary history (*PAA* 11). The poetry that makes up these collections, labelled 'fugitive' verses, are any that cannot be fairly placed in a more authentic contextual collection of works.

Most of the chapters in the pamphlet (excluding the last one and the conclusion) take a broad view of poetry, lamenting the indignities facing individual poets – and even the general conception of poetry – caused by the market forces which lead publishers into uncritical selections of the more popular verses. Most publishers, Riding and Graves argue, want at least one book of poetry on their lists; yet publishing individual poets does not pay, so the publishing firm must find its own more marketable strategy. The ideal anthologist must 'be merely a barometer of fashion' and 'will also have to appreciate the economy of book-producing', both of which are harmful to the independent poet (*PAA* 51–2). They list examples of mutilated poems, of anthologists engaged in rewritings and miscontextualizing, of anthologists engaged in historical reconstructions and contriving strange selections for volumes claiming to include the 'Best Poems'.[41] But it is only with the last chapter, 'Anthologies and the Living Poet', that attention is turned to the authors' own contemporaries and their use of the anthology. The modernist anthology becomes their final subject and it is here that they seem most concerned with the encroachment of external factors into poetry reception.

The authors address first the problem of the self-consciousness caused by the existence of influential anthologies acting as arbiters of public taste and marketability. Living poets, they suggest, must choose either to write 'toward the anthology or away from it' (*PAA* 159). This is the first recognition that the compilation of anthologies affects not just the perception of poets but also the writing of poetry. Those who write towards the anthologies are accused of targeting the audience that an anthology affords by fulfilling the criteria which anthologists look for. Riding and Graves are not discussing weaker poets here, but those they find of value who simply cater too much to the demands of anthology readers and compilers. Edith Sitwell is criticized for accommodating her poetry towards 'the pleasure of being popularly received' (*PAA* 160–1). James Joyce is also criticized for writing his *Pomes Penyeach* (1927) in reaction to the successful appearance in anthologies of poems from his earlier *Chamber Music* (1907), whereas his 'Ballad of Joking Jesus' is a prime candidate for a 'True Anthology' because of its fugitive nature within the larger narrative of *Ulysses*. Eliot is mentioned as well, since it was *The Waste Land* which ensured his presence in many anthologies, yet they note that he is rarely represented by that poem – by his own design, as we shall see – but with earlier poems or later ones, such as 'Journey of the Magi' which, they imply, was written specifically to further his 'anthology career in earnest' (*PAA* 162).

But Riding and Graves, as might be expected, are just as interested in those who are forced to write 'away from' the anthology. To write with the anthology in mind at all causes problems for the living poet, regardless of whether the poem is directed 'toward' or 'away'. They explain: 'Anti-anthology poets often overreach themselves, inflicting self-protective distortions on their work – as parents in old Central Europe often deliberately maimed their sons to save them from compulsory military service' (*PAA* 159). The implication here is that even those who do not write 'toward the anthology' are ruined by the existence of a culture of anthologies, since they must make their poems entirely incapable of being anthologized. This anthology culture can be seen as representative, in this case, of the wider institutionalization of literature since, as we shall see in the following pages, the anthology represented the meeting point of individual writers and the broader literary context of publicity, production and the market. There is a recognition here by Riding and Graves, in common with other modernist latecomers, that a simple rejection of the institution is not enough, since even that rejection allows for the cultural power the institution has over literature. In this case, Riding and

Graves seem to suggest that anthologies will succeed in destroying poetry whether the poets play along or not, since it is the existence of the anthology game that matters rather than how it is played. The only hope is to forget the existence of anthologies, since 'the problem of remaining outside the anthology system should be to the poet no other than the problem of writing as it is best for him to write' (*PAA* 159). Yet the system is so pervasive that Riding and Graves suggest 'in the long run it is almost impossible to hold out against the anthology'.

That the greatest obstacle for poetry caused by anthologies is the intrusion of market forces is made explicit by the last few pages of the chapter. Even in the more fairly selected anthologies, those which include poets on critical evaluation rather than public appeal, the editors cannot pay contributors. Yet this poses a problem when the critical selection includes living poets with a mass appeal who demand a fee, and since their presence is vital to the success of the anthology, 'Each "name" is paid for according to the owner's awareness of its exact market-value' (*PAA* 175). If an equally worthy poet does not have a 'name', they are paid nothing to reflect the absence of a market value, and if they demand payment, Riding and Graves tell us, they are 'punished' by omission. Thus even anthologies which are not governed by popular demand are tainted by the intrusion of market forces.

Riding and Graves wait for their conclusion to produce ideas for solutions to the problems they identify in the contemporary literary field. They conceive of the need for an 'impartial committee' to govern the creation of 'a new standard *English Poets* to be published co-ordinately in England and America' – a 'Corpus' to consist of 'perhaps thirty large quartos' (*PAA* 182). The idea is to bring together everything by every poet in a single standardized work, thereby inhibiting the emphasis placed on fashionability and market value enjoyed by certain authors or, just as importantly, by certain authors' more widely anthologized works. There would be room at the back of the text for anthologists' recommendations, so that readers could still follow 'Best Poems' compilations if that interests them, but there would be no compulsion to select only the fashionable verse or verse writers. The committee's emphasis would be very much on inclusion, even incorporating those poets upon whom the committee cannot agree; and once a poet was included, his or her relative merit within the greater body would not matter, as there would be no preference of order, representation or critical comment. Riding and Graves argue, 'With the Corpus, students would be able to discard such text-book lies as "the Age of Shakespeare," "the Age of Dryden," "the Age of Wordsworth."

Poetry would show itself to be not a sequence of fashions, but of individual poets who are poets only to the extent to which they are outside the sequence of fashions' (*PAA* 184). Again, this has implications for high modernism, a period for the first time completely associated with the fashionability of up-to-date literature, and in searching for a more democratic reflection of poetry, Riding and Graves are taking a decidedly late modernist position. The upshot for poets like them, entering the period as latecomers, is that there would then be no 'Age of Eliot' or 'Pound Era' within which they either conformed or failed to conform to the period fashion.

Yet Riding and Graves are wary of applying the Corpus to their contemporaries. The Corpus would necessarily be 'removed by at least a generation from the politics of contemporary literature', and only later editions would include 'more recent [poets] who had just passed through the thirty years' purgatory qualifying them for admission' (*PAA* 188, 186). There are several reasons for this. One is the authors' fear of a contemporary Corpus providing an 'order which was qualitative rather than quantitative, a liberal order of taste' (*PAA* 188). It may seem strange that they prefer quantity to quality, but clearly, as poets writing outside of the period's fashions, they desire as wide a range of poets working in any epoch as possible. There are also financial considerations, since living poets naturally wish to be paid if their verse is sufficiently commercial, complicated by the fact that 'the value of contemporary poems varies with critical wire-pulling and first-edition speculation and unaccountable fashion' (*PAA* 190). An even more significant problem involves the committee required to make selections, one which must be 'representative of all legitimate tastes in contemporary poetry: the same economic forces that govern the publishing of poetry at the present time would also govern the definition of legitimacy'. The inescapable problem, according to Riding and Graves, is that commercial interests inevitably affect critical interests, and therefore questions of value would inevitably encroach on a contemporary list of 'legitimate' poets even when the goal of making such a list would be widespread inclusion.

During their time together Riding and Graves appeared in a number of anthologies.[42] Graves had appeared earlier in the series of *Georgian Poetry* from 1917 and Riding in the more recent *Fugitives* (1928) – anthologies which are singled out in *A Pamphlet* as being among the best of a bad breed, particularly thanks to the role of their editors in keeping free of coterie politics or commercial considerations. Yet even these early anthologies are criticized, along with the imagist anthologies, for the long-term effects they engendered – the institution of fashions and the difficulty for group poets of shaking off the label (*PAA* 192). But there are examples of Riding and Graves refusing their permission to appear in highly influential and reputation-making anthologies, as evident in Yeats's introduction to the *Oxford Book of Modern Verse*, where they are the only two poets named among those who are 'absent from this selection through circumstances beyond my control'.[43] The choice of anthologies to which these poets would contribute seems to be based on whether or not a list of criteria was met by the soliciting anthologists and their publishers. This is most obvious in Michael Roberts's *The Faber Book of Modern Verse* (1936), an anthology they considered to be 'exceptional' and, for the first time since *A Pamphlet*, worth making an exception for. Yet it was not a straightforward decision, as Janet Adam Smith, Roberts's wife at the time, makes clear.[44] Roberts received thirty-nine letters, two postcards and a telegram from Riding and Graves during the year he was preparing the anthology, most of them aimed at an investigation of Roberts's intentions for the book and suggestions as to its underlying principles, its contents and the tenor of his introduction. Smith relates how neither poet was impressed with his choice of the other poets, but recognized that any anthology of a contemporary period would be an inharmonious 'Noah's Ark catalogue'. Roberts had to reassure Riding and Graves, aiming to

overcome their fear that he was too much concerned with contemporaneousness; to convince them that he was not promoting a literary gang, that he was including politically committed poets – Day Lewis, Spender – because he thought they were good poets, not because he happened to share many of their views; that he was not tying labels around Riding's and Graves's necks, nor making them march under any flag, nor using them to promote a view of poetry they disapproved of.[45]

These fears all seem typical concerns for Riding and Graves, and to an extent of the late modernist in general. Yet Roberts was, from the start, the ideal editor to oblige them. Smith reveals that Roberts agreed to undertake the anthology (at Eliot's request) only if it 'was not to be a comprehensive anthology of the "best poems" of an age', that 'poets chosen must be given proper space to show themselves', and he 'was not going to include himself' – all types of intrusions against which Riding and Graves had argued in *A Pamphlet*.[46]

But even though Roberts succeeded in corralling Riding and Graves, Smith's description of the making of the anthology reveals that it was still beset by the very type of commercial considerations that they saw as inhibiting contemporary poetry. Eliot features largely in the history as both editor at the publishing house and central poet of the selection, showing great diplomacy in allowing Roberts free reign while at the same time evidently attempting to shape the book according to his own preferences. There is correspondence between Eliot and Roberts concerning the selections of Eliot's work, along with other poets published by Faber. Eliot is concerned on behalf of Faber that including too much of his own work and that of Herbert Read and Stephen Spender would risk giving people the 'feeling that they have got all they need of us', thereby harming the sales of Faber books. Eliot goes on to explain, 'I have always in the past refused to allow "The Waste Land" to be used either in part or whole in anthologies. To take a part mutilates it, and to take the whole means taking what I regret to say is the only one of my poems which most people feel it necessary to read.'[47] Eliot then suggests that Roberts looks for something from *Murder in the Cathedral* (1935), presumably a fragment which will encourage sales of his more recent work. Roberts answers firmly that 'a selection which omits "The Waste Land" is a misrepresentation'.[48] In his view, 'if the anthology as I see it is accepted, it is bound to have a notable opinion on public taste. It will be the standard book of this kind for ten or twelve years, and should add to the number of people who will buy your *Poems 1925–1937*.' Clearly, Roberts is an ideal anthologist, reassuring all contributors that their needs will be met, even when they seem somewhat conflicting. *The Faber Book of Modern Verse* was engineered in such a way that it appeared to reinforce the centrality of the most central poets while simultaneously accommodating those on the periphery by playing down that centrality within the book itself. Anthologies were never merely literary endeavours, but always also commercial, political or, as was recognized as early as 1920, social institutions.[49]

Roberts succeeded in including Riding and Graves primarily because he convinced them that his anthology was sufficiently removed from contemporary politics and institutional poetics. Nevertheless, they seemed to remain wary of any compilation of contemporary poets where the autonomy of poetic value was debased by intruding issues of commercial, social or institutional selection. Both poets became known for their insularity (Roberts even intended to use Graves as an example in his introduction of 'the insular tradition') and their desire to keep poetry as free of contemporary comment and distortion as possible.[50] The final paragraph of *A Pamphlet* signals this:

For the worst fate that contemporary poetry can have is to have any fate, however unarbitrary, with its contemporaries. If the popular anthology, if contemporary poetry in general were removed as a subject of journalistic reference, and the magazines devoted to such reference removed as well, there might be nothing left but a few plainly printed volumes, to be found out by those who were meant to find them out, exercising no persuasion but that of being between their two covers, from line to line and page to page, for whoever should happen to open them. (*PAA* 192)

Evidently, in the opinion of Riding and Graves some anthologies are better than others, but the best outcome for modernist poets is to be left alone by the contemporary publicists, vendors and shapers of public opinion. As evidenced throughout her career, from the earliest essay to the last, Riding's enduring ambition is to free the poet from the system, whether that system take the form of group politics, literary magazines and anthologies, critical commentary or an intruding sense of history. For these two poets, anthologies are only one more example of the influence that fashions, markets and social groups exert over poetry on the page, particularly as instituted during the high modernist period.

Many decades after Riding had given up on poetry, in the last years of her life, she was still drawn into making public statements on the subject. In a 1980 article entitled 'Literary News as Literary History', she makes one last attempt to ensure that her poetry, if it must be read at all, should not be read in the context of contemporary literary gossip. Although it takes Riding thirteen pages to reveal the real reason she is writing, it becomes clear that this is a response to a brief comment in an interview with Tate, where he comments, 'The last I heard of Laura she was picking grapefruit in Wabasso, Florida.'[51] This offhand remark leads Riding into an almost embarrassing tirade, informing the reader in some detail about the truth about her 'fruit-shipping work', summarized finally by, 'My home is not in a grapefruit grove; nor did any grove we owned, or our fruit-shipping business, fail, as this news-and-better-maker's tale has it.'[52] But while the article seems based on a petty matter, Riding success-fully couches her argument in a wider context, raising more important issues of how literary history eventually comes to be written. The chief complaint brought forward by Riding is that the 'literary-world distinc-tion between straight literary material and the varying forms of literary journalism, with literary history and literary criticism and literary news splashed about generously in indiscriminate profusion, has hardly any reality for ordinary reader-publics'.[53] Not only is there a lamentable demand for literary news, in the form of gossip, there is too rarely a distinction made between the myths built up surrounding literary matters and genuine literary production itself.

The problem becomes even greater when gossip begins to form the substance of more permanent literary histories. Riding states early in the article, 'Literary "news" is a commodity practically identical with literary "history".'[54] The fact that these two are equated is as much of a problem as that they are seen as commodities. Her central concern seems to be over the prominence of literary reputations – it makes no difference whether based on rumour or 'history', since they are the same thing – in establishing values within the literary world. She suggests that

> the identity 'literature' has lost even historically conventional reality. The literary-minded human inhabitants of this world in its contemporary existence live in it with no sense of literature-values other than those of a scale of importances, ever-fluctuating, applied to the existing course of literature as itself an ever-fluctuating production of news of itself. The dusty air of this lends to it a false appearance of ever-accreting historical significance.[55]

Riding's desperate attempts to correct perceptions of her fruit-shipping business hereby take on the more important purpose of attempting to resurrect more appropriate values for use by literary commentators. Although Riding had renounced poetry, she clearly still feels that a poem should represent itself rather than be subjected to the irrelevancies of the poet's involvement with citrus produce. A poet's reputation, Riding suggests, has taken prominence over poems themselves, and those who claim to have an interest in literature are really only interested in hearing who is 'important', who is 'eccentric' or who is doing something 'new'.

Despite writing in 1980, Riding suggests that the problem began with the introduction of modernism early in the century. Stein is taken as an illustration – probably because Riding finds a number of critics over-emphasizing, in her opinion, the connection between the two modernist women writers. Once a close friend and admirer of Stein, she suggests that her fellow expatriate American's 'reference-value' in the contemporary literary world was due more to her 'news-value', which built up around her 'eccentric personality, and [her] association in the circuits of literary and journalistically general gossip of the time with . . . the literary "new"', rather than being due to the real value of her literary works.[56] There were those aware of this at the time: Elliot Paul, a colleague of Eugene Jolas, recognized in 1926 that Riding was one of the only critics to assess Stein's literary worth directly, rather than discussing her eccentric personality or her celebrity.[57] Riding goes on to suggest, in 1980, that Stein's work is likely to deserve 'a place in the history of twentieth-century literature', but that it is difficult to establish the value of her work and what place she should take in it because her works have been 'obscured in the confusion of literary news', which is attracted by innovation in literary style and personality rather than poetry or prose alone.[58]

But this is precisely the problem. With the modernist period, innovation and newness *became* timeless qualities, so that what is 'news' goes down as what is 'history'. Riding informs us, 'The identification of literary news with literary history began to be made early in this century, in the efforts of critical commentators on its literature as "new" – the literature of a new century – to give it historical standing.'[59] Thus modernist critics were historicizing their contemporaries (even, often, themselves) through the journalistic institution. Riding concludes:

The resultant distortion of the natural sense of literature . . . has made twentieth-century chronicling of twentieth-century literature, in its regions of historical report and reference, a chaos of critical and historical irrelevancies and rashnesses of allusion, comparison, tracings of influence or work-character trend, with neglect of the actually relevant, critically and historically, embedding the chaos in a consolidated immunity against correction.[60]

There are several issues here which are key, coming from a modernist forty years after her attempted escape from the misrepresentations of the poetry world. Riding seemingly rejects the notion that the period's literary history was allowed to form according to the merits of its literature in its own time, being distorted by the contemporaneity of the authors and their 'chroniclers'. Yet it is not just a problem of literary reputation and gossip, but that of premature connections and alliances being drawn between writers with little in common on the page, or arbitrary conclusions drawn about literary influence and trends of style or thought. There is a sense of futility in the fact that the distortions of an age historicizing itself before its end results in 'a consolidated immunity against correction'. Unless one becomes a news writer oneself, there is little hope of breaking down the established notions of literary alliances, influences and historical progression. The 'plain reader' is an irrelevant entity in a literary age that packages itself complete with reputations, affiliations and literary gossip that serves as literary history. In fact, for Riding at the end of her career, there is no distinction between the plain reader and the poet except that most poets seek to maintain a distinction between them – normally by establishing their own importance to the literary field.[61]

As a late modernist, Riding found herself out of fashion with those who were focused on keeping 'up to date'. She realized early that any coherence she might hope to find with other poets would have required her to compromise her own poetic convictions in some way. That she was not prepared to do so, and suffered a certain 'existence only unto herself' for her decision, tells us almost as much about the literary values of the period as they do about her. The last lines of *A Pamphlet Against Anthologies* reflect her desire to see poetry reside only in printed lines in individual volumes, not being forced to engage with literary institutions, commercial or historical. Yet Riding never seems capable of remaining free of the modernist industry's emphasis on modes of fashion – the efforts of her contemporaries to turn innovation into a commodity, immortalized by incorporation into self-conscious constructions of literary history or tradition. There is no one danger to modernist poetry, according to Riding – it can be destroyed by the self-conscious correction of a figure like Eliot, the excessive commercialism of anthologies and their editors, or even the celebrity innovation, the newsworthiness, of a figure like Stein. But there is only one thing, seemingly, that can save it. Riding's futile attempts at isolation give us a clue, as she searched for a more simple relationship between poet and plain reader. Ultimately, she found that she could, in fact, exist only unto herself, albeit outside the canon and bereft of readership.

CHAPTER 3

The immolation of the artist:
Henry Miller and the 'hot-house geniuses'

'The transition from Ezra Pound's cantos to the bed is made as simply and naturally as a modulation from one key to another; in fact, if it were not made there would be a discord.'

Henry Miller, *Tropic of Cancer*[1]

The transition from high modernism to late modernism is one marked out, to some extent, by the institutional success of the former. Wyndham Lewis, we have seen, took part in the revolution that brought high modernism into being; yet it was the success of this 'new fashion in art' and its perceived failure to produce lasting change which sparked his decades-long critique of its shortcomings. Likewise, Laura Riding, too late for the successful institutionalization of the new, felt herself alone in lamenting the closed structure of the literary field – writing a series of works against premature literary history, group politics, and the inflation of literary celebrity gossip. Henry Miller can similarly be drawn into their company, though few critics these days seek to find his place in literary modernism. We forget that *Tropic of Cancer*, published in 1934 by an author only three years younger than T. S. Eliot, brought Miller almost immediately into the literary spotlight. For a time it appeared he would gracefully enter the modernist canon, especially when writers with influence over literary institutions – including Eliot and Ezra Pound – took favourable notice.[2] But Miller would continue to publish books for forty more years, books of uneven quality which rarely point back to his somewhat modernist beginnings but look forward to Beat writing and other postwar literary fields.

Having so far examined writers who throughout their careers have made a point of struggling against high modernism and its perceived institutional power, we now move to a different kind of modernist latecomer. This is not to say the modernist ascendancy presents no challenge for the remaining authors in this study, but that the writers seek to find opportunistic ways of working around these challenges. Nor would I like to suggest that this opportunism always pays off for these writers, as it still proves difficult to fashion a career under the shadow of 'Modernism Triumphant'. But the fact that Miller is so rarely a part of modernist literary history – despite his best works being written within its cultural sphere – reveals that it was possible for the modernist latecomer to borrow the 'modernist tradition' while developing a distinct aesthetic. The notion of inheriting a relatively unified sense of modernist tradition will be discussed in detail in the last chapter, but this chapter seeks to find a context for Miller among a wide array of high modernist authors, including Lewis, Pound, James Joyce, Marcel Proust, Gertrude Stein and the Surrealists. The complicated picture this sometimes presents serves only to reflect the difficulty facing the late modernist writer who must seek to recognize modernist innovations while attempting to move beyond them. Miller's attempt to both borrow and desecrate the high modernist position likewise led to a career with a remarkably polarized response – complete with many fans and many detractors, but little objective engagement with the texts.

It may strike one as unfair that critics of Miller, whether supporters or detractors, tend to target the man behind the books much more than the books themselves. If it is a fault, however, it is the fault of the author. Miller, as we will see, deliberately encouraged this confusing mixture of man and mythology. In creating a fictional protagonist for his novels with the name Henry Miller, the author blurred the distinction between art and life. Miller's readers may be forgiven for not knowing how much fact appears within his fictions, and even the biographers seem incapable of determining how much fiction infiltrates the 'facts' of his biography. These several incarnations of Henry Miller are certainly all related, and it is not the purpose of this chapter to extract biographical truth from the myth built up around the man. Yet the nature of that myth and the career that spawned it – involving paradoxical and simultaneous desires to preserve and destroy the elevated position of the artist – together illuminate the most crucial twist in the breakdown of high modernism.

This contradictory emphasis on creation and negation, on individual freedom and determinism (curiously enough, Miller claims for himself an equal debt to Oswald Spengler's *The Decline of the West* (1926–8) and Lewis's *Time and Western Man* (1927), though the latter was written in opposition to the former) is comprehensible only once we restore Miller to a late modernist context in relation to the successful high modernist revolution. By the 1930s, books were beginning to appear which looked back with nostalgia to the two previous decades of high modernist art; volumes like Malcolm Cowley's *Exile's Return* (1934) and Robert McAlmon's *Being Geniuses Together* (1937), tended to cap off the period of modernist ascendancy by romanticizing and historicizing the artists involved. This was itself a signal of the shift from high modernism to late modernism, as Aaron Jaffe has pointed out. After Jamesian artist-heroes gave way to the Joycean artist as character, late modernists increasingly found the subject matter enticing but complicated by the precedent.[3] Increasingly, late modernists had to find new language to describe the high-art world. As McAlmon himself would write, "While it had not been passionately the fashion to be an artist or a genius in 1920, certainly it was by 1929. Both on the Continent and in America, every second college boy, radical, or aspiring writer wished to start a magazine, and some of them did."[4] If high modernists had instituted the fashion of 'being a genius', it was the late modernists who refined it, extended it and subverted it. Even Stein – whose career, despite beginning during the initial modernist revolution, reveals a number of reference points to Miller's own – both pushes the cult of genius in the 1930s and simultaneously devalues it, most clearly by writing *Everybody's Autobiography* (1937).[5] Miller would take a similar approach, unlike Riding, who had denounced Stein's flirtation with celebrity and eccentric personality.

It is into this era of late modernist memoir-writing – a reinjection of personality, with discussions of biography, autobiography and celebrity genius – that Miller's somewhat belated career is eventually launched. In fact, Miller's literary position is largely defined by his attempt to write his own memoir-style history of a literary career not *in response* to that career or active involvement in literary circles, but by making a memoir out of the first book he would publish. Miller's memoirs were not retrospective, simultaneously trying to write the history of a life he was living, always looking forward first in order to look back from a posthumous vantage. Much of Miller's career, as we will see, was focused upon, on one hand, the death of literature as it passed into literary history and, on the other, more personally, his own eventual death, leaving him consumed with the idea of prepackaging his biography in order that the Henry Miller myth might survive. As he wrote in an early draft of *Tropic of Capricorn*, 'Here is where I create the legend where I must bury myself.'[6] Miller is perhaps unique in his eagerness to write his own epitaph at the start of his career.

With an author so firmly in opposition to institutional literature as Miller, the question must be posed why he was so intent on transforming his personality into a series of books and building a place for himself in a future literary history. The answer must involve Miller's cultural context, entering relatively late in life a field of literary activity already, to some extent, concluded. Proust and Joyce had seemingly ended the possibilities of the literary novel, while Eliot and Pound had not only invented modern poetry, but also issued a complete critical programme to codify its place within literary tradition. With the high modernist emphasis on form becoming the dominant aesthetic, literature in general seemed in danger of losing relevance to life and wasting away. Miller, by furnishing his books with his own personality, hoped to breathe new life into what he considered a fading art. 'Our literature,' he wrote in 'Un Etre Etoilique' (1937), a piece as much about himself as Anaïs Nin, 'unable any longer to express itself through dying forms, has become almost exclusively biographical.'[7] Miller recognized many of the same problems that Riding had described within the modernist literary field, where the cult of the author began to eclipse writing itself. But Miller reacted very differently. He was preparing his life, even from the beginning of his career, for his biographers, as we shall see, embarking on one of the most highly self-conscious literary careers of the twentieth century. The man who prophesied the end of all literature hoped, by building his novel around an invented persona bearing his own name, to write one 'last book', and thereby position his name within an enduring, if ultimately degraded, literary history.

The beginning of Miller's career fits the pattern established by Lawrence Lipking, who describes the beginning of a poet's vocation as both an original act of self-making and an act of inheritance of the very idea of a poet.[8] While Miller is responsible for the myth of the author he built around himself, he owes his conception of the 'author' to his heroes and his modernist contemporaries. The first evidence of his recognition of a modern movement in the literary arts comes as early as March 1922, before he ever genuinely tried to write himself. He comments on this to his friend, Emil Schnellock: 'Say, many thanks to you for introducing me to Ezra Loomis Pound. I have him and the whole tribe of modern poetasters on my desk . . . And what's more, I can understand it, that's the mystery! Sounds like stuff I say to myself all day long. Maybe, Creeping Jesus, I'm another Lindsay or Masters or Bodenheim, eh?' (*LE* 4). This is Miller's first recognition that there is a 'tribe', and the first hint of interest that he might join it. Miller's devotion to pursuing a literary future would grow steadily stronger, though he always took his cues from the past.

Although Miller became aware of Pound in 1922 and other high modernists a short time after, he was at that point a long way from joining their ranks. In fact, his hope that one day he might become 'another Lindsay or Masters' reveals that his career plans involved little more than vague ambition to be considered an author. Still new to modern literature, he had learnt nothing yet about the relative programmes and critical groups having formed themselves around Pound and the other high modernists. He seems, at this stage, more interested in *posing* as a writer, treating it as a hobby while working odd jobs to support his first wife and their child. Miller's casual approach to literature can again be witnessed in another letter to Emil in which he writes. 'In other words I am free as a lark all day and night till any hour. Let's celebrate and write literature and draw funny pictures' (*LE* 11). This attitude towards 'writing literature', resulting less in an accomplished work of art sanctioned by readers and institutions than in the instant creation of a joke for a friend, was the precursor to his later antiliterature campaign and his devotion to writing 'unrehearsed' texts. With this unceremonious attitude, 'literature' was something to be played at like a game, not to be taken seriously as the modernists might, just as the funny pictures casually drawn by his friend might count as 'art'.

A paradox began to emerge in Miller's approach to writing which he would struggle with for the rest of his career. A gap became apparent between his ambition to become an author, a direct descendant of a long tradition of literary heroes as viewed from a historical perspective, and the obvious enjoyment he found in the present, in writing light-hearted and unfinished pieces for his friends. Whether this distinction is entirely artificial or not, it was enough of an issue for Miller to make him self-conscious every time he sat behind his specially purchased author's desk to write 'literature'. Even Pound and 'the whole tribe of modern poetasters', who can be identified as a group already published and institutionalized by the public library, were producing something completely different from the type of sketches he could churn out in a single night for an audience of one. Miller, for all his ambition, felt unqualified when faced with the task of becoming the next Joyce or Proust. How could he, 'just a Brooklyn boy', write a classic? Such a production required a specific literary style, a better education than he had, or the backing of a group or literary institution. A distinct division arose in Miller's mind between what he could write off the top of his head and what required a special literary refinement or style. The former was writing; the latter was Literature.

Such a division is perhaps best theorized by Roland Barthes in 'Authors and Writers', where he distinguishes between those who 'want *to write something*', labelled the authors, and on the other hand the writers, who simply '*write* (intransitively)'.[9] Barthes reveals the social pressure placed on the author which the writer is able to ignore:

> The author is the man who *labors*, who works up his utterance (even if he is inspired) and functionally absorbs himself in this labor, this work . . . Thus is born the myth of fine writing: the author is a salaried priest, he is the half-respectable, half-ridiculous guardian of the sanctuary of the great French language, a kind of national treasure, a sacred merchandise, produced, taught, consumed, and exported in the context of a sublime economy of values.[10]

Barthes makes clear that no one is entirely either a writer or an author, but some form of combination. Yet with Miller, the writer seems so aware of the author's preeminence in some future posterity that he becomes inhibited and self-conscious. The application of Barthes's distinction between author and writer in the context of Miller's career bears resemblance to Jacques Derrida's distinction between what he calls 'good and bad writing: the good and natural is the divine inscription in the heart and the soul; the perverse and artful is technique, exiled in the exteriority of the body'.[11] As we will see, the principal dichotomy for Miller's career ambitions lies between this first type of writing (Miller called it writing from the 'solar plexus') and the 'artful' technique of the author, as exemplified perhaps most thoroughly for Miller in the work of Joyce, Proust and other high modernists. Miller's desire to be considered an author would persistently conflict with his inability to write that type of sacred, highly laboured or produced literature that Barthes describes as the output of the author. Yet at the same time, his focus on free and unlaboured writing, on the other hand, was always inhibited by his acute awareness of the elevated position held by the artist figure in contemporary society.

Early in his career, Miller was too inhibited by literary history and institutions to write publishable work. But it is significant that, even after Miller had found some success with *Tropic of Cancer*, his favourite genre remained the letter to a friend, since presumably a private correspondence could escape the pressures of form, style and publication. Erica Jong notes that Miller's letters, especially those to his friend Emil, are highly significant because the author can be entirely himself within them.[12] But it is rarely pointed out that even Miller's letters show how deeply self-consciousness infiltrated his writing. Letters addressed to his closest friends often carry announcements of his wider audience, like 'Copies to Ross, Stanley and posterity'. The idea that Miller's letters are unselfconscious – or in the words of the editor of Miller's letters to Nin, written 'without the filter of art, the conscious ordering and rearranging of incident' – is simply not true.[13] For Miller, the letter *is* the art, and there is no going backstage, as it were, to the less polished, more unconscious self. Despite writing hastily and often spontaneously, Miller could never fully forget the author figure he was creating for a future literary posterity. For example, he announces in a letter to Emil that 'this is a sentimental outburst in an introspective vein. Perhaps a sly leaf inserted into my future memoirs' (*LE* 12). Miller's work in general could be said to incorporate continually the conflicting qualities of the spontaneous outburst and the studied memoir. Almost everything Miller produced was for the benefit of some future biographer – perhaps himself – to look back at his life from some historical vantage.

But Miller, beginning his career in the 1920s, could not avoid being conscious of the type of 'art' which had made giants of such contemporaries as Joyce, Proust, Eliot and Pound. Watching secondary criticism build up around *Ulysses* (1922) a mere ten years after it appeared as a book, for example, Miller was already speaking of publication of his letters before he had anything else to publish. A year before *Tropic of Cancer* properly launched his career, he writes to Emil:

Very little of me will ever be squeezed between covers – in my lifetime. I know that. I'm reconciled to it. But the minute I'm found dead – it will be the old story of art dealers. 'Have you got one of Miller's letters around the house – any little scrap will do?' I know that before I kick off, and I'm enjoying it in advance. I may not have a fine funeral, but I'm one guy who's enjoying his own funeral. (*LE* 107)

Such self-conscious confidence reveals how back-to-front Miller conducted his literary career. Posterity came first, complete with collectors and posthumous celebrity, while the 'art' to make him a writer worthy of collecting seems only peripheral. No doubt this is partly due to Miller's personality, but we can also see it as characteristic of the late-1920s literary scene in general – a scene whose participants were fixed on notions of genius, as McAlmon described. While it had long been recognized that writers could gain celebrity within their own lifetimes, as Charles Dickens and Alfred, Lord Tennyson had shown in the previous century, it was not until the high modernist era that the academy and the cultural market had caught up to such an extent that they existed simultaneously to the authors they dealt in. The immediacy of cultural longevity meant that Miller, before he had published a single text, could speak of enjoying his posthumous fame in advance. He was, in essence, writing letters – his favoured art – specifically for the collectors and historians he was sure would one day appear.

But while Miller dreamed of his funeral and the acclaim afforded the author he aimed to become, it was his second wife June who first taught him how to play the role within a present context. She moved Miller from Brooklyn to the bohemian art world of 1920s Greenwich Village, where everyone, whether productive or not, might call themselves artists. June's revulsion towards what she termed 'the bourgeois' in Miller's personality first led him from being a working-class dreamer to fulfilling the stereo-type of the starving artist. It was June who forbade Miller to hold a regular job, supporting him by trading on her overt sexuality – 'platonic whoring' Miller called it – so that he could write full time.[14] It was not precisely what he wanted. Besides not approving of June's methods of supporting him, his working-class ethic made him unhappy to be unemployed. Still, the fact he was unemployed and lived in a shabby apartment made for the type of romance one could read about in the biographies of artists. Miller would exaggerate these conditions later when looking back upon this phase of his life. As Robert Ferguson points out, the romantic notions of himself as a starving writer suffering for his art actually had no relation to his failure to find success as a writer early in his life.[15] Yet such fantasies have everything to do with the making of an author, if not a writer. Miller had always had the impetus to write, and was by definition 'a writer' from an early age; but June's knowledge of the links between art, commerce and sexuality brought a new sense of artistic sensibility to Miller's career and helped turn him into the thing he had always thought he wanted to be: an author.

June knew that bohemian life in Greenwich Village during the second and third decades of the twentieth century had become a marketable commodity. The artists of the area had begun attracting tourists in the early 1910s, and, as a result, a new breed of agents and 'artists' emerged to capitalize on this. As Steven Watson illustrates, this part of New York in 1917 saw its inhabitants respond to increased interest from outside the Village, finding ways to parody their own pretensions.[16] Watson goes on to provide examples, like Guido Bruno, who advertised and charged admission to his own artist's garret to up-towners, rooms filled with easels and free-verse-reciting poets.[17] Similarly, June quickly took charge of marketing Henry Miller, the starving writer. He would sketch out short pieces, roughly a page long, which were sold, door to door or café table to table, as 'mezzotints' – a type of impressionistic piece, some of which bordered on Surrealist automatic writing, though he was not, on his own admission, familiar with the movement at this point. June soon learnt that they commanded better prices if sold under her name. In this way, Miller became a mere literature factory, producing 'works of art' which were packaged, marketed and sold by his wife under her own brand label.

It was only when June left for Paris that Miller saw how his wife had nurtured his ambition for authorship but intimidated the unstudied writer in Miller, to the point where he could not sit at his typewriter without thinking first of art, reputation and literary history. While Miller was not quite ready to shed the self-conscious literary pretensions which burdened his writing, he was beginning to redefine his goals, focusing again on being a writer rather than the producer of commodities behind the contrived 'author' his wife had invented. Yet Miller never abandoned the tactics of turning the myth of the artist-author to his advantage as a writer. All his works from this point become distinctly autobiographical, finely focused on the personality of Henry Miller, even when that persona was an invented one. Perhaps most significantly, June's calculated shaping of his personality into the mould of a marketable genius left him with a permanent distaste for the concept of literature. Miller would go on writing for decades, growing remarkably prolific after finally being pub-lished in 1934, but his breakthrough novel opens with these sentiments: 'A year ago, six months ago, I thought that I was an artist. I no longer think about it, I *am*. Everything that was literature has fallen from me. There are no more books to be written, thank God.'[18] Yet he continued his pursuit of authoring further books, and inventing his author-self. Some-how Miller formed a long literary career out of insistently rewriting – as *Tropic of Cancer* was originally entitled – *The Last Book*.

It was his experience of writing material for June to sell that led Miller to realize just how contrived his writing style was. In 1928 he found himself, while writing his first novel, *Crazy Cock*, conforming to a preconceived idea of literature, planning extensively with wall charts and comprehensive notes, spending large amounts of time creating what he considered to be a specifically literary style – an approach perhaps partly inspired by Joyce's construction of *Ulysses*, famously (even at the time) written according to an elaborate schema. *Tropic of Cancer* was designed to subvert this notion of carefully constructed and systematized literature. Writing to Emil while finishing *Crazy Cock*, Miller says:

This book, for example, has been so carefully and painstakingly plotted out, the notes are so copious and exhaustive, that I feel cramped, walled in, suffocated.

When I get thru I want to explode. I will explode in the Paris book. The hell with form, style, expression and all those pseudo-paramount things which beguile the critics. I want to get myself across this time – and direct as a knife thrust. (*LE* 71)

Although Miller had not yet abandoned his attempts to construct a deliberate author-myth around himself, he was finished with failed attempts to produce the work of 'the author' in Barthes's sense of the word. There was a difference between the presentation of himself as an artist in his books and the man who wanted simply to write: 'a very plain, unvarnished soul, not learned, not wise, no great shakes in any way you look at me – particularly "*comme artist*." What I must do, before blowing out my brains, is to write a few simple confessions in plain Milleresque language' (*LE* 64–5). *Tropic of Cancer* was the result – what he called 'the Paris book: first person, uncensored, formless – fuck everything!' (*LE* 80).

Writing uncensored, first-person prose without a prescribed form was, in Miller's view, the best way to avoid an official manner of writing he could only condemn as 'literature'. It was Michael Fraenkel, a Paris acquaintance, who helped Miller realize that this was the adversary he had been battling in each previous attempt to write. As Mary Dearborn points out, it was Fraenkel who not only recognized that Miller's talents lay in unsystematized writing, but gave him the principle behind his pursuit of it: his hatred of 'literature'.[19] Miller's new form of autobiography, not only first person but also using his own name in the text, implied that any literary device or style would only make the portrait less true. Spontaneity would take over where the critical faculties let him down, since Miller himself admitted, 'As a critic I'm lousy' (*LE* 74). With this realization, he knew his only chance of producing something worth notice was to free the writer from the critic and author, and hope that instinct and candour alone would merit an audience. In order to remain true to his vision, he decided the next novel would not seek to revise or polish either the prose, the subject matter or the tone.[20] While this may have been the original plan, several years of delays in publication in fact forced Miller to revise *Tropic of Cancer* extensively.

Yet there is little doubt that Miller's decision to emphasize the spontaneity of his writing – a composition method based on his admiration of Surrealist 'automatic writing' – was a result of his antagonism towards what he called 'literature'. Miller's career would hinge upon his uncertain position between being a writer or an author; the Surrealists would be as important a correlation for him in this as the high modernists like Joyce or Proust. Which is not to say Miller wished to belong to either group.

In 'An Open Letter to Surrealists Everywhere', he would clearly announce that he thought the movement's distinguishing characteristics too universal, in geography and history, for the kind of group character they sought to promote.[21] But Miller would appreciate the instinctual, unconscious impulse, a type of writing 'from the heart' which was in direct opposition to the more formulated style he had tried to adopt from the high modernists. Especially writing autobiography, Miller was encouraged to escape from the realism that had made *Crazy Cock* a failure, since, as the Surrealists had discovered before him, through exploring the effect of imagination, desire and the unconscious on reality, a more powerful image of life could be derived.[22] Miller's new career would be focused more firmly on this type of impulsive writing, finding creative outlet through that which was filtered through his unconscious as much as what was consciously and deliberately built into a finished work of literature.

If Miller was against literature, though, what – and why – was he writing? He announces early in *Tropic of Cancer*, 'This is not a book. This is libel, slander, defamation of character. This is not a book in the ordinary sense of the word. No, this is a prolonged insult, a gob of spit in the face of Art, a kick in the pants to God, Man, Destiny, Time, Love, Beauty.'[23] In other words, it is unrehearsed rhetoric, intent on provoking its readers by attacking anything they might hold sacred, whether religion, chastity or (capital-A) Art. Miller's narrator provides commentary in a philosophical tone in between anecdotes of his friends and acquaintances. There are many allusions to other literary works, including modernist texts by Eliot, Joyce and Pound, but on the whole, Miller's main focus is 'to get off the gold standard of literature'.[24] The novel itself does not share modernist interests in form or style, since 'I wonder if style, style in the grand manner, is done for'.[25] This is *The Last Book*, as Miller calls it within the text, and it will 'exhaust the age'.[26]

Tropic of Cancer was not actually given the title *The Last Book*, perhaps because Miller wanted to write another one, or perhaps because he was coming to the view that other modernist texts had already exhausted the age before him. His opinion of *Ulysses*, for example, was changing. Where Joyce had once been one of Miller's models as author, *Ulysses*, a novel based heavily on detailed attention to form and style, was increasingly seen by Miller to be a dead end. Along with Proust, Joyce was enough of an influence that in Miller's book on D. H. Lawrence (written at the suggestion of Miller's prospective publisher in order to show he was a 'serious' writer and not a mere pornographer), Miller felt the need to exorcize these literary demons. As he wrote to Nin as early as October 1932, 'I want to exhaust my ideas on these two men [Lawrence and Joyce], and have done with them for all time.'[27] Although Miller's *World of Lawrence* was never published, expanding over a number of years into an unmanageable pile of notes, a key section (what Miller called a 'coda' to the work as a whole) was published separately as 'The Universe of Death' in *Max and the White Phagocytes* (1938). It was here that Miller tried to come to terms with the supremacy of Joyce and Proust in the world of modernist literary fiction as 'the two literary figures who seem to me most representative of our time'.[28]

If Miller had needed Fraenkel to provide the principle behind which he could denounce the type of literature he was no good at writing, Miller turned to another writer to provide his principles for attacking Proust and Joyce. 'The Universe of Death', though featuring only one direct quotation from Lewis's *Time and Western Man*, is riddled with paraphrases and allusions. Miller admired Lewis, as he told Lawrence Durrell in 1937.[29] Lewis's attack on Joyce and Proust is echoed throughout Miller's article, suggesting that they 'elected to identify themselves with the historical movement', and merely '*reflect* the times'.[30] Joyce is criticized for his character 'types' and labelled an 'encyclopedic ape'.[31] Proust is considered to be self-embalmed in 'living death, for the purposes of dissection'.[32] However, though Miller owes a debt to Lewis for his terms of abuse, the main emphasis of 'The Universe of Death' is not precisely that of Lewis's 'The Revolutionary Simpleton'. Where Lewis focused on the sinister 'time-cult' and their attack on space, lamenting the Bergsonian influence on 'interior' art, Miller is more concerned with the absence of 'life' or vitality in these two writers. 'Proust had to die in order even to commence his great work', Miller writes; 'Joyce, though still alive, seems even more dead than Proust ever was.'[33] Miller appears to favour Lawrence's vitalist approach to Joyce's obsession with form and stylistics or Proust's insistent backward gaze.

Miller is perhaps typically avant-garde in his preference for a practical application of art to life over an art-for-art's-sake aesthetic. But while sharing with the Surrealists and other avant-garde groups the view that art was an expression of, rather than a distancing from, personality and spontaneity, Miller's chosen approach to the elevated position of the artist remains closer to that of the high modernists. For this reason, one of Miller's earliest critics, George Orwell, placed Miller in the company of Eliot and Pound, considering the *Tropic* books as belonging to the 1920s rather than the 1930s. This is primarily because Miller is more concerned with the artist-hero than the politics of the wider world. It is owing to this insulation (what Peter Bürger calls the autonomy of the modernists) from politics that Miller is branded 'inside the whale' – alone and unaware of the greater circles in which he moves.[34] Miller himself admitted his insularity, providing Orwell with the whale image some years earlier in 'Un Etre Etoilique'. Miller was proud to stay clear of movements, declaring to Emil in 1934, 'I feel free of all cults, isms, movements, countries, latitudes, and philosophies. I am alone, a man, an artist, by Jesus, and I want nothing to do with these sap-heads – Putnam, Gillespie, Bald, etc. *Cripes!* Nor with Pound or Eliot or Joyce' (*LE* 152). Writing on 1920s subjects in the 1930s, Miller clearly found the need to manoeuvre between the first group (all acquaintances of his in Paris) and the latter three, the high art heavyweights (then and now) of 1910s and 1920s modernism.

Miller's emphasis on a personal art-life praxis stems, perhaps, from this awkward position, following on the heels of the ascendant modernists. While Miller occasionally appears to take an anti-art position, his continued devotion to art, believing it was produced merely through being alive, was simply distinct from his contemporaries. Although a novelist, Miller considered his books a mere by-product of the art of living. In a similar way, he considered all the artefacts produced by his life to be works of art, establishing a type of scrapbook method, holding up 'ready-mades' – train tickets and menus – alongside his novels as works of art. Even while Miller was writing the novel which would make his reputation, he was storing away scraps of paper he considered almost equally important. Several letters from 1933 written to Emil reveal that Miller was worried about a 'great mass of data, invaluable to posterity, which [June] in one of her morphine moods may throw on the fireplace' (*LE* 112). He had already sent Emil a collection of 'souvenirs of Paris' for safe-keeping, hoping his friend might want to 'make books of them for yourself' (*LE* 111). Not only, it seems, was Miller himself capable of transmuting his daily litter into art, but he had ambitions that his life would spread to become the basis for books by several different authors. Miller had a strange attachment to these souvenirs, viewing them not only as the product of his artistic living but also as vital elements of being. Describing his archives of letters and notes, he wrote to Emil, 'I would give the world to recover these things – half my life hangs there in those papers' (*LE* 119).[35] Although Miller would continually disparage 'literature' as falling short of real life, he still clearly placed priority on those aspects of his life which had been documented and made tangible.

But Miller's artistic stance is problematic, owing to, on the one hand, his uncritical collection of every ticket stub and note scribbled on a napkin, which seems to place him in the Surrealist camp of found art, and on the other, his insistent vision of his career within a high modernist paradigm of literary tradition – a future literary history which would feature his works within the tradition. This paradoxical stance leads many critics to take Miller less seriously. For example, he is often criticized for his unselective approach towards publishing, an approach which produced a multitude of texts, many of which found their way into print only because a cult had built up around his personality.[36] But rather than dismissing Miller as a writer incapable of extracting the perfectly polished text out of a steady stream of drivel, it is important to recognize that Miller was taking a stance against established notions of the literary text. Even if this position played to Miller's personal strengths, it must be recognized that such a stance stemmed from conviction rather than mere carelessness.

Probably Miller's most explicit statement of his aesthetic is found in a book he did not author. *Art and Outrage* (1959) is subtitled *A Correspondence about Henry Miller,* a correspondence between two of Miller's closest literary allies, Lawrence Durrell and Alfred Perlés. Despite the formal and self-conscious tone of the letters, the exchange seems an innocent discussion of Miller's legend, his intentions and his unliterary approach. But Miller intrudes, incapable it seems of ever allowing anyone to form an opinion of him without his help, and two letters, one to each of his friends, are published towards the end of the volume. It is here that Miller himself, provoked by his friends, takes up the issue of his intentions, which prompts Durrell to label these two letters 'the Preface to his collected works no less'.[37] Miller admits, in his letter to Durrell, 'Where the writing is concerned, I did nothing consciously. I followed my nose. I blew with every wind. I accepted every influence, good or bad. My intention, was there – as I said, merely to write. Or, *to be a writer,* more justly.'[38] This distinction is key, as it reveals the contradictory nature of Miller's writings. Writing seemingly according to instinct or whim, yet dedicated less to automatic expression than to the goal of *being* a writer, Miller portrays himself as simultaneously instinctive or impetuous while fully self-conscious.

In his letter to Perlés, Miller explicitly outlines his view 'that the highest art is the art of living, that writing is but a prelude or form of initiation for this purpose'.[39] This is the conviction which drives Miller to publish every fragment of his writings – even encouraging the publication of other people's letters and stories when they are centred on him. Miller views writing as a means to an end – 'the art of living' – rather than an end product in itself, and therefore attempts to subvert the modernist aesthetic of the *mot juste* and the cultivated masterpiece. He prefers compiling scrapbooks of scribbled lines and indiscriminate recollections – preserving even what is crude or uncultured, even mistakes and improprieties – to the carefully prepared work of literary art. Continuing on this theme, Miller writes, 'But even from a limited, academic, hide-bound point of view, the traditional art view, how silly it is for critics to be disturbed about slag, excrescences, drift and scoriae. How little they understand the role of the so-called non-essential, the commonplace, the ugly, the unartistic.'[40] This reaction to the 'traditional art view' links Miller even closer to the Surrealists, perhaps; yet he refuses to emphasize his similarities with other artists, preferring to define himself in opposition to the high modernist aesthetic. This is not the only instance, either, where Miller reveals his distaste for the carefully pruned and cultivated work of art. Decades earlier, before Miller could even be called a writer, he had written to Emil about Henry James's aim of weeding out nearly a third of his first draft of a novel. Miller comments, 'What precious offal, what divine excrescences must have been contained in these unique Jamesian "droppings"' (*LE* 6). This attitude reveals Miller's difficult relation to his modernist forebears, following their lead in focusing on the commonplace and, sometimes, the ugly, but refusing to use his role as writer to transmute the ugly and inartistic into a polished work of art. For Miller, unlike Joyce and Proust, the work of art is not intended to reflect life, transforming the banal into the epic and mythic, but to invest itself in life. For Miller, art exists only to augment the personality and convert myth into a new reality.

Miller recognized, though, that his belief in the importance of artistic refuse and his distrust of the refined and edited work flew in the face of highly cherished contemporary notions about art. Having spent so much of his career cashing in on the popular conception of the bohemian artist in 1920s and 1930s narratives, he never forgot that his best asset was personality, and that his dedication to art, superficial at the best of times, was only playing up to an institution which allowed him to express that personality. After discussing in *Art and Outrage* the superiority of life over any other form of art, Miller explains:

The fear which writers or artists in general have when confronted with such an issue is that art would disappear. Dear Art! As if anything could destroy it. How do you destroy the cornerstone of life? Why worry? True, we may eliminate the hot-house geniuses – but on the other hand we might, once again, endow everything we see, do, touch or think about with art. We may all become, or re-become artists! There is a kind of immolation (of the artist) I believe in.[41]

This desire to sacrifice the role the artist commands by endowing each person with their own art form – that of simply being alive – is perhaps typically late modernist, though certainly stretched to its furthest extreme. In labelling those artists he would like to eliminate 'the hot-house geniuses', it is clear he is taking a deliberate stand against any writer who makes use of the contrived, heightened atmosphere of institutional Art to promote their own genius. Miller's democratic view that art is the product of any living being reveals a deeper antagonism towards those who favoured aesthetic authority, raising the artist above life, and rejecting personality in favour of a historical fatalism.

Miller's often-contradictory remarks, though, do not always supply the best evidence of what his career means to twentieth-century literature. Durrell, for example, sometimes provides a clearer and more level-headed understanding of Miller's significance, even if, as Miller's friend, he takes a partisan perspective. Durrell's opening essay to the first tribute book about Miller, *The Happy Rock* (1945), recognizes in Miller certain qualities the author might never perceive in himself. It is here that Durrell places Miller some distance between the 'literary gents' of modernist aesthetics, who begrudgingly allow, according to Durrell, that Miller's prose is the work of a genius, and the ordinary reader who can recognize Miller's honesty and 'Brooklyn predilections'. Durrell is perhaps not alone in seeing Miller as the missing link between the high cultural world of intellect and autonomy and 'the "proletarian" literature of the future', as Durrell phrases it in another book.[42] This view leads Durrell to the conclusion, 'In Miller you have someone who has crossed the dividing line between art and *Kitsch* once and for all.'[43]

Although Durrell was writing in 1945, the books with which Miller crosses this 'dividing line' were written at a time when the term 'kitsch' was undergoing discussion by a number of theorists. Norbert Elias's essay 'The Kitsch Style and the Age of Kitsch', for example, was first published in 1935, just when Miller was being praised by high modernists like Eliot, Pound and Herbert Read. Elias defines the term 'kitsch' as 'an expression for this tension between the highly-formed taste of the specialists and the undeveloped, unsure taste of mass society'.[44] Miller, then, is a kitsch writer, since each of his books is written across the divide between intellect and instinct, literary allusions mingled with dirty jokes. Miller appealed almost simultaneously to serious critics and Second World War soldiers. Yet the tension between the high and the low is flaunted by Miller instead of hidden, and he almost celebrates his awkward position between T. S. Eliot and G. I. Joe. It is perhaps surprising that in catering to the coarser tastes of the mass market and readers of pornography, Miller did not alienate his audience of serious cultural critics. But as Alison Pease has shown, modernist writers like Joyce and Lawrence had already established for the first time a serious audience for novels involving the obscene, engaging with elements of mass culture while maintaining their high art status.[45] But Miller has no high art status to preserve. The reason Miller's early novels were adopted by the literary elites he disparaged is perhaps best provided by Norbert Elias, who suggests that the kitsch artist 'is never only something antagonistic existing outside the true creators, but is also a basic situation within them, a part of themselves'.[46] The high modernists were ready to accept Miller, not only because he took the artist as his subject, as Orwell says, nor simply because he wrote in a fluent prose style, as Durrell says, but also because, in his concurrent promotion of low culture next to high, and in accommodating himself to a mass audience, he helped perpetuate the 'height' of high modernism.

Theodor Adorno, in a contrasting piece, sees 'insufferable kitsch' as the result of the determination of authors to continue narrating when there is no longer a story to be told. In 'The Position of the Narrator in the Contemporary Novel', Adorno, who would never have followed Elias in his positive definition of kitsch, considers mass culture responsible for the death of the novel when he suggests, 'Just as painting lost many of its traditional tasks to photography, the novel has lost them to reportage and the media of the culture industry, especially film.'[47] Miller, in spite of this pronouncement, should be seen as a novelist who embraced the culture industry, compiling his novels out of raw 'reportage' from his life, and avidly supporting the expanding film industry. Durrell recognizes Miller's ability to use what other artists hold in contempt, as he says, 'His line of vision is not obstructed by derived canons of art and life. Everything registers with pristine clearness. His interest in films and newspapers strikes a note of refined horror in the literary men who admire him.'[48] In fact, there was very little that Miller disdained, apart from artists who held themselves distant from common life. While Adorno states, 'For telling a story means having something *special* to say, and that is precisely what is prevented by the administered world, by standardization and eternal sameness,' Miller might counter with the argument that any person is capable of saying something which remains 'special', regardless of its common nature, simply by expressing a living personality.[49] The resulting product, which Adorno calls a 'cheap biographical literature', is exactly what Miller thrived on.

The nature of autobiographical literature, though employed from Augustine through Jean Jacques Rousseau to Proust and Joyce, had not been fully theorized by the time Miller was exploring his own form of auto-novel. The problem of self-expression was key to a writer who placed living above writing yet continued to publish frequently, attempting to sustain the portrait of himself as author. There was an inherent conflict, revived each night, in Miller's chosen role, between whether he would stay in his room to write or escape the confinement of literature to gather experience. There is irony in the picture of Miller the writer, a man who celebrates 'life' to such an extent that he wants to grasp it with both hands, but who is burdened wherever he goes with typewriter and writing desk. Miller wants life so fervently that he must fix it in the one place – language – where it is no longer unadulterated life but mixed with self-conscious reflection. In recognizing this dilemma, though, Miller is not alone among the modernists, as we have already seen with the Surrealists. In a similar vein, Stein's work in the 1930s, despite the fact that she had sustained a career of several decades by the time Miller was first published, presents an interesting context for Miller's autobiographical works. She, too, was experimenting with her own autobiographical forms and raising her own questions about the nature of what we might call a 'common genius', as well as sharing Miller's interest in the problem of simultaneously living in one moment and writing the moment down for posterity.[50]

This is the traditional problem of the writer who attempts to seize the present instant – something Miller would have been aware of from his reading of Henri Bergson's works. Any single observation can be perceived only with the passing of time and the registering of the observation in memory – thus making perception a historical activity, complete with subjective contextualization, rather than pure objective observation.[51] This is what Miller criticizes in high modernists like Proust, who lives only through his memories, putting life wholly behind him as he immerses himself in the art of his autobiography. But it is not a problem Miller could fully escape either, so long as he insisted on expressing his life in books. The pen (or the typewriter) is always slower than the eye, just as recording an action takes longer (most times) than the action. It is for this reason that Wilhelm Dilthey, the philosopher credited as the founder of modern studies in autobiography, distinguishes between 'direct awareness' and 'representing' as separate but linked activities.[52] For Miller, the conflict between the two is evident in phrases he uses, describing himself one minute as 'a man living out of his solar plexus', repudiating the 'big shots, with their theories and their white ink' and those who are 'highly conscious and deliberate' – then the next moment describing himself as 'always aware', proving himself one of the most self-conscious writers of the period.[53]

Miller would address the problem specifically only very late in life, after a combination of fame and age had brought his writing career to an end. Miller says in his 1972 memoirs:

The first time you do something, you're not conscious of it, as it were. You don't look at yourself in the mirror. Then, when you are writing, it's just like looking in a mirror and watching yourself doing it all over again . . . And you *know* you're performing this time. That's the difference between the conscious and the unconscious act.[54]

Yet it is important to note that this comes late in Miller's career, since it is at last acknowledging a problem he spent many decades trying to ignore, an idea which echoes Bergson's formulation of the 'intellectual effort'.[55] Much earlier, Miller had used similar terminology to criticize Nin's diaries, saying, 'The whole drama of her life is played out before the mirror. If she is sad the mirror reflects her sadness; if she is gay the mirror reflects her gayety. But everything the mirror reflects is false, because the moment she realizes that her image is sad or gay she is no longer sad or gay.'[56] At the height of his career, Miller still believed he could avoid the entanglement with self-consciousness that he saw evident in the diary form. What he seemed not to realize was that, in being as much a central protagonist of Nin's diaries as she was – diaries which he was reading as they were being written – he, too, was guilty of turning his life into mere performance. The intrusion of his self-conscious awareness of Nin's unfailing diary-keeping would, according to his own account, falsify his emotions and passions, corrupting the spontaneous approach to life he had originally promoted. The conflict is, on a smaller scale, that of literary modernity in general as described by Paul De Man, where he discusses writing as both the act and the process of interpretation that trails behind the act itself.[57]

Miller seems particularly naïve in his dealing with the conflict between the act of living and that of recording life. The irony is evident, for example, in *Tropic of Capricorn* (1939), where Miller contrasts himself with those, 'disguised as artists', who 'in order not to become victims of that insomnia which is called "living", . . . resort to the drug of putting words together endlessly . . . *I wanted to be wide awake without talking or writing about it, in order to accept life absolutely.*'[58] That this sentiment is expressed in the third of his many books seems to reveal the frustration of his goal. Clearly, regardless of what Miller might say about living without reflection, he is not fully satisfied with mere life unless it has been transformed into words and transmitted to an audience. Paul John Eakin identifies this as the primary debate in autobiographical theory: should the self be seen as autonomous and independent or contingent upon communication with others?[59] Although Miller often speaks in spiritual terms of the autonomy of the self, he plainly cannot escape the notion he inherited from an early age – that his task was to follow his literary heroes in the attempt to fix the transcendence of life to the page. In this, he cannot shake the tradition he was born into, subscribing to the view shared by many other autobiographers, that without language there is no identity or self.[60] Even if, as Miller discovered early in his career, his personality was his one advantage, it was valid only if it could be recorded.

This need to lay down in language all the spontaneity he found in life, compounded by his lifelong aim to be thought of as a writer, led Miller to the same problems he criticized in others. In 1939 Miller wrote to Nin, announcing, 'You have chosen not to create but to record creation.'[61] It is a fitting observation of Miller's own career, one which began with the composition of an autobiography of a writer who had at that point published no works. *Tropic of Cancer*, more than any other Miller book, tries to record the present as it happens, writing on the typewriter with one hand about what the other hand is doing. Miller gave up, after this, on the experiment of recording the present, realizing, as the writing of the novel spread across many years, that one could only fix the present within a constructed past. With *Tropic of Capricorn* he becomes much more Proust-like, revisiting a former period in detail. He wrote to Emil to say, 'My "anecdotal life," as Zadkine puts it, is finished' (*LE* 143). Miller felt that he had collected enough experience to build out of each successive book a new mythic life.

It is in the letter to Nin describing her tendency to record creation rather than create that Miller comes closest to finding a resolution to the conflict between living and recording life. He tells her, 'Writing is life, but what is written is death.' This equation is key, echoing Stein's comment from three years earlier that 'a thing goes dead once it has been said'.[62] Miller, not unlike Stein, is able to associate the *act* of writing with living life, but temporality is crucial, since the collection, publication or simple reading of these texts can only be associated with a perished tradition – with death – in much the same way he associated high modernists like Joyce and Proust with a dead form of literature. The high modernists, with a few notable exceptions, like Stein, had mostly aimed to retain some detachment from the life being recorded – had written, as Miller had first tried to write, according to a structure or some elaborate form, or as an escape from personality. Now that Miller had moved to a more spontan-eous, formless and personalized type of writing, he saw the need to escape also from history, the impending time which would render the life captured on the page into something dead. What Derrida would go on to say in 'The End of the Book and the Beginning of Writing' is wholly relevant to this issue, one which was a key response to the high modernist aesthetic: 'What writing itself, in its nonphonetic moment, betrays, is life. It menaces at once the breath, the spirit, and history as the spirit's relationship with itself.'[63]

If Miller's views on the death of literature and the life only available in the moment of writing could be somehow removed from Miller's publi-cation record, this principle might be seen as the key to Miller's position. It goes some way to explain Miller's distaste for institutional literature or, phrased differently, his preference for Barthes's writer, who is simply engaged in writing, over the author, whose name is printed on the spine of a book. Literature was a collective term for all that had been written in the past; life was action in the present, even if merely sitting at a typewriter, putting all that one knows about oneself on to the page. This also reveals why Miller was interested in the Surrealists, believing that a limited sense of reality could be surpassed only by the work of art's ability to engage with the surreal.[64] But regardless of what Miller may have told Nin, it is clear that he was not able to resist the urge to be known as an author, publishing his own contributions to the finished works of Literature – always with an eye on some future posterity which would, he reckoned, judge him as an author, an artist, and not just one who wrote. Miller appreciated automatic writing so far as it was 'an effort, at bottom, to return to the original vital source, which is in the solar plexus' – or it was 'meant to exhibit thinking rather than a finished thought', since this suited his personality.[65] But he could never let go of the role that an established history or finished text played in making masterpieces, according to the high modernist model he had inherited.

The tension between these positions would never go away, but they are almost certainly most acute while Miller was writing his first published novel. The clearest example comes, once more, in a letter to Emil, written in 1933 after hearing that June, whom he had been avoiding, had been seen with another man. Jealous and drunk at his typewriter, he announces, 'This may sound mad, but it is absolutely sincere, sincere as a man can be who is weeping and at the same time examining the carbons to see if they are inked enough!' (*LE* 120). With one eye blinded by tears and the other making sure this expression of emotion would be preserved for the future editor of his collected letters, Miller finds himself straddling the divide between art and life that he spent so much of his career trying to break down. In taking such special care, even when drunk and upset, to keep a copy of every letter, he does not seem to believe his own pronouncement that writing is life and what has been written is death – unless, of course, Miller is more obsessed with death than his celebration of life would indicate. In the same letter to Emil, he writes:

Maybe I'm not an artist, as the world judges art and artists. But in my soul I know that I am – though there is very little to prove or justify myself. Anyway, the few who knew me can testify as to whether I was one or not.

I lapse unwittingly into the past tense. I am writing at top speed. *I was!* Read what you like into that. (*LE* 122)

Miller seems to catch himself – perhaps as 'unwittingly' as an 'always aware' author can be – thinking of his career once more from a posthumous date. In considering himself as an 'artist', it seems enough that he knows it, but only for a moment, until once more he pushes the present into the past, rendering his writing into literature.

After the letter dissolves into drunken misspellings and sentences trailing to nothing, it is continued, dated '12 hours later', once Miller has sobered. He writes, 'You can disregard the enclosed letter. Read it for your own amusement . . . This morning I read it over and laughed my head off. Never trust the author, trust the tale. If I say my heart is breaking, never believe me. It is just literature' (*LE* 126). What was, to the best of his ability, sincere the night before is now not to be trusted, according to his paraphrase of Lawrence. Perhaps Miller, feeling vulnerable, wishes to cover up his expression of emotion; but by branding it literature, a transformation which seems to have happened overnight, Miller is recognizing the effect that temporality has on the written word in eternalizing a transient impulse. Whatever it is, the written text is no longer something Miller identifies with – his life having moved on beyond the literary. But a month later, once Emil had received his letter and praised its contents, Miller again changes his mind, writing, 'You said you were touched by the letter about June. Christ, yes! I was *real* for a half-hour. Falling apart. I hope some time to describe those sensations in full. It was very "Albertine." *Very*' (*LE* 133). Seemingly after a little encouragement from his sole reader, Miller seems once more ready to acknowledge that sincerity is an author's virtue and that a recording of feelings present could be as significant as a later remembrance of things past. More importantly, Emil seems to have confirmed to Miller that writing is not valuable only at the moment it is written, but that being '*real* for a half-hour' can remain real a month later, if the language is preserved and transmitted to others. Again, we are faced with a Bergsonian idea of present and past in Miller's autobiographical approach, since this stretching of the present instant – expressed as 'life' – into a posthumous and unceasing history seems to be Miller's dual purpose as writer.

It is a *dual* purpose primarily because Miller insists it is one, though only by emphasizing one moment that he is a writer and another that he is an author-historian. Miller seems equally intent on establishing monuments to succeed him after his death as he is on writing 'for the moment'. This is not unusual among autobiographers, or writers in general. De Man describes the writer as a mixture of one who acts and one who records actions for posterity, 'a combination that would achieve a reconciliation between the impulse toward modernity and the demand of the work of art to achieve duration'.[66] This statement clearly places the tension between action and reflection at the centre of literary modernity, as illustrated in the period here discussed. And as John Sturrock suggests, autobiography is rarely written without the author first identifying the need to reveal a 'life-task' after the passing of time and the effort of reflection.[67] Miller often appeals to this passing of time in order to be redeemed by future readers, even when, at other times, he is willing to equate the finished text with death. Miller finds himself continually in the grey area intrinsic to autobiography, what De Man calls the 'convergence of aesthetics and of history'.[68] The core of autobiographical theory lies here, coming to terms with authors who create art simultaneously as writers (or those who act) and historians (or those who record action), aiming to reconcile imagination with reality, or creation with critical reflection.[69] Miller's literary position is clearly situated here, cultivating a modernist author persona only in order to draw audiences to the uncultivated writing he continued to produce.

Miller always managed to surround himself with avid supporters, receiving constant reassurance – from fans of his personality as well as of his books – that he would be remembered long enough to be included in a future literary history, a reassurance which seemed integral to his continued literary production. But contrasting with his enthusiasm for surrounding himself with his supporters, he still maintained his distrust of the official literary institution each time it sought to accept him. This resulted, as one would expect, in a sharp suspicion of Miller on the part of the academy and in a simultaneous cult growing up around his personality. Philip Rahv notes this as early as 1949, suggesting:

With few exceptions the highbrow critics, bred almost to a man in Eliot's school of strict impersonal aesthetics, are bent on snubbing him . . . His admirers, on the other hand, are so hot-lipped in praise as to arouse the suspicion of a cultist attachment. They evade the necessity of drawing distinctions between the art of exploiting one's personality and the art of exploiting material, from whatever source, for creative purposes.[70]

The 'necessity', however, of drawing this distinction is perhaps suspect, certainly in this context. What is the difference between extracting 'art' from the author's life and simply making the author's life into 'art'? Miller himself was never convinced that such a distinction needed to be made, ready to exploit anything if it could be in some way called 'art' – which according to his definition, almost anything could. For this reason, Miller's career took a very different shape, in terms of secondary works springing up around the artist, than that of any other modernist. For instance, Miller not only answered letters to ordinary collectors of his books, but even published his entire correspondence with one of them.[71] Yet this does not reflect a straightforward desire on Miller's part for *any* publication surrounding his life or works; when Richard Ellmann was interested in writing a biography, he was persuaded to abandon the project because Miller was so uncooperative.[72] Always intent on maintaining full control of his public image, Miller was ready to accept disciples that other authors would have resisted, while also ready to dismiss supporters that other authors would have relished having.

While his tactics were perhaps perverse, Miller was doing nothing very new in trying to sustain a certain image by limiting his audience.[73] His attempts to find Miller enthusiasts among his general readers started in earnest in the 1940s. His fame, by this point, was established enough that fans and collectors were beginning to search him out; the more obsessive even chose to move near his home in Big Sur. Happier with devoted followers than mildly approving critics, Miller recognized a new market among the author-cult devotees. The collectors especially, he found, were willing to pay large amounts of money for limited editions. Miller used his fame not only to help himself but also to promote his friends. For example, a chapter from *Black Spring* (1936) was illustrated by his friend Bezalel Schatz, and sold as a coffee-table book for $100 a copy. Similarly, a book was produced in 1944, reprinting a chapter from *Black Spring* and including an 'original water colour' and 'several photographs of himself in the act of painting', all of which, priced at $50, was produced 'in a spirit of homage by friends of Henry for his friends'.[74] While many earlier modernists might have been friendly with their critics and reviewers, Miller rather chose his friends from among collectors and disciples.

This did not help Miller's already tenuous relationship with the literary establishment, as some critics are eager to point out. Orwell, though he considered *Tropic of Cancer* an 'important' novel, predicted at the end of the 1930s that Miller would eventually surrender his talent to literary 'charlatanism'.[75] The label stuck, as the 1940s saw the *Tropic* books give way to productions like *The Happy Rock*, a type of fan magazine, and the *Henry Miller Miscellanea* (1945), which was, it claimed, 'assembled and published to aid biographers of Henry Miller, to foster greater interest among the collectors of his work and to raise funds for the publication of his many manuscripts'.[76] Although *Tropic of Cancer* had sold extraordinarily well among American soldiers by the end of the Second World War, Miller failed to capitalize on his newfound popularity, allowing his $40,000 in royalties to be devalued in postwar French francs. Even if Miller was by no accounts wealthy until the *Tropics* were published in America, he found he could trade in on the myth he had carefully built around himself. His accountant, for example, received a signed watercolour as payment for his services.[77] Surrounded by collectors and fans, Miller could get most things he needed simply in exchange for a signed letter or a hastily drafted piece of 'literature'. In this way, Miller survived the 1940s and 1950s on the credit of his future worth as an artist.

By the end of his life, Miller was growing less critical of representations of himself. The shape of his mythical character swelled out of control by the 1970s as he allowed books like *Henry Miller: My Life and Times* to be distributed by the Playboy Press, complete with pictures of him, more than eighty years old, playing table tennis with naked models. Erica Jong suggests that the author begins, towards the end of his life, to caricature himself.[78] While most Miller biographers strive to point out where the 'authentic' Henry Miller differs from the invented character of the books, Jong chose to keep the myth intact, feeling empathy for Miller as a friend and fellow writer. She writes, 'I *expect* a writer to "lie" in order to get at a deeper truth. I take for granted that imaginative writing exaggerates and rearranges "facts" in the name of a higher fiction. I also understand how hard it is to survive one's own fame.'[79] The last sentence is the most suspicious, though, since Miller never intended to survive his fame. Even when Miller praised life over art, most of his career was a performance directed towards the biographer. Miller was one of the first writers to gamble everything on the validity of the idea that, as Jong laments, 'we live in an age when literary biography is more read than literature. Writers' lives tend to have more commercial viability than their own books.'[80] This fact, even if an exaggeration, was in fact the key to Miller's success, beginning his life work from the point of his death, always looking backwards from a future posterity. *Tropic of Cancer* perhaps succeeded only because it was written as if that future was an assured historical certainty.

Miller fits well into the role of modernist latecomer, at least in the 1930s. Bound to be impatient after the certainties of the previous decade's literary history – the seemingly unmovable and unliftable monuments left by Joyce, Proust and Eliot-influenced depersonalization – late modernists also had to come to terms with the uncertainties of a dark future, an imminent war and the promised end of literature. Although Miller wrote nothing in the 1920s, even then he considered himself a writer, and consequently watched his generation closely as it produced highly wrought, calculated works of art. From this point, Miller's main priority was to build his own work of art out of the raw experiences of his life. In writing books based on the past and present incarnations of 'Henry Miller', there was little fiction left for him, apart from the invention of the personality to support these narratives. He knew the power of the author-myth, having lived in Paris, where anecdotes of Joyce's and Proust's eccentricities were passed around with frequency. He was self-conscious, as well, of the value of each scrap of writing a genius produced. Miller's career got properly under way not with the first two completed novels, but with the collection of artefacts from his daily existence in Paris, recording, preserving and constructing the myth of his life, less concerned with art or literature than with destroying the distinction between the artist and the ordinary guy.

But if Miller was the first writer to cross the dividing line between art and kitsch, it was because he was incapable of wholly abandoning the high modernist belief in the myth of the artist; nor could he fully invest himself in producing highly formulated works of art, preferring the automatic and the ready-made, the visceral over the cerebral. Miller championed 'the human document' over 'the consciously or technically finished work', yet he insisted that every 'human document' was still the work of an artist, and deserved to be recorded for some future posterity.[81] Even if Miller held the democratic view that every person alive was a type of artist, he tended to elevate himself to the position reserved for celebrated authors.

Although he was an 'ordinary guy' himself, he saw fit to publish his correspondences with other 'ordinary guys'. He even made use of his elevated position among followers and fans for his material gains and to further personal interests. Despite what Miller wrote to the contrary, his actions reveal that he was never able to expel the idea, formed early in life, that the artist commanded an exalted position in society, and could claim esteem, honour and an eventual fame.

The contradictions and paradoxes evident throughout Miller's career provide evidence of the difficult position in which modernist latecomers often found themselves, attempting to come to terms with a concluding high modernism and the mystery of what might succeed a historical period so completely identified with the up to date. In *Tropic of Capricorn* Miller remembers his early efforts to fit his thoughts into an acceptable literary style, which makes him conclude, 'Nothing is accomplished by sweat and struggle . . . Everything I had written before was museum stuff, and most writing is still museum stuff and that's why it doesn't catch fire, doesn't inflame the world.'[82] One can understand why Miller, caught in the wake of museum-bound monuments left by the high modernists, positioned himself as an antagonist to the careful aesthetic of Eliot, Pound, Proust and Joyce. Yet Miller's one dream from the beginning of his career was to be, like those just listed, admired as a writer. There is no doubt he achieved this admiration to a certain extent. By the end of his life, the only way researchers could gain access to the Henry Miller Collection at UCLA was to petition the author himself, making out of Miller a type of curator of the museum of his works, a position he evidently relished. He wrote hundreds of letters to collectors to ask if they had found some limited-print publication of his, doling out 'human documents' and conversational revelations of his 'unrehearsed' life. The unconscious and 'automatic' aspects of a writer loosely tied to the Surrealists and later the Beats had ultimately been taken over by the backward-looking stewardship of the established author. Miller found himself to be, by the 1960s and 1970s, what he had always wanted to be, a fully established and renowned author. The irony lay in his method of achieving this goal – a method involving an explicit rejection of the manufactured genius grown in the 'hot house' of institutional literature, though simultaneously constructing his own biography under the most artificial and self-conscious conditions, manufacturing a mythological figure as seen from the vantage of a largely predestined future posterity.

CHAPTER 4

Investing in the modernist legacy: Objectivist adventures in the 'Pound tradition'

'The older generation is not the older generation if it's alive & up . . .
What's age to do with verbal manifestation, what's history to do with
it . . . I want to show the poetry that's being written today – whether
the poets are of masturbating age or the fathers of families don't
matter.'

Louis Zukofsky, letter to Ezra Pound (*P/Z* 67)

Henry Miller, marginal modernist though he may now seem, spent the
1930s finding room for himself between the high modernists, the Surrealists
and mass-market fiction. This may seem an unusual position to be in, but
it is not entirely unique, as examples from the same period of Gertrude
Stein's career might illustrate. The late modernist period, in fact, often
found individual writers struggling to accommodate their writing within
an ever-changing literary field. When contrasting the birth years of some
authors discussed – Stein was born in 1874, Wyndham Lewis in 1882,
Miller in 1891, and Laura Riding in 1901 – it becomes clear that this is
not purely a question of age or generation, but a specific problem facing
those who are defined in relation to the programme of innovation that
had been instituted in the 1910s and 1920s by the high modernists. Yet the
question of generations which seems to hang over the heads of many
modernist latecomers is one which must be examined from their own
point of view. For one, the definition of a literary generation must be
established, as it is possible to distinguish succeeding generations by any
one of several categories, including historical formulation, marketability,
aesthetic innovation, influence and even something so simple as the age of
the writers involved. In this study of second-generation modernists, the
factors of age, influence (at least in Harold Bloom's sense of the word)
and innovation have been neglected – Lewis's inclusion alone indicates
this – in favour of questions regarding the relations between market forces
and historical narratives. So the question of generations for late modernists
becomes one of whether an artist can exist without first finding a position

within the existing cultural field, historical narrative or market of literary production. In the cases presented in this study, the artists must infiltrate each of these as latecomers.

The group of poets loosely connected under the name 'The Objectivists' were just as susceptible to the challenges facing other modernist late-comers in terms of literary markets, politics and cultural fields. What makes them particularly fascinating, however, is the connection they maintained, in spite of these cultural and institutional issues, to certain high modernists in aesthetic matters. Where many late modernists tended to cast themselves in reaction to the highly aesthetic doctrines of their precursors, the 'Objectivists' tended to maintain the belief that poetry was an autonomous art, and that the masters to be examined and imitated included their immediate precursors, especially Ezra Pound and William Carlos Williams, but even, to a limited extent, T. S. Eliot and James Joyce. Yet rather than adopting the highly self-conscious historicist mind-set of many modernist contemporaries – both high and late – who often hoped to be the beginning or the end of some distinct literary era, this group of poets, somewhat vaguely assembled, tended to blur the lines between historical designations. In fact, some of the 'Objectivists', as we shall see, while recognizing that Pound and Williams were among their direct predecessors, would find it difficult to think in terms of literary gener-ations at all, failing to see why it was so important to Pound that they come 'after' the initial high modernist revolution.

In his essay on 'George Oppen, Charles Olson, and the Problem of Literary Generations', Stephen Fredman focuses on the question of whether Oppen and Olson really belong to two distinct and successive post-Poundian generations, as often proposed, or should be considered merely to be slightly overlapping contemporaries. In doing so, he writes of their shared literary parent, Pound, who first taught them that a gener-ational model was an effective method of gaining an audience for them-selves.[1] But what Fredman does not investigate, despite his attempt to argue 'not for the abolition of literary-historical terminology but rather for a more nuanced historicizing of poetry', is the way in which even Oppen's and Olson's shared patriarch cannot be confined solely to the previous generation of poets. In the correspondence between Pound and Zukofsky cited in the same article, Zukofsky questions the benefit of relegating Pound to the corral of older poets while he is still writing innovative and energetic poetry. Although Pound eventually got his wish not to be included in the 'Objectivist' issue, the fact that modernist poets found such terms of position-making and poetic lineage worth consideration is significant, especially as it has direct bearing on our own inherited notions of literary history.

Pound was a natural choice as literary forefather for poets such as the Objectivists, since his critical essays of the 1910s and 1920s had established the foundation of image-based poetry and his own poems had provided the model for working upon this foundation. However, Pound was also a primary figure in the 1930s literary field, a promoter of young poets within publishing and critical institutions and a proponent of the maintenance of a poetic tradition. But just what was Pound's vision of a poetic lineage, and how far did he foresee the emergence of a 'Pound tradition'? For an artist like Pound who consistently placed his own work and his own time into a larger historical framework, it must have been clear that, while fitting one's work into a past tradition establishes a place for a new poet, it becomes increasingly important to find a forward lineage as well, effectively making out of oneself a vital link in a chain stretching through many ages. The nature of the Pound tradition is something which has been investigated, notably by Marjorie Perloff; and earlier on, Pound's legacy was perhaps most effectively remade for an entire generation in Hugh Kenner's *The Pound Era*.[2] But what did it mean for the poets themselves to exist within such a thing as the Pound tradition? Did this tradition exist in the minds of the Objectivists, either as a debt to a precursor or as an identifiable historical connection from one poet to another? And what might an inheritance of such a tradition mean in terms of marketability, identification and production?

Any history of the Objectivist movement finds itself under pressure from the beginning, burdened with a name that none of the parties involved is quite happy with. Zukofsky was forced, he reported, to choose a name by Harriet Monroe, editor of *Poetry*:

[W]e'd better have a title for it, call it something. I said, I don't want to. She insisted; so, I said, alright, if I can define it in an essay, and I used two words, *sincerity* and *objectification*, and I was sorry immediately. But it's gone down into the history books; they forgot the founder, thank heavens, and kept the terms, and, of course, I said *objectivist*, and they said *objectivism* and that makes all the difference.[3]

Whether the suffix makes any difference or not, Zukofsky *is* now remembered as the leader of the Objectivist movement, as well as of Objectiv*ism*, even if such a thing never existed. As Zukofsky seems to acknowledge, he has no control over our perception of literary history. Yet even Zukofsky's reluctance to name the movement is a historical reconstruction, since his own correspondence with Pound – not only Zukofsky's mentor but a great one for forming and naming movements – shows the younger poet casually throwing out a great number of suggestions for names, including '*Poets, 1931,* or *The Twelve,* or *U.S.A. 1931,* or *606 and after*' (*P/Z* 69). *Objectivists* was his own favourite, and since Pound did not disagree, the movement was born and branded.

But exactly *who* was branded with this label would be a question posed by literary historians for decades after the initial christening. As Zukofsky acknowledges, very little about the Objectivist movement was decided by any of its contributors, nor by Pound, nor by Monroe; the idea of a movement quite simply resulted from that which had 'gone down into the history books'. What begins as a list of contributors to one issue of a well-established poetry magazine gradually evolves into a critical designation for a select group and a point of reference for poets and critics when discussing this group. Michael Heller, for one, points out just how far the literary grouping is and was accidental and arbitrary.[4] In fact, the list of names of original contributors to the 'Objectivist' issue of *Poetry* has undergone many revisions, with one addition and numerous deletions, until we have reached the select permutations of group members labelled 'Objectivist' by contemporary critics. These almost always seem to include Zukofsky, Oppen, Carl Rakosi and Charles Reznikoff, with Basil Bunting and Lorine Niedecker acting as alternates. What must be remembered, though, is that this short list has little to do with 1931; instead, each member owes his or her place in the group to the critical formulations of the 1960s or after. As Fredman rightly points out, the reconstruction of the Objectivist group in the 1968 interviews with Professor Lawrence Dembo are perhaps as significant in establishing their position in literary history as their essays and publications of the 1930s.[5]

What is most interesting about the Objectivists' return to attention in the 1960s is, as Andrew Crozier suggests, that a problem is created – 'an abhorrent vacuum' between Pound and Williams and the New American Poetry – to which only they can provide the solution.[6] This vision of Objectivists as a 'missing link' is essential to any generational construction, but perhaps misleads in that it disrupts the chronology of poetic development itself. In other words, the Objectivists, though first conceived in the 1930s, the decade to which they have lately been restored, must still in some way belong to the 1960s, the decade in which they first managed to find a significant audience. As Crozier summarizes:

There would be no problem, needless to say, had their reemergence been a matter merely of critical rediscovery, or had they reemerged as revivalists of a period style; but, as we know, critical rediscovery followed their reemergence as poets of late maturity. And this is the key to the embarrassment they have induced ever since, for with this second flowering they reemerged discontinuously, it would appear, from a prior history that nevertheless – for it was there to be investigated – provided the only terms in which they could be thought. They were interviewed half to death as witnesses to their own pasts.[7]

In other words, the Objectivists are a group coherent only in retrospect. Crozier's choice of phrasing indicates just how far their complication of the modernist literary field stems from their failure to register a generational leap upon their first emergence in the 1930s and their belated reclamation of a largely forgotten literary position. Whatever renown they received as 1930s poets was largely showered on them because of their 1960s positions – because they could show a highly developed poetic stance which could be fully understood only if literary history could resurrect their former positions.[8]

The primary interviews referred to are those published in the Spring 1969 issue of *Contemporary Literature*. In a decade when few poets or critics discussed the term 'Objectivist', Dembo was a man who, as Niedecker recognized, 'wanted very much to understand Objectivism', assembling the four most central members, as he saw it, in Madison, Wisconsin.[9] These interviews reveal a critic eager to define a movement which the poets involved are incapable of defining. Rakosi, for example, when Dembo relates Williams's history of the movement as told in his 1951 *Autobiography* (in which Zukofsky, Reznikoff, Oppen, Bunting and Williams sit down to lunch in 1928 to found the group), responds, 'That is not correct. Williams did not get together with those men to found the objectivist movement. And I doubt whether it is a movement in the sense in which that word is generally used. The term really originated with Zukofsky, and he pulled it out of a hat.'[10] The others similarly play down the idea of coterie beginnings, though often apologizing for betraying the aura of the myths built up around the 'movement'. Reznikoff admits he could not understand much of what Zukofsky was saying in his founding essays.[11] None of them encourages the interviewer to view the four of them sharing more than friendship, mutual respect and a desire to be published. Oppen is asked, 'Why was it called "Objectivist"? Was there any sense of movement?' and answers, 'That was Louis' term, as far as I know . . . What I felt I was doing was beginning from imagism as a position of honesty.'[12] Each member plays down his role, even attempting, as in this case, to minimize all that distinguishes the Objectivists from the antecedent poetic group, suggesting there is little difference between themselves and the movements of the previous generation.

This is not rare in post-Poundian poetics. As Christopher Beach makes clear, poets in the Pound tradition are keen to foreground their debt to their precursors, emphasizing the level of influence rather than seeking to escape it, as they might within Bloom's model.[13] Reznikoff, for example, when asked about the origins of the group's name, vaguely remembers, 'We picked the name "Objectivist" because we had all read *Poetry* of Chicago and we agreed completely with all that Pound was saying. We didn't really discuss the term itself; it seemed all right – pregnant. It could have meant any number of things.'[14] He goes on to say, 'I think we all agreed that the term "objectivism," as we understood Pound's use of it, corresponded to the way we felt poetry should be written.' It is instructive that Reznikoff remembers incorrectly, attributing the word to Pound, who was in this instance silent. The Objectivists are keen to claim Pound as father, even if by suspect retrospection. But as Michael Heller asserts, history, for the Objectivists, is not a lesson there to be learned as much as it takes the form of 'a pressure'.[15] And in terms of literary influence and identity, Pound was the constant pressure shaping their literary positions.

For each member of the group, this pressure would have been different. For Zukofsky, who was in direct contact with Pound at least until the war, it would have been immediate and concrete. For someone like Niedecker, however, whose poetry was dismissed by Pound, he represented little more than the spirit of an age – the haunting image of a dead grandfather. But for all the Objectivists he represented a master poetic theorist, a figure around which to align themselves, and even, at times, a kind of warning. Rakosi phrased it like this:

First, I had better admit I believe that Pound's critical writing – particularly the famous 'Don'ts' essay – is an absolute foundation stone of contemporary writing. But in his own work I think he's been disastrous as a model . . . He pretends that his material is epic when it is only a device to achieve grandiosity at the expense of the reader . . . But that's Pound's song, and once a person has been exposed to Pound's aura, it is difficult not to succumb. After all, who doesn't want to be great?[16]

It was more, though, than just Pound's epic scope or (more importantly) the value of his critical writings which made him a figure around whom the Objectivists were happy to position themselves. It was also his stature within literary institutions, perhaps particularly his influence within publishing circles and his vision of a consolidated poetic society (as evident in his persistent desire to bring all his literary allies together within a single publishing institution).[17] Pound, in other words, beyond being an example and a theorist for the Objectivists, provided a cultural context, complete with literary contacts, knowledge of the field and the likeliness of fulfilling his long-term ambition to be remembered by future literary historians.

The English poet Bunting, though sometimes excluded from the Objectivist camp by those emphasizing the American or Jewish character of the poetry of the others, was the first to search out Pound and make demands on his attention. Always proactive and bold as a young man, Bunting had already spent time in prison for resisting military service in the first World War, then found his way into bohemian circles in London, where in 1919 Nina Hamnett first showed him Pound's recent work.[18] 'Homage to Sextus Propertius' made such an impression on Bunting that even thirteen years later he would call it 'the most important poem of our times, surpassing alike "Mauberly" and "The Waste Land"'.[19] Following many of his friends who would divide their time between London and the continent, he left England for Paris in 1923, where he first met Pound. There is little record of their contact during the first few months, until the autumn when Pound famously sprang Bunting from prison, having found him in his cell reading François Villon after a night of heavy drinking and confused confrontation. Pound set him to work for Ford Madox Ford on *The Transatlantic Review*, where Bunting began to mix with some now-famous literary figures.

However, a letter Bunting wrote shortly after his arrival in Paris reveals a proposed joint venture between him and Pound even earlier than the Villon prison episode. Writing to his friend and fellow poet J. J. Adams, Bunting discusses money that he and Adams had saved to start their own literary magazine, given the tentative title *Timon's Cave*. He writes:

I've been talking to Ezra Pound. Amongst other things, I told him about Timon's Cave. I get on very well with that fellow . . . he suggested as follows: – If he can raise a little wind to pay contributors, some Americans will guarantee four numbers of the 'Little Review,' under his editorship. There is a ready-found audience. Why not hand over the Timon's Cave fund & become the collaborators of Joyce, Lewis, Pound, Eliot (unless the Criterion begins to pay better) & others? But there arises this difficulty. Pound demands complete control. Consequently, the right to reject our work . . . If he likes it, the Little Review continues, plus Adams, Vines, Collier, & Bunting. For myself, I would be content. For you, it would involve a measure of abdication. Let me set out the pro's & con's on a new sheet of paper.[20]

Bunting's summary makes him sound inclined towards joining *The Little Review*, listing seven positives and five negatives. Included under 'Pro Pound's Scheme' are the arguments: 'Prestige of names of Joyce, Lewis,

Pound, Eliot, Cocteau, Picabia . . . Advertisement wider than any we could achieve unaided, except by rather wanton aggressiveness.' Under 'Contra Pound's Scheme' Bunting puts down, 'Adams no longer editor . . . but before Timon parts with a penny he knows exactly what Pound intends to do with it' and 'Lack of cohesion. Timon's Cave had a central idea. Pound's contributors are from the breakup of Vortex & Dada. We may be overwhelmed by the well-known names, & by the flashiness of the Dadaists.'

Although there is no mention here of what that central idea of *Timon's Cave* is, it is worth noting that Bunting considers Pound's proposed *The Little Review* to lack cohesion, especially given our own knowledge of Pound's efforts towards the consolidation of his literary allies into a distinguishable movement. For a decade Pound had been searching for a single unifying banner to bring coherence to the writers he believed in, even if it was no more than the title of a magazine in which they could all appear. As early as 1917, he had written to Margaret Anderson about his plans for *The Little Review*: 'I want an "official organ" (vile phrase). I mean I want a place where I and T. S. Eliot can appear once a month (or once an "issue") and where Joyce can appear when he likes, and where Wyndham Lewis can appear if he comes back from the war.'[21] In 1923 Bunting, having spoken with Pound, echoes this list of names, though things had clearly changed by that time. Lewis was, of course, back from the war and focusing on painting rather than writing, while Eliot and Joyce had both produced their monuments of modernist literature the year before. While these four were still well known mainly in artistic and highly cultured circles, their publicity value in those circles would have been high, and they quite likely would have been considered as forming a central core to a coherent literary movement. Becoming 'collaborators' with these four writers, as Bunting puts it, would have meant signing on to an already established literary project – to become, in a certain sense, venture capitalists in the business of modernism. This is not to suggest it was completely about money, since Pound's own prerequisite was that he approved of his contributors' poetry. But there is a sense of investment behind the proposal: if Bunting and friends invest money in *The Little Review*, *The Little Review* would in turn invest its established cultural credit (based on, if nothing else, the earlier publication of *Ulysses*) in their poetry.

That Bunting was lucky enough to be faced with either of these options – to start up his own magazine and movement or to join an already existing one – is also lucky for us, since it clearly illustrates the choices facing any second-generation modernist. As Bunting acknowledges, publicity for an unknown was available only either through highly aggressive tactics, which might never prove effective, or through joining those who already commanded a wide audience. The dilemma was how best to find one's own literary position. As with entering any cultural field, an artist was forced to define himself or herself in relation to the dominant literary figures. To take a stand at all meant to stand *with* the established group or *against* it. Although Bunting may never have seriously considered taking a stand against Pound's or Eliot's literary dominance, he knew that one had to be careful with any alliance entered into. While finding a 'ready-made audience' cut through years of hard work in making one's voice heard, it also meant that that voice could be drowned from the beginning by a wider group's preestablished agenda. Bunting recognized quickly as well that, although the prominent literary figures attracted the spotlight, they also cast the longest shadows. The same 'flashiness' that would draw attention might also 'overwhelm' the novice poets. Both options contained a type of gamble: to start on one's own meant the likelihood of never being heard by more than a handful; yet to enter the modernist slipstream and allow oneself to be dragged into prestigious company meant relinquishing much of the control one had over the direction of one's own career.

Although Pound continued to appear under 'administration' for *The Little Review* until the Autumn/Winter number of 1924, neither Bunting's poetry nor his prose was ever printed in that journal. Whatever reason there may be for this – whether Adams dismissed the scheme or the younger poets were let down by those on Pound's end – we can still see in Bunting an early willingness to seek out the literary reputation makers. His contact with Pound, though not leading him immediately to print, secured him an important ally. It was largely on Pound's recommendation that Bunting was taken on as a secretary to Ford at the *Transatlantic Review*. A little later, when Pound moved permanently to Rapallo, Bunting followed, perhaps partly because he understood that Pound could offer a young inexperienced poet a platform and links to a ready-made audience. There is no doubt Bunting had his own friends and collaborators, but Pound had a special talent for organizing poetry with a coherent public presentation. One of Pound's most valuable gifts to the poets who surrounded him was the ability to champion the group or the collective movement, allowing poets with little access to the public sphere or the literary institutions a platform on which to gather.[22] Bunting knew that he would never be the kind of poet who could both write verse *and* manage the political game of the period's literary institutions. Pound was someone who could help manage the latter.

However, at this time, Pound as an ally had perhaps as many negatives as positives. Despite his position near the centre of the movement, it is important to keep in mind that he was gradually *losing* some of the cultural authority he had worked so hard to obtain from 1909 to 1922.[23] As Pound handed back to Eliot the edited version of *The Waste Land*, helped it get published and earn the *Dial* award, he was also, as it turned out, handing over the position he had held up to then within the literary establishment – that of the arbiter of cultural worth.[24] Pound, it should be said, never *chose* to lose his role as cultural authority, but it was increasingly a struggle throughout the 1920s to find an audience for his chosen disciples. What is instructive is that by 1925, Pound was engaged in editing Bunting's own first major poem, *Villon*, much as he had done with *The Waste Land*, and helped in having it placed in an important periodical.[25] Of course, Bunting was not Eliot, and these two poems are not directly comparable, but it is also true that Pound in 1925 was not Pound in 1922. He could no longer command the cultural power necessary to draw to *Villon* its deserved attention or to establish Bunting's reputation as he had for Eliot with *The Waste Land*. Eliot, whose cultural power in the literary circles of London was increasing as Pound's was decreasing, never believed sufficiently in Bunting as a poet, and would not publish him until the late 1930s, and even then only with one poem.[26] Arguably, if Bunting had been solely interested in a patron-poet, he chose the wrong one.

But Bunting was much less interested in the power shifts of the literary establishment than in what he saw to be the proper way to write verse. This is evident in his open criticism of Eliot's literary politics, including the 'international disaster' of *The Criterion* and the religious turn Eliot takes in the 1930s. But in spite of this, Bunting still admires the careful music of many of Eliot's lines.[27] We can gather that Bunting, as he would make explicit later in life, already considered the value of poetry to be completely separated from its subject matter and the values of its creator. The importance of this belief would grow in significance as the 1930s progressed, and Bunting remained an ally of Pound despite an increasing irreconcilability with his mentor's chosen subject matter in poetry and prose. As Pound's fascism and obsession with economic theories grew more intense, he became more of a liability to those in his camp, and that Bunting remained a firm advocate of Pound's poetry (despite some inevitable critical response) offers testimony that Bunting had not joined the Poundian school simply for the credentials a member might receive.

In fact, apart from appearances in *Poetry* and other small Pound-influenced publications, Bunting failed to find any 'ready-made audience' because of his association with Pound, at least not until late in life, when critics began to reconstruct Pound's influence. As late as 1951, an influential critic like F. R. Leavis would state, 'If we ask what other poets Pound backed [other than Frost and Eliot] the answer is that it is hard to remember, because on the whole they matter so little.'[28] This would begin to change only in the 1960s, when Pound's reputation would be reestablished – first by an emerging group of poets and subsequently by the academy – to such a degree that by 1971 the modernist period could be compellingly branded *The Pound Era*.

This rapid resurrection of an entire 'tradition' is worth noting in its own right, but when discussing the reputation of the Objectivists it becomes an integral part of understanding the notice the movement commanded. For Bunting, it is often commented that his entire poetic work might have been forgotten if various circumstances had not led him to write *Briggflatts* in the mid-1960s, a modernist poem arriving just as the retrospective critical view of modernism was changing. But while it was this poem that secured his place in literary history, it was once more having an audience that encouraged him to write the poem. To a certain extent, the resurrection of the 'Pound tradition' – first by poets of the period and only later by literary critics – was the crucial factor in encouraging him, after a long period of infrequent publication and little or no poetry, to begin writing once more. And it was only with *Briggflatts* that Bunting once more became a poet in his own right instead of a man who had simply lived his life around poets. There had always been a type of celebrity by association which haunted Bunting, nearly always overshadowing his recognition as a poet. Russell Banks, for example, remembered asking himself when meeting an elderly Bunting for the first time, 'What do you say to a man Pound sprung from a Paris jail?'[29] This emphasis on history rather than poetry would plague Bunting much of his life, as he disapproved of the 'charlatans', 'the bogus' and 'all those who sold their talents for money'.[30] Yet it was this same association with literary celebrities which gave Bunting reassurance from the beginning that he was writing poetry which would eventually be widely read. Just before his death, when Bunting was asked if he had ever been concerned that his poetry would never be noticed at all, he answered, 'I was quite confident it would be done sometime. If you have practically no readers, but those readers were people like Yeats and Pound, and Eliot, Carlos Williams, well, you're pretty confident some notice will be taken sooner or later.'[31] Although confidence is always easier with hindsight, Bunting's statement reveals just how far confidence in one's promoters, or even in one's audience, can turn into confidence in oneself.

In choosing Pound as his literary precursor, then, Bunting was not only placing his confidence in him as a long-term investment, but also making him a type of target audience. There were times in Bunting's career when Pound was the only audience his poetry received. Imitation was inevitable. Later, Bunting would admit that many of his statements from the 1920s and 1930s were merely 'echoing Pound's ideas', and that, as a literary figure, he was 'a little overwhelming'.[32] Pound, as has been stated earlier, was most useful to young poets as an umbrella of ideas and positions, as well as a promoter and publicity agent. But having a spokesman meant quite often relinquishing one's own voice to the collective movement, even when that movement was forever shifting its constituent parts. In other words, Pound could act as a stabilizing centre only if the members of the circle were willing to follow him wherever he went. As Pound's ideas grew more focused on economic theory and centralizing governments and less based upon the principles of poetics, Bunting, for one, found he was unwilling to follow. It was Pound's anti-Semitism, as expressed in letters directly to the Jewish Zukofsky, that caused the initial break in Bunting's relations with the older poet. Bunting wrote a fierce letter to Pound in late 1938 and the two seldom communicated directly after it, using Pound's wife as an intermediary. Bunting would never abandon his belief in Pound's principles of poetry and, to a certain extent, his poetic example, but what was increasingly clear was that Pound's sense for good poetry could be clouded by the prejudices embedded in his mind.

In that same year, Pound published his *Guide to Kulchur*, a prose work dedicated to Bunting and Zukofsky. Bunting's own copy of Pound's book reveals, within the notes Bunting wrote in the margins, the thrust of the younger poet's criticism of his one-time mentor. Bunting primarily takes issue with the passages in which Pound tries to unify knowledge and history into broad principles. On the first page, where Pound quotes the Analects, '*Said the Philosopher: You think that I have learned a great deal, and kept the whole of it in my memory? . . . It is not so. I have reduced it all to one principle*', Bunting writes, 'A very dangerous and deeply ignorant thing to do: impoverishing language.'[33] Later, when Pound discusses the importance of medieval scholasticism for anyone who seeks to set their ideas in order, Bunting comments, 'A man who wants to set his ideas in order wants to kill them: and that is what he will achieve via this misconception of scholasticism.'[34] When Pound suggests, 'You can write history by tracing ideas, exposing the growth of a concept', Bunting responds, 'You falsify it so.' Bunting summarizes the whole first section of Pound's book with the observation that it 'seems a thin kind of civilisation that appeals to E. P. One with anemia; or chlorosis. An adolescent's rather priggish, very egocentric dream.'[35] Although these sentiments were never made public, they still reveal Bunting's distaste for Pound's vision of a centralized cultural institution. This was, of course, what had first drawn Bunting to Pound, that the older poet was willing to be a stable central authority figure to the young and voiceless, but as Pound's vision stretched to the point of placing himself as the stabilizing centre of history and universal knowledge, Bunting realized how constraining and false this vision was. While Bunting would continue until his death to defend Pound's contribution to the poetry of the period – for example, stating that 'Pound has provided a box of tools . . . and a man who is not influenced by Pound, in the sense of trying to use at least some of these tools, is simply not living in his own century' – he could never accept Pound's abstract and unifying theories of history, culture or knowledge.[36]

Throughout Bunting's career, his greatest concern regarding the work of his contemporaries was the descent into abstraction. For Bunting, who believed in poetry only as long as it was a direct result of experience, some of the other members of the modernist enterprise were too intent on theorizing life rather than living it. Zukofsky was one of these. From the first moment Bunting and Zukofsky were placed next to each other in print, Bunting recognized this vital difference between the two Objectivists. In response to Zukofsky's essays on Objectivist doctrine in *Poetry* and the anthology, Bunting wrote an 'Open Letter to Louis Zukofsky' in which he criticizes his friend for trying to theorize a new kind of poetry. He uses the metaphor of hat-making to criticize Zukofsky's abstraction:

If I buy a hat I am content that it should fit, be impermeable of good texture, and of colour and cut not outrageously out of fashion. If I am a hatmaker I seek instruction in a series of limited practical operations ending in the production of a good hat with the least possible waste of effort and expense. I NEVER want a philosophy of hats, a metaphysical idea of Hat in the abstract, nor in any case a great deal of talk about hats.[37]

Bunting was never comfortable with Zukofsky's manifestos. But it is not just Zukofsky, since Bunting makes clear he does not trust even his own criticism. The open letter goes on to say, 'I have no alternative *principle*. I do not think anything can be simplified . . . A movement, a religion, is no substitute for clearsight, even if it be a much better religion than those recently current amongst writers.'[38] In deliberately *not* devising or promoting his own critical programme, Bunting seems to take on the role of late modernist in a similar way to Riding, in contrast to his fellow late-modern Objectivist, Zukofsky. In viewing this 'new' principle for poetry as no real improvement, Bunting seems ready to count himself out of the gamesmanship infiltrating the very notion of progressive poetry as established by his modernist forebears.

Criticizing his contemporaries is one thing, but Bunting was not afraid to stand up to the modernist patriarchs on this issue either. His criticism of Eliot's religious and moral stance has already been noted. But even Pound, who had initially contributed the founding principles on which Bunting's own poetry rested, was guilty in Bunting's view of descending at times into mere abstraction. The whole modern movement, of which Bunting found himself part, was built upon deliberation rather than activity, Bunting suggested to Pound in 1934:

But the literature of the last – how long? – has all of it been psychological: people talking or thinking about things they didn't do, or would like to do, or why and why not . . .

It occurred to me a long time ago that this indirect business had gone about as far as it would go without degenerating. Nobody is going to do it better than you for a hell of a long time, and Zuk can only introduce further complications of method that remove it from the possible reader, step by step, until somebody will arise who will . . . be totally unintelligible.[39]

This was Bunting's great fear, and his most significant criticism of modernism. He is willing to accept that Pound succeeded in his efforts in exploring the subjective, but worries what will result from repeated attempts at recreating the modernist innovation he calls 'indirectness'. Bunting wants to be seen as a man of action and reproaches those who are content to simply reflect and speculate. In a late essay, Bunting asserts, 'Very few artists have clear, analytical minds. They do what they do because they must. Some think about it afterwards in a muddled way and try unskillfully to reason about their art. Thus theories are produced which mislead critics and tyros, and sometimes disfigure the work of artists who try to carry out their own theories.'[40] Bunting seems to favour an instinctive approach, or at the very least a theory left implicit rather than produced explicitly as explanation.

It is worth noting, though, that with the production of his acknowledged masterpiece, *Briggflatts*, we find Bunting for the first time engaged in his most careful analytical thought. In an interview looking back on the composition of the poem, he describes the elaborate pictorial and thematic structure used, and he seems aware of the poem primarily as an example of 'how to make a poem'. In fact, the poem might never have been written had not Tom Pickard, on the suggestion of Jonathan Williams, approached Bunting for advice on how to write poetry. The result was a much more self-conscious poetic experience than Bunting seems to have engaged in before. He admits, when speaking of *Briggflatts*:

> I have a clearer notion of how I wrote that than of how I wrote other things, because Tom Pickard was looking over my shoulder, so to speak, and I was all the time thinking of how this could be made useful as a lesson, to a very very young poet just beginning. So that I'm aware of things that I'm not aware of in other cases.[41]

A reversal of roles seems to be the main cause of Bunting's increased self-consciousness. For the first time, Bunting was the mentor, and in stepping into the role he had reserved for Pound, he perhaps emulated the more highly theoretical qualities of the older poet. After the publication of *Briggflatts*, his opinions suddenly began to matter to what must have seemed to him odd acquaintances: students of poetry, journalists, literary critics. Although Bunting would always maintain that abstraction was the primary enemy of poetry and that excessive thinking would harm quality verse, he was increasingly willing, after *Briggflatts*, to take the role of lecturer, theorist and even at times critic.

   While Bunting could be said to have eventually succumbed to the peripheral literary institutions he avoided for decades, the belatedness of the recognition he deserved makes it possible to see his inherent distrust of the authoritarian views that the other, more famous, modernists had earlier accepted. In 'A Note on *Briggflatts*', he states, 'Hierarchy and order, the virtues of the neo-Platonic quasi-religion, were prime virtues to Yeats, Pound and Eliot. They are not virtues to me, only expedients that chafe almost as vilely as the crimes they try to restrain.'[42] So even after his only unmistakable literary success, Bunting remained wary of the establishment of any 'official' system or order. Yet despite his criticism of the three core poets of modernism, upon his death Bunting was memorialized as 'a poet uncompromisingly married to the modern move-ment as that movement had first defined itself in the poems of Pound and Eliot in the 1920s'.[43] There can be little doubt that Bunting was a poet firmly in the Pound tradition, and learnt much from Eliot and Yeats as well. Yet, despite the fact that at his death it was necessary to emphasize Bunting's position *with* the modernists because of the uncomfortable gap between the 1920s and the 1960s, it has now become so commonplace to see him next to Pound that his criticism of certain main tenets of modernism is often ignored.

The term 'uncompromisingly married' certainly allows no room for his distaste for modernist abstraction or the myth his precursors built up around themselves. In a late lecture he would say,

So much has been written in recent years about Yeats and Pound, Eliot and Joyce . . . that I sometimes have difficulty in recognizing the men I knew when I was young.

And even those men themselves, when they write about their youth, seem often to be more concerned with amusing or picturesque exploits than with the real roots of what happened. We hear a lot about the Imagists, and about F. S. Flint or T. E. Hulme or other people of no importance.[44]

There was a time when this ability to shape literary history compelled Bunting to seek Pound's help, hoping to be one of these peripheral figures in the Pound circus, even if it meant being overwhelmed by the immensity of the legend being written. As we have seen, the umbrella of Pound's movement was attractive to a young and unestablished poet who wanted an audience without the need for aggressive publicity. But while Bunting's investment in Pound's literary fame eventually seemed to pay off, he never managed to escape the centrifugal pull of the Pound circle. Bunting may have never fully wanted to escape, but there is a sense that he felt himself a victim of the pressure of literary history, that he had no control over his own poetic career since each of his poems would be removed from its factual world and placed within an emerging critical and theoretical framework. There was no escape from abstraction, from those who would construct a simple order and hierarchy out of the world in which he had simply tried to live. This was implied within his modernist inheritance, something he could never escape from the moment he first chose Pound as his literary father figure.

Though Zukofsky was first introduced to Pound much later than Bunting and spent much less time in his company, the two Americans perhaps have more in common in their poetic endeavours. They were both active in formulating literary groups and in theorizing the type of poetry written by those groups. While Bunting chose the role of the maverick, the impulsive wanderer and adventurer, Pound and Zukofsky, as I hope to show, invested themselves in the business of forging twentieth-century poetics through careful manipulation, not only of words, but of reputations and perceptions.[45] Towards the beginning of his career, Zukofsky, like Bunting, sought to position his career in relation to Pound.

Through early publications in 'little magazines', he came into contact with both Pound and Williams, which immediately provided the ambitious young poet with literary precursors. Zukofsky was quick to align himself with his two father figures, eager to learn not only from their example, but from their opinions of his work and from their institutional contacts. The further value of such an alliance, beyond what Zukofsky might have learnt in his formative years, was simply to be surrounded by prominent figures of the literary world. As Robert Creeley tells us, 'My first information of Zukofsky was in the dedications of two books crucial to my senses of poetry, Ezra Pound's *Guide to Kulchur* ("To Louis Zukofsky and Basil Bunting strugglers in the desert") and Williams' *The Wedge* ("To L.Z.").'[46] Such instances of prominent name-placement for a largely unread poet would be key to finding Zukofsky the place he now commands with the poets of the generation after his.

But the question of generations, even for a poet like Zukofsky, who readily adopted Pound as a father figure in letters, is made complicated by the view of history held by the Objectivists in the early 1930s. In the extensive correspondence between Pound and Zukofsky regarding the February issue of *Poetry* which the younger poet was to edit, it is clear that the two, while both intent on promoting the same group of poets, view the positions of generations in different ways. Pound, in adopting Zukofsky as his 'Deerly beloved son', desires to cultivate his poetic lineage, not only by choosing an heir but also by extending, through his son's efforts, the movement he had first propagated (*P/Z* 101). As early as February 1928, Pound was writing to Zukofsky to say, 'Somebody OUGHT to form a group in the U.S. to make use of the damn thing now that I have got it in motion' – the *thing* meaning the magazine *Exile* specifically, though the sentiment could be applied to Pound's poetic movement in general. Pound gives Zukofsky very specific advice on how to conduct meetings for such a group – 'choose a restaurant the indigent can afford, and that wont too greatly disgust the opulent' – and those not to be included in it – 'NOT too many women, and if possible no wives at assembly' (*P/Z* 13–14). But Pound is careful not to say who *should* be invited, hoping that Zukofsky will provide Pound with new converts. Pound is clear that the established writers are not to be included: 'To keep the group pure in heart, I think one must avoid tired and out worn personalities. I wont invidiously give a list. But some of my contemporaries have so institutionalized themselves' (*P/Z* 13). It is clear Pound hopes that Zukofsky might bring 'new blood' into the ageing modernist movement.

But the institutionalized are precisely the ones Zukofsky is most eager to meet, preferring the already established group of modernists to a fresh gathering of the uninitiated as Pound envisions. Zukofsky responds to Pound's prescriptions for a 'good' group with, 'I'd like Cummings – so would Bill (he had him out once). Both shy, they wd. take long to thaw. Marianne [Moore], yes, but would she? I'll ask Bill. Add myself – and you have four – three arrived, and one to keep in touch with the younger generation' (*P/Z* 16). To Zukofsky, this would look like the ideal society for him to keep, one young acolyte learning at the feet of the three most acknowledged modernist masters living in the New York area. There is no more effective way to assure a young poet's eminent arrival than to associate with those already arrived. But Pound has quite different goals for the group he wants Zukofsky to organize. Having carefully tried to maintain his position at the centre of all poetic activity for two decades, Pound was by the 1930s ready to see a new generation form itself, independent of his own, in order that he could relinquish the responsibility of keeping in touch with each new poet arriving on the scene. In Zukofsky he found a disciple who could be relied upon to raise a group which might look towards Pound for a literary progenitor, without any need for Pound himself to engage in nurturing and facilitating. It was for this reason that Pound arranged with Monroe to have Zukofsky edit his own issue of *Poetry* magazine, hoping that Zukofsky could establish himself as Pound's deputy director of a second phase of his own brand of modernism.

Pound gives Zukofsky the same detailed instructions for the magazine as he had for the literary meetings. It is evident from the letters that Pound is very much invested in the *Poetry* issue, yet wants to keep the fact hidden, suggesting, 'I see NO reason <for you or for me> to tell anyone that I have had an indirect participation . . . The fact that it will be hard for you to satisfy yourself among yr. con'empraries is all to the good' (*P/Z* 50). Pound, in hoping to force Zukofsky to win over his own generation, prefers to remain behind the scenes, rather than openly endorsing his protégé. In fact, while Pound had previously advertised his activity as orchestrater of poetic movements, in the case of Zukofsky he is always careful not to appear too close – indeed choosing *not* to publish work by the younger poet in case 'our detractors . . . wd. suspect me of being influenced by gang feeling. Which I am not. (at least in this case)' (*P/Z* 3). In giving Zukofsky advice, he constantly emphasizes his own age, and that the *Poetry* issue is to be filled with those much younger. He writes, after much fatherly advice, 'For the rest, it is up to you to tell me.

I can NOT be expected to know wot the young are doin" (*P/Z* 50). This is not, however, a gesture of humility so much as an acknowledgement that, in his present cultural position, too much responsibility is placed on him in the task of successfully bringing together the movement of modern poets:

I WANT a new list of men NOT chosen because they have already got in touch with me . . . I can not damitall MY recommendation now means too much.

You can make twenty bad guesses and have 30 expectations without doing yourself any harm and without injustice to the men you omit. (*P/Z* 52)

Pound's intended role for Zukofsky in the organization of a new generation here becomes clear. There is a sense that Pound no longer feels capable of sustaining the cultural legacy he has built for himself and his contemporaries. He appears to desire a group of poets who are no longer *his* contemporaries, but those of a younger generation which might look up to him as a precursor, and push him into the position of ancestor, perhaps even the position of the *classic*.

Pound had a better sense than most of his contemporaries of how literary generations worked. He knew the importance of an artist making a name as a proponent of the 'new' in order that, as fashions changed and a new 'new' took over, literary history would commemorate the former artist's work as an example of his or her age. Much of Pound's cultural prestige, for example, came from his founding of 'imagism', a movement which seemed so distinctly to break with the poetry of the preceding generation that even when it was no longer new or radical, it was remembered as an important event in the history of poetics. Pound remembered this nearly two decades later, as he coached Zukofsky in founding his own movement, telling him, 'Take your time and you can produce something that will DATE and will stand against Des Imagistes' (*P/Z* 45). Pound advises his disciple to engage with the past he himself instituted, in order that Zukofsky might create his own occasion, which will in turn require engagement from the next generation. In urging Zukofsky to succeed the imagists, Pound was urging his 'son' to follow the path which had first led him to the position of cultural power he then commanded. Rather than simply building Zukofsky's reputation on Pound's more typical tactics of preface-writing, alliance-making and media exposure (if 'little' magazines can be described as exposure), Pound rather hoped to encourage an entirely new generation built in effect upon the precepts he had established in his youth, but positioned *against* or *next to* his own movement in a sequence of generational displacement.

One theoretical model for such displacement of generations, as outlined earlier in the Introduction, is that elaborated by Pierre Bourdieu's study, 'The Field of Cultural Production, or: The Economic World Reversed':

The ageing of authors, schools and works is far from being the product of a mechanical, chronological, slide into the past; it results from the struggle between those who have made their mark (*fait date* – 'made an epoch') and who are fighting to persist, and those who cannot make their own mark without pushing into the past those who have an interest in stopping the clock, eternalizing the present stage of things.[47]

When speaking of *faire date*, Bourdieu might easily use Pound as an apt illustration, since the poet was concerned from early in his career with not only making a name for himself, but also creating a poetic stance which would make its place in history. One example can be found in his *Active Anthology*, a collection from 1933 which included many of the Objectivists, in which he claims, 'If ten pages out of its two hundred and fifty go into a Corpus Poetarum of a.d. 2033, the present volume will amply be justified.'[48] This focus on a future history, as we have seen, is characteristic of the self-conscious modernists, and Pound is perhaps foremost among them in placing a date upon every utterance, thereby charting his contribution to the historical progression of the period.

But Pound, while revealing an understanding of how poetic generations work, does not fulfil the role expected of him within Bourdieu's pattern. Throughout his correspondence with Zukofsky, Pound accentuates his own placement within the older generation, yet encourages Zukofsky and the younger generation in their upheaval and rebellion, even when the younger poets see no need to rebel. While Bourdieu outlines the tendency of the older generation – the 'consecrated' writers – towards conservation of the status quo and the preservation of the moment, Pound reveals himself eager to be superseded, and have his own generation relegated to the past. Pound's intention, in fact, seems as much centred upon his own encounter with the history books as it is upon seeing Zukofsky take his position in a new potential ascendancy. Bourdieu describes how this occurs: 'When a new literary or artistic group makes its presence felt in the field of literary or artistic production, the whole problem is transformed, since its coming into being, i.e. the previously dominant productions may, for example, be pushed into the status either of outmoded [*déclassé*] or of classic works.'[49] This is similar to the idea held by both Eliot and Pound on the effect the new work of art has upon the tradition it enters.[50] Obviously, Pound is counting on the Objectivists establishing him as *classic* rather than *déclassé*, since he is helping to fashion their movement in his own poetic lineage. But what is clear – especially with Pound's continual advice that 'the number ought to be NEW line up. You can mention me and old Bill Walrus [Williams] in the historic section' – is that Pound was actually intent on becoming a monument of the past, despite his continued presence near the centre of certain 1930s poetic circles (*P/Z* 51).

Zukofsky was clearly perplexed by Pound's efforts to have himself relegated to the history books at such a premature stage of his career. The younger poet had just begun to enjoy the proximity (if not always physical, at least on the same poetic platform) of his literary mentors, and was not willing to watch them disappear as a result of his own emergence. Zukofsky goes to great pains to remind the older poet that the names Pound and Williams still belong to the living generation and that they are still active in writing the most significant poetry of their age. Zukofsky is mystified at Pound's intention to insulate himself within the 'historic section', writing to ask, 'what's the use of preserving names if they don't represent literary capacity – didn't know you favored literary history' (*P/Z* 66). He goes on to advise Pound,

Don't think there'll be need for historic section – unless you send me The Return or something to reprint. If you send new work – it's obviously contemporary . . . Bill's Alphabet of Trees no more than 2 pages & not history – tho it'll go down into the anthologies. Define history as a story which it takes time to tell (Roger Kaigh) – but we deal with duration, the instant, NOW etc. (*P/Z* 71)

The question of Williams's poem is significant, since Zukofsky considers it a prime candidate for historical preservation, *but only after the passing of time*. Rather than getting ahead of himself by viewing poetry, like Pound, from the view of some future literary history, Zukofsky would rather present in his issue of *Poetry* the best poems he can find to represent that instant in time, whether they are produced by poets already established and 'classic' or by those who were only newly finding their voice.

Williams's career provides texture for the distinction between high and late modernism. His name surfaces in Michael Whitworth's introduction to a collection of essays on the subject of 'Late Modernism' – referring particularly to Robert Kern's question in 1978: 'Is Williams a late modernist, or an early postmodernist?'[1] In attempting to answer a question posed this way, one is naturally led away from reading Williams as a high modernist himself, despite his position in the poetic revolutions of the 1910s and 1920s. It has been shown as well that, despite his antagonism to

Eliot's *The Waste Land* and its influence, his aesthetic position on form, politics and auratic art was more in line with the autonomy of high modernism than either late modernism or postmodernism.[52] But perhaps most fascinating is what happened to Williams as high modernism itself became historical – as Williams's centrality to literary history was renegotiated by the academy and by his influence on later poets, notably the Objectivists and the Beats. It is the latter group that positions Williams towards the centre of literary modernism and literary celebrity as Eliot, Pound and Joyce had experienced decades earlier. For these reasons, in the months leading up to the introduction of the Objectivist group to the reading public, Williams would have had little of the desire that Pound expresses for pushing his own poetic career into the past. Williams is part of the present, the 'now', in a way that Pound seems incapable of, so long as he is conscious of his role in a future poetic genealogy.

Pound, as we have seen, took much more responsibility for the general progression of a poetic tradition than either Williams or Zukofsky. Where Pound concerned himself with both contemporary and enduring reputations, as well as the general notion of progress in the arts, Zukofsky merely wanted to show what could be produced in any given moment. In response to Pound's advice on making a stand against imagism in order to make a 'date' for his movement, Zukofsky reminds him, 'The only progress made since 1912 – is or are several good poems, i.e. the only progress possible – & criteria are in your prose works. Don't know <my issue> will have anything to do with homogeneity (damn it) but with examples of good writing' (*P/Z* 65). It is hard to know whether to read the phrase 'damn it' as regret or emphasis, but it is clear that Zukofsky realizes the importance of homogeneity for Pound's vision of a progression of literary generations succeeding one another like clockwork; but Zukofsky respectfully insists that he is unconcerned with movements, reputations or even literary periods. He openly admits that he wants to include some of the original imagists within his own group.

Think I'll have as good a 'movement' as that of the premiers imagistes – point is Wm. C. W. of today is not what he was in 1913, neither are you if you're willing to contribute – if I'm going to show what's going on today, you'll have to. The older generation is not the older generation if it's alive & up – Can't see why you shd. appear in the H[ound] & H[orn magazine] alive with 3 Cantos & not show that you are the <younger> generation in 'Poetry.' What's age to do with verbal manifestation, what's history to do with it, – good gord lets disassociate ijees – I want to show the poetry that's being written today – whether the poets are of masturbating age or the fathers of families don't matter. (*P/Z* 67)

Zukofsky clearly cares little about differences in membership or pro-gramme between the former imagist generation or the latter Objectivist, and only wants to show, nearly two decades on, that poetry is still being written in new and significant ways. For him, there is no need for antagonism between generations or movements, nor does he want to exclude those he considers to be the best poets of his period, even if they also belong to an earlier period. He goes on to say, 'Of course, you shd. appear merely as one of the <u>contributors</u> not as <u>favver</u>.' Zukofsky misses Pound's point, since this is exactly what the older poet wants: appearing in the historic section as a forefather, rather than 'merely' as a contributor. But Zukofsky, unwilling to dismiss or displace those of the former generation, is also unwilling to provide them with any preferential hand-ling. In other words, Zukofsky wants to be an editor, not to play the role Pound himself is trying to pass on, that of cultural arbiter and formulator of history.

   Pound's response makes some concessions, but he still refuses to allow that there is anything but a generation gap between himself and those he wants included in Zukofsky's magazine. He writes,

Am trying to write Cantos 31 to 35 and am not anxious to disguise myself as my grandson . . . my existence can be 'covered' by statement.
   In 1913 les jeunes did not respect their papas. In 1930 there are a few middle aged bokos that we can afford to let live. (*P/Z* 74)

Pound would perhaps see it as a compromise that he should let himself live, but such existence, for Zukofsky, remains insufficient, since it allows Pound to escape his responsibility as active contemporary. Rather, Pound's is a ghostly presence, one which can be 'covered' by a statement, as if persisting only through a profession of belief by the younger generation that the absent father is still present in spirit. But perhaps even more significant is the rationale Pound gives for his absence, evident in the insinuation that his present work on the Cantos would not somehow fit with the basic substance of Zukofsky's magazine. Pound reveals that he still thinks in homogenizing partitions, and that he cannot be part of a group writing 'youthful' poetry, even if Zukofsky does not even want the distinction of being a 'group'. Pound is incapable of sharing Zukofsky's perception of the magazine issue as an assembly of the best poetry of the moment, regardless of the contributing poet's age, level of celebrity or political affiliation. In his opinion, the only chance of fitting with the young, uninitiated and unrenowned would be to somehow disguise himself and his work.

The February issue of *Poetry* was eventually published with contributions by Williams, McAlmon, the four major male American Objectivists (Zukofsky, Oppen, Rakosi and Reznikoff) and Bunting, as well as a company of now-obscure names; there was only a small paragraph at the back regretting the absence of Pound, announcing, 'Mr. Pound gave over to younger poets the space offered him.'[53] But Pound's influence is still very present in the issue, particularly the belief that one poetic generation succeeds another. Monroe, for one, was unable to read Zukofsky's magazine without reproaching her chosen editor for his rebellion against his precursors, a rebellion that perhaps Pound had initiated on Zukofsky's behalf, against his wishes. Responding in the following issue of *Poetry* in an editorial entitled 'The Arrogance of Youth', Monroe writes, 'Certain attributes of youth are a continual surprise to the elder world, and none is more astonishing than youth's violent rebellion against the immediately preceding generation.'[54] Looking back at Zukofsky's editorial statements in the February issue, we can find only what might be called a mild hint at rebellion, only explicit really in a phrase Zukofsky borrowed directly from one of Pound's personal letters to him: 'Implied strictures of names generally cherished as famous, but not mentioned in this editor's *American Poetry 1920–30* or included among the contributors to this issue, is prompted by the historical method of the Chinese sage who wrote, "Then for nine reigns there was no literary production."'[55] Monroe is perhaps rightly indignant that Zukofsky should consider any poet who does not write according to his programme ('because there was neither consciousness of the "objectively perfect" nor an interest in clear or vital "particulars"') not to exist at all, but she is mistaking Zukofsky's statement of *support* for those few older poets he does believe in, particularly Pound and Williams, for that of a demolition-hungry avant-garde revolutionist. She writes, 'With one grand annihilating gesture this young exponent of a "new movement" sweeps off the earth the proud procession of poets whom, in our blindness and ignorance, we had fondly dedicated to immortality.'[56] But we must remember that it was at Pound's and Monroe's own insistence that this was ever a 'new movement', and that in stretching the boundaries of his group to include the older generation at all, Zukofsky was not being as rebellious as Pound had wanted him to be.

On this topic of Zukofsky's break with the preceding generation, Marjorie Perloff adopts Monroe's phrase – 'A few familiar names get by, though often by severely wrenching Mr. Zukofsky's barbed-wire entanglements' – to argue that Zukofsky's generation of 1930s poets should be viewed as separate and distinct from the high modernists who came before them, despite Zukofsky's evident wish to minimize this distinction.[57] But Perloff goes on to suggest that this difference mainly results from the fact that 'the relationship between tradition and the new had become vexed' – as has been suggested of all 'late modernists' discussed in this study.[58] The very fact that Zukofsky was unwilling to take up the role Pound had prescribed for him – that of the new proponent of the 'new' – meant that he was, perhaps unwittingly or unwillingly, advocating a new approach to the established view of poetic development. In other words, coming after the generation that shouted 'Make it new!', Zukofsky's insistence that there was no need to supersede the old generation might now be viewed as strangely radical. Even if the sentiment resulted from a conservative desire to retain links with a modernist giant like Pound, Zukofsky's stance certainly initiates a new way to view the problem of literary tradition and influence.

Zukofsky had made this clear even before he had reluctantly chosen the name 'Objectivist' for the group that would succeed the imagists. In his essay 'American Poetry 1920–1930', for example, Zukofsky reveals his belief that imagism 'never started merely with the image (1913)'.[59] This may not be a profound observation, but in stripping the 'movement' of its distinguishing principle, he opens space for himself to manoeuvre within the legacy its exponents had left. He continues, 'They are thus not a gang-plank for a younger generation to step onto. Or if they are, their individual rungs matter, and Cummings is maybe on shore or sometimes certainly on board.' This is an important statement regarding categorization and generations. Zukofsky seems uncomfortable with the idea of one generation relying on its predecessor's platform, and is willing to accept such an inheritance only if the case of each poem is taken on its own merit. He prefers the image of the ladder to that of a springboard, and every poet who has gone before, though possibly on a higher rung, is still on the same ladder, rather than offering their backs for the younger generation's feet. This view, as Andrew Crozier points out, was expressed in response to an essay by Zukofsky's friend René Taupin in which he establishes a theory of the evolution of literary generations, yet it still allows Zukofsky room to believe in the idea of development within the field of poetry.[60] He answers, 'New writers had perhaps better be given a chance to find their own forbears. Varying from possibly evolutionary implications of statement one may study the progress of individual work rather than its use in an "evolution" of poetry.'[61] Zukofsky is here still concerned with the idea of influence, but rather than focusing on one generation influencing another, he emphasizes the individual influences which can be found amongs contemporaries regardless of their age or which literary category they have previously belonged in – influences which are often simply, as he phrases it, 'in the air' at any single moment.

Zukofsky's short article of 1930 entitled 'Influence' is a key statement in this respect. In building a list of properties that affect the way one poet influences another, influence is seen, on the one hand, as a 'conscious choice or rejection of a literary tradition', but also, and on equal footing, as a 'presence in the air: sometimes the proximity of a poet's edified literary acquaintances, however conscious or unconscious a poet may be of the almost literal drafts around him'.[62] The more conscious decision to either embrace or dismiss an entire tradition is evident throughout Zukofsky's theoretical writings, where he establishes his predecessors by creating lists of poets significant to him, and also where he ignores other poets, regardless of their reputation, as if they never existed. But the less conscious influence, that which is 'in the air', seems also of great concern to Zukofsky and is a concept vital to an understanding of Objectivist doctrine as it engages with history. Throughout Zukofsky's critical writings there is a focus on the poet's interaction with the widest possible sense of tradition, including both the classical texts (Eliot's monuments) and what Bourdieu calls 'the ideas and problems which are "in the air" and circulate orally in gossip and rumour'.[63] This leads Michael Heller to make a distinction between 'Poundian and Objectivist poetics' based upon the fact that with the Objectivists there is always a focused sense 'of one's time'.[64] Although Pound exerts much effort in influencing the contemporary institutions, these are based upon a macrocosmic view of tradition, extending from a classical past into a vision of the future, engaging with the present often only in terms of how the present will look once it is past. Zukofsky, on the other hand, tends to equate the terms 'classical' and 'contemporary' fully in his critical writings, going so far as to suggest in *A Test of Poetry* (1948), 'The lasting attractions in the words of a poem and its construction make it classic and contemporary at the same time.'[65] What is important for Zukofsky is the production of 'good' poetry, and for him, that production results as much from what is hanging 'in the air' as it does from tradition, history or principle.

The fact that Zukofsky equates influence with 'the almost literal drafts' becomes more poignant when we look to the end of his life when the poet increasingly suffered from hypochondria. There are cases where Zukofsky's fear of 'catching' something seem directly related to his conception of his own poetry and that of his contemporaries. For example, when his friend Bunting returned to New York upon finding a renewed public enthusiasm for his work in America, he hoped to share his first public reading with Zukofsky. But the American poet, as Peter Makin relates, would not attend. After a brief private meeting, Bunting described Zukofsky as 'very bitter and, strangely, very jealous. A painful hour. He did not go to the reading because of "drafts". Yet I rank as his oldest friend.'[66] Zukofsky's hypochondria was, no doubt, acutely real, yet the metaphor is his own – the link between 'almost literal drafts' and the idea of influence, those intangible elements which hang 'in the air' in every age and have as much effect upon a poem as the weight of tradition and history. Bunting himself seems to link the idea of poetic 'jealousy' with the hypochondriac fear of draughts. This is not to suggest that Zukofsky, even unconsciously, neglected to support Bunting's reading because he was afraid of being influenced by him or by anyone else. Instead, Zukofsky's hypochondria is used here to illustrate just how conscious he was in later life of what could be carried invisibly through the atmosphere of any given time or place.

Yet Zukofsky's obsession with 'drafts' was not simply the product of old-age neurosis. As his wife Celia points out, 'I think Louie was born suffering from hypochondria. I never knew Louie not to complain of drafts.'[67] In many ways, this anxiety over what was 'in the air' helped Zukofsky develop a doctrine for the group he called the Objectivists – that each poem is quite simply an object, growing out of the particular moment in time in which it exists. There is a distinction to be made here between the high modernist view of a new work finding its place among the existing monuments, which suggests the present grappling with – even changing – the past, and the Zukofskyan idea that all times are hanging in the air of the present. For him, 'It would be just as well when dealing with "recencies" to deal with Donne or Shakespeare', since, as he states it, 'the good poems of today are – as jobs – not far from the good poems of yesterday.'[68] The only reason that 'the really new work' can be recognized as such is that historians, whose existence Zukofsky finds pertinent, resurrect 'language structures' and traditions ('Pound from the Troubadours, Eliot from Webster, etc.').[69] And while the conscious acceptance or denial of an inherited tradition is important to Zukofsky's idea of poetic influence, equally important is the idea that all poets are simultaneously contemporary and classical, sharing the influences which can be found within the 'almost literal drafts' of a specific time or place. It is for this reason that Zukofsky felt it did not matter that Pound was of an older generation than him, since as long as the two existed within some kind of shared context or 'tradition' they would be subjected to the same poetic influences, and no distinction would need to be drawn between one generation and the other.

Pound and Zukofsky's affectionate father/son relationship did not last for more than a decade. By the mid-1930s, the two were openly squabbling over a number of issues. In a particularly heated exchange of letters during 1935, Pound berates Zukofsky for being behind the times, saying, 'If you are too god damn dumb to read what is being printed/ and insist on sticking in 1927 ... thass thaaat ... I can't hold the boat FOR you' (*P/Z* 162–3). Pound's claim is based on subject matter, though, rather than poetics, and since Pound's next anthology was to be 'econ/ conscious', Pound says Zukofsky will be left out. Zukofsky answers criticism with criticism, claiming that Pound's latest poetry had done 'nothing to move the cockles of my heart or the network of my brain' and that, without Zukofsky's input in his anthology, there would be 'nothing in it'. The relationship quickly turns businesslike and sometimes hurtful. Pound complains, 'I shd/ have been better employed on Fenollosa, during the past 25 minutes or whatever. how many hours per day ... etc. are you worth' (*P/Z* 170; ellipsis Pound's). The tendency to put a symbolic value upon the poet's work and their friendship is continued in Zukofsky's reply:

Not a minute of yr. time if you can produce anything to equal in value the first Canto or the opening of the XXXeth; maybe a good deal more of yr. time than you can imagine I'm worth, if you continue to say the same things, after de Gourmont, you said 20 years ago, having forgotten by now what they meant. (*P/Z* 172).

The letter closes with the line, 'And a new life to you, Z'. After this, the correspondence is much less frequent.

That Pound and Zukofsky were busy assigning values to the time spent on each other and to their respective poetry according to how up to date it was reveals how completely these two poets immersed themselves in the business of poetry. In contrast, we can look at the career of another Objectivist, Lorine Niedecker, who also happened to play a role in the above dispute which unravelled the father/son relationship. Pound had published Niedecker on the advice of Zukofsky in his guest-edited issue of *Bozart-Westminster*, but immediately wrote to Zukofsky to tell him, 'I don't think yr/Niedecker is so hot/ ... It got by, because I printed one tadpole on each recommendation of qualified critics' (*P/Z* 163). Niedecker had approached Zukofsky a few years earlier just as Zukofsky, in some ways, had originally sought out Pound. Zukofsky defends her only partially to Pound, saying, 'Nor have I swallowed Miss Niedecker's mental stubbornness. However, her output has <u>some</u> validity, <u>some</u> spark of energy, which the solipsistic daze=maze of <u>Mr. Kummings</u> hath not' (*P/Z* 165). We see here for the first time Zukofsky in the role of mentor rather than disciple, though he admits he cannot 'swallow' her 'mental stubbornness' – a pursuit of traditions other than those in which Zukofsky had himself invested.

By this time, Zukofsky and Niedecker were two years into their affair. Niedecker, a poet from rural Wisconsin who had received little support in her literary endeavours, was attracted to Zukofsky as the leading figure in a brand-new movement of poetry after his organization of the Objectivist issue of *Poetry*. She wrote to him and he encouraged her, helping her get published. Niedecker spent some time with Zukofsky in New York before returning to Wisconsin, the affair permanently over by 1939 when Zukofsky married Celia Thaew. But Niedecker had found much more in Zukofsky than a lover, and their relationship continued through correspondence and occasional meetings for the rest of her life. Zukofsky provided Niedecker with a desperately needed poetic theorist and critic, as well as someone experienced in the institutions of literature. Even more important, Zukofsky provided a link to the tradition of poets who 'mattered' – something Niedecker was quietly concerned about her entire career. Zukofsky and Niedecker even shared their poetic subject matter, telling each other stories or phrases which the other would incorporate into their poetry. It did not matter that they rarely saw each other, Zukofsky told Niedecker in an unpublished letter (paraphrased by Jenny Penberthy), since immediate contact was not so important as 'what was in the air of a time' (*NCZ* 47). In this respect, their shared poetic was typically Objectivist and mutually influencing.

Although Niedecker is now often placed (when discussed at all) near the boundaries of the Objectivist group and in the Pound tradition, it is important to note, as Peter Nicholls has shown, that Niedecker's earliest poetry – that which showed her 'mental stubbornness' in not conforming to Pound's and Zukofsky's doctrines and tastes – was written in the Surrealist tradition.[70] Niedecker herself did not realize this was the case until Zukofsky filled in the gaps in her knowledge of recent literary history. Her distress over the fact is evident in a letter written to *Poetry* magazine, as she discusses a poem she has recently submitted; 'The one, "Progression", was written six months before Mr. Zukofsky referred me to the surrealists for correlation . . . [I]t's a little disconcerting to find oneself six months ahead of a movement and twenty years behind it.'[71] This is a crucial concern for a poet of the modernist period, where being up to date and 'of one's time' was the primary distinction of the 'important' poet. But she is right to call herself 'six months ahead' of Surrealism, since she had developed her own poetic technique independently of the movement's influence. Yet Zukofsky, who is somewhat dismissive of Surrealism, makes sure she is aware that she is falling behind her own time in following poetic currents he claims – a clear exaggeration – to be twenty years old. Niedecker's phrase 'Zukofsky referred me to the surrealists for correlation' perhaps best provides the critical terms with which we might understand her position in her own literary field. While the poetry of this rural poet took her environment and its 'folk' for subject matter, her entire career was focused intensively upon her primary point of reference within the literary world, Louis Zukofsky, and it was he who provided some kind of correlation with literary tradition. It should be remembered that our own placement of Niedecker among the Objectivists is a late construction, and that she would not have had the comfort of belonging to a 'group' which the others, simply in having been published together, might have enjoyed. Early in Niedecker's career, Zukofsky provided the only literary connection to anything outside herself.

Much has been made in contemporary criticism of Niedecker's chosen stance of anonymity and marginality.[72] The question of how to reconcile her at times uncultured 'folksy' persona with the sophistication of her poetic creation is thus resolved in the elaboration of a heroic figure who chose to defect from the avant-garde circles and institutions of high culture in order to produce poetry untainted by commercialism and literary partisanship. But whether Niedecker chose to remain free of literary institutions, following the example of Emily Dickinson, or was simply excluded from them, she is unique among late modernist poets for being so far removed from the centralizing forces of the Pound tradition while still being very much identified in conjunction with it. In many of the letters she wrote to Zukofsky and Cid Corman, Niedecker reveals a distinct – possibly formulated – naïvety when it comes to matters of publication, from copyrights to publicity, and a persistent misunderstanding of a range of literary politics, from constructions of literary history to common opinions held about her contemporaries. In other words, all the things Pound specialized in offering a young poet were withheld from, perhaps by, Niedecker.

What is it, then, that positions Niedecker among the poets in the Pound tradition when she began her career unknowingly writing Surrealist verse, and was so far removed from – even disliked by – the great arbiter of literary reputations himself? The obvious answer is that, as a pupil of Zukofsky, who was himself a pupil of Pound, Niedecker inherited certain Poundian principles without ever having contact with Pound himself. There is little indication of when she first became aware that Pound was in many respects the founder of the type of poetry she was writing, but it is almost certain that again Zukofsky was responsible for her 'correlation' with the movement. This is not to say that she was forced to write 'Poundian poetry' by a domineering Zukofsky, or to underestimate her own formulation of her poetic; conversely, she was keenly aware of her place in writing 'new' poetry. Late in life she would recall, at the age of eighteen, reading Wordsworth and being 'vaguely aware that the poetry current (1921) was beginning to change'.[73] This is Niedecker's kind of poetic awareness – based upon instinct and impression, rather than concrete knowledge of movements, circles and histories. In 1967 she would write to Corman discussing a new kind of poem she wanted to write: 'the kind of thing I mean is in the air, Cid, it will be done by somebody else if I don't . . . [Zukofsky] & I have always gone neck to neck in sensing things.'[74] Yet her intuition seemed to lead her, in 1921, to a vague awareness of the innovations being made at that time in more cosmopolitan parts of the world.

What is difficult with Niedecker, as with many other private authors, is to understand her own conception of the literary field within which she wrote, especially given Zukofsky's lead on most matters of literary tradition and doctrine. So while it is important to allow Niedecker the anonymity she seems to have wanted, we must simultaneously investigate the problems posed by her introduction, in the mid-1930s, to the group of poets working with or around Pound, a literary figure she neither knew directly nor seemed interested in corresponding with. Even if we manage to mute our own posthumous constructions of her career within literary histories of the period, we are still perhaps reassured that her contemporaries viewed her poetry within the Pound tradition. Edward Honig remembers in the late 1930s Niedecker feeling 'vitally connected with poetry in the Pound school', and he goes on to say, 'It seemed pretty clear that most of Lorine's reading of poetry, science, political and music theory came directly from Zukofsky and Pound, a paideuma I was not ready to follow.'[75] By 1951, she was enthusiastic about reading the new collection of Pound's letters, remarking to Zukofsky, 'Oh me, those were exciting days, the 30s and what we knew of the time preceding thru Pound. I got a lot out of letters that spoke of what to read altho I have

Pound's How to Read' (*NCZ* 177). There is certainly, even in Niedecker's own mind, a sense of inheritance from Pound, who, though only eighteen years older than Niedecker, strikes a grandfatherly figure, being far too distant to take on the more primary role of literary father. This space was reserved for Zukofsky throughout her life, and Pound remained a shared mythology built on poetic dogma and stories of 'exciting days'.

Yet questions about the haste with which Niedecker attached herself to an entire poetic lineage cannot be quickly answered, even given her detachment from theoretical conceptions of literary history. There is no doubt Niedecker was as widely read as her context allowed her to be, yet she attaches herself so fiercely to the Pound/Zukofsky tradition that, when confronted by literary acquaintances with differing opinions on the importance of these two, she seems genuinely astonished. From her first perception of Zukofsky as chief Objectivist and figure of authority within poetic circles, she seems to have retained an inflated image of his influence among his contemporaries. Similarly, when accepting Pound as a figure-head for the current of modernist poetry she found herself caught in, she fails to grasp the idea that it is possible to deviate from that stream. As she writes to Zukofsky as late as 1958:

Wyndham Lewis (Time and Western Man) on Pound etc ... yes, I see it all much better now – sometimes it takes a person years to really understand a thing if you miss out on some little explanation in the beginning. Lewis is not at all friendly to P. Whereas I thought P had a great regard for Lewis and that therefore there was no real criticism of Pound in that early day – mid-twenties. (*NCZ* 244; ellipsis Niedecker's)

Niedecker reveals herself to be the victim of a rather limited vision of literary history, unaware of alternate traditions through her correspond-ence with and directed reading from Zukofsky. Even now it seems common to come across literary histories which place Pound at the centre of a dominant movement of poetry to which there seems no alternative 'serious' poetic development. With Zukofsky as her only 'correlation' within the literary field, Niedecker had already made her choice to inherit the tradition in which we still read her verse.

This is not to suggest her work should be extracted from the context of the Pound-focused Objectivists. If this is a case of mistaken identity, it is her mistake, and not the responsibility of literary criticism to seek independence for a poet who did not herself desire it. But the question of literary inheritance and indebtedness adds a new context at times to Niedecker's poetry – verse which takes as its own theme a desired escape from the legal side of legacies and ownership. For example, an untitled poem is suggestive of this:

> The death of my poor father
> leaves debts
> and two small houses.
> To settle this estate
> a thousand fees arise –
> I enrich the law.[76]

The end of the poem finds Niedecker contemplating her own death and legacy – a book of Chinese poems and a pair of binoculars – seeking to find that little something left behind after the legacies are stripped away through indebtedness. Niedecker's grandfather and father appear regularly in her poetry, as does the land she inherits from them. A poem entitled 'Foreclosure' suggests, 'Leave me the land/Scratch out: the land' – an action which renders the line simply 'Leave me'. Foreclosure appears in at least two other poems, and her inherited property becomes a recurrent symbol of inheritance and debt.[77]

Still, for all those who will argue for a new history to be written which features the Niedecker who commendably retained a quality of verse independent of the influence of her male colleagues and the literary field she fitted into only problematically, Niedecker's own choices, and her own voice, must figure within our own posthumous constructions. And while recognition for a deserving poet is always preferable to neglect, an alteration of history is a different matter. Even if we were to remove Niedecker from the 'narrative of pathos' which Rachel Blau DuPlessis sees as a danger, how does one read an 'anonymous' poet? One can read an anonymous *poem*, but in configuring Lorine Niedecker, with name intact, as an anonymous poet, she takes an impossibly precarious position without points of reference, and we miss the essential context which Niedecker herself had a hand in constructing. Niedecker acknowledged as much to Zukofsky, after reading Jonathan Williams's review of her book, *My Friend Tree*, saying, 'And you, my mentor and champion, he [Williams] says – true, but I was very careful this shdn't come from *me* so's not to embarrass you . . . I wdn't know how to write poetry without Zukofsky and J. wdn't know how to review me without Zukofsky!' (*NCZ* 321). This declaration of dependence is no doubt part exaggeration, since we know that Niedecker was capable of retaining her own poetic voice and style, and brought something new to Objectivist verse. But the second point is the more relevant, since Niedecker's poetry had by then been so rooted in Zukofsky's paradigm that to discuss her work out of this context would be to miss its fundamental framework. That a poem needs a framework becomes apparent, as Niedecker learns, only when it is published and reviewed – in other words, when it is fitted into existing traditions and institutions.

There is certainly a point to be made that Niedecker, as a rural and unconnected poet, should be allowed to remain free of our imposed structures, whether institutional or merely practical. After all, in the words of DuPlessis, 'She made no "literary career".'[78] Yet a poet without a career rarely gets read. Niedecker knew that Dickinson was an exceptional case in receiving a posthumous reputation as a major poet, despite an entire lifetime of silence. Niedecker wrote to Corman, discussing the fact that one could, if one chose, withdraw from literary circles and institutions, suggesting, 'Also that there is such a thing as silence – and the great, everpresent possibility that our poems may not get read.'[79] This equation of silence, a quality she valued, with a permanent lack of audience, a situation she feared, probably best reveals why she allowed her 'literary career' to centre around Zukofsky, a poet with relatively slight readership, but one Niedecker had faith would eventually find fame.[80] And as she once remarked to Corman, dissatisfied with the length of time it took Zukofsky and her to find publishers for their work, 'Well, we are the long range people, you included.'[81] This is, of course, not dissimilar to Bunting's belief that he would find an audience eventually because of his connection to Yeats, Pound, Eliot and Williams. Success comes eventually to those who are tied to poets already bound for the history books. As Bourdieu has outlined in an essay called 'The Long Run and the Short Run', the most significant difference between 'commercial' and 'cultural businesses' is the length of time they are willing to wait for their investment to pay off. Where the commercial business hopes to meet 'a pre-existent demand', and allows for the 'built-in obsolescence' of their product, the cultural business engages in an 'entirely future-oriented production'.[82] Niedecker, without acknowledging the poetry 'business' directly, admits that she is invested, along with her allies, for 'the long run'.

This, then, should be acknowledged as Niedecker's chosen 'literary career', though she certainly put less effort into reputation-forming and infiltration of literary history than some of her contemporaries. To quote DuPlessis once more, 'Poets alone can rarely put themselves on the scholarly or critical agenda; to do so they must write criticism, give interviews, network, make movements, perform acts of cultural flourish.

Niedecker did not. For instance, she wrote only three reviews, two of Zukofsky, one of Corman.'[83] This is at once true and misleading: it is actually common enough for poets to take the initiative required to gain them scholarly attention. That Niedecker opted out is to a certain extent true, in that she showed *less* initiative in establishing a critical position for herself than other poets, but she was not silent, nor completely unconnected with a critical or institutional framework. In the three reviews Niedecker wrote, she left us a kind of clue, as if directing our gaze first to her mentor (Zukofsky) and then to her contemporary and supporter (Corman) for correlation. The Niedecker we glimpse in her letters to these two associates shows far too much concern over her own and her contemporaries' reputations, particularly in the 'long-range' future, to be considered fully invested in anonymity. She may have been detached from any company of poets and deliberately naïve as to the 'business' side of poetry, but we must not imagine her to be unaware that the 'business' was going on, or that to be read, she must position herself within a literary tradition in such a way that, in some distant future, she would be a significant figure, even if it was, as she imagines, '500 years from now' (*NCZ* 303).

Pound's brand of modernism, when viewed through the careers of some of the Objectivists, can be read simultaneously in terms of inheritance and investment. What we now so readily term 'the Pound tradition' was partly formed by these younger modernists who were eager to attach themselves to some shared ancestry, finding in Pound established poetic doctrines, a ready-made audience and a sense of being involved in an evolutionary succession of poets. Yet it was a long-term investment, and not an insured one, as Pound himself knew. He wrote to Zukofsky many times asking the younger poet to strengthen his [Pound's] reputation wherever possible, as in May 1932: 'Also the fact that I have a crikikul METHOD ought to be rubbed into the blighted pubk/and that yawp (started by Aldington; about Eliot beink the more seerious schorlar or crik or whatever, ought to be spiked. fer the sake of everybodys future income' (*P/Z* 126). We can guess who is included in 'everybody' – clearly Aldington and Eliot are not – and it is easy to understand Pound's concern for himself and for those invested in his programme and reputation. Any young poet coming into a career in the 1920s or 1930s was faced with the question of position-taking in the bipolar literary field of Eliot and Pound, twin giants of publicity and arbiters of cultural values. If the poet had no desire to stand completely alone, in defiance of the emergent and ascendant modernism, as an apostate, there was little choice but to invest in one heritage or another, selecting one's ancestors and eventual inheritance.

Niedecker, we have seen, was twice removed from the generation of Eliot and Pound yet can still be firmly cast in the modernist tradition, beginning her career in the 1930s and adopting Zukofsky as her literary guide. But because she chose to invest herself in the poetic lineage of Pound and Zukofsky does not mean she had great faith in her own poetic pedigree, or even in every member of the genealogy. Niedecker's faith in Pound in particular was tested on a number of occasions as she grew aware that Zukofsky's vision of his mentor was not shared universally. She was shocked to read of Pound admitting his errors, and even questions the validity of the interview with Grazia Livi in which he states them.[84] And in one of her last letters to Corman, she would reveal her devotion to Pound to be less based on affinity or affection than on a sense of duty, saying, 'I'm a little bunch of marshland violets offered to the crooked lawyer – O no . . . how could I refer to Pound in that way??? – I owe so much to him as most present-day poets do.'[85] But Niedecker was well experienced in problematic inheritances. Her Wisconsin property, to which she often drew parallels with her poetry, had been inherited from her father greatly diminished by payoffs to keep peace with a neighbour whose wife he was sleeping with, leaving only a small strip of land ravaged each year by spring floods. Niedecker, speaking of this situation, might just as well be speaking of the doubts she had about her modernist inheritance, when she says, 'You live with the knowledge that this land where your life and your money are completely tied up is a lost cause and it must be kept secret otherwise you're totally sunk' (*NCZ* 246).

Niedecker saw hints within her own lifetime that she would find a readership in the long run, but she did not live long enough to confirm that her investment had paid off. She is still finding readers, not yet widely, but in her own right, as well as grouped with the Objectivists. Even towards the end of her life she was already a witness to the appropriation of the other poets in her 'tradition' by critical, academic and publishing institutions. She was amused to see, with the publication of Zukofsky's shorter poems, that he was becoming, as she phrases it, 'Respectable at last!' (*NCZ* 347). But with respectability came absence. Zukofsky grew more careful and withdrawn, even from his closest friends. He would not give Niedecker permission to publish a selection of his letters, even heavily excised, nor to ever mention his son, even in conjunction with her cycle of poems dedicated 'For Paul'. She watched as poetic institutionalization began to change Zukofsky, as she would comment in December 1965: 'so much in LZ's life is being revised'.[86] What hurt Niedecker most was Zukofsky's concessions to the universities, particularly the University of Texas. In 1963 Zukofsky wrote to Niedecker asking her to return some of the books he had written which, over the years, he had sent her; he wanted the Humanities Research Center to have a complete collection of all his works. Niedecker responds, 'You ask me to return some of your books. I wish you'd ask me to return some hair or flesh. This really hurts' (*NCZ* 335). But Niedecker submitted in the end and sent the two volumes she had been asked for – *Le Style Apollinaire* and *55 Poems* – since Zukofsky had insisted, feeling it was an essential part of his literary legacy and the final investment in his own poetic career. As Penberthy points out in a footnote, though, these two books do not make up part of the present Zukofsky Collection at the university.

It is perhaps the most lamentable aspect of the 'business' of poetic inheritances that a legacy might grow in value by so much that poets are tempted into selling their birthrights. Niedecker, as we have seen, was a victim. She wrote to Zukofsky a year later to say, 'I ought to be shot for parting with that Feb., 31 Poetry. And I remember the evening you reached up on your shelves and handed it to me to keep' (*NCZ* 352). The construction of 'Objectivism' – false as it may be – was beginning by this time to transform a simple gift from one poet to another into a valuable artefact, commemorating the birth of a new generation, even if that generation had never conceived of itself as such. Likewise, about this time, Zukofsky was trading off his own received inheritance, selling the letters Pound had sent him over the years – by now valuable commodities – in order that the University of Texas might publish his *Bottom: On Shakespeare* when no one else would.[87] Is he to be blamed? No. It was the most practical method of having one of his most important critical texts published. Niedecker was even more practical perhaps: when Zukofsky would not allow her to publish a selection of his letters to her, she sold them to the Humanities Research Center as well, and with the money built a garage on their property which she and her husband named the 'University of Texas' (*NCZ* 103). It is a fitting end to her career. So much of Niedecker's poetry is based upon her native territory, her inherited ancestry, yet it was her share in the modernist inheritance which brought her enough money to finally give something back, erecting a monument to the business-side of poetry production on the very site that produced her own innovative offering to the tradition.

CHAPTER 5

The last word: or how to bring modernism to an end

'The rear-guard . . . advances towards 1914, for all that is "advanced" moves backwards, now, towards that impossible goal, of the pre-war dawn.'

Wyndham Lewis, Blasting and Bombardiering (BB 256)

The problem for the high modernists was how to create a sense of the new that might endure beyond the period of its innovation. Some were so successful that their names are still associated with what is 'advanced' despite the fact that they have been considered classics for nearly a century. Ezra Pound's and T. S. Eliot's conception of tradition – where 'the really new work of art' takes its place among the 'existing monuments' – relies as much on a view of future histories as it does on history itself; it is a position which reaches simultaneously forward and back and, paradoxically, towards revolt, renewal and reconciliation. Eliot's career is most often taken for an example of this somewhat contradictory position, where on the one hand his poetry seems exceedingly new and modern, while on the other hand his criticism seeks to gain a traditional footing for this poetic modernity. Patrick Parrinder, in assessing critical authority, even goes so far as to wonder if Eliot's critical position lost 'its sense of purpose once the modernist literary revolution was completed?'[1] Yet implicit within this question is a whole new paradox, that of a modernist revolution which *can* be completed. Parrinder no doubt refers to Eliot's success in turning his brand of 'making it new' into an established position, complete with critical authority, influence within publishing institutions and the endorsement of a Nobel Prize for Literature. Yet the question must remain: how did modernism – focused as it was on the production of new works of art – ever find itself completed?

Part of the answer, of course, lies in the dual nature of high modernism. As Djuna Barnes wrote, 'Man makes his history with the one hand and "holds it up" with the other', a useful portrayal of the problem facing the modernist artist, as I hope to have illustrated in previous chapters.[2]

Modernists were not just engaged in writing the literature of the period, but were often simultaneously acting as critics and historians of their own movement. This self-preservation had two main effects. On the one hand, it meant that the new could instantly become historical – not just engaging with, but *becoming* history. Gilbert Seldes, for example, in an article entitled 'Nineties – Twenties – Thirties' in *The Dial* in 1922, was able to identify contemporary works (specifically 1922's *Ulysses* and *The Waste Land*) 'which will be "modern" for the next generation'.[3] This is an important statement, coming in the very same issue of *The Dial* in which Eliot's *The Waste Land* was published in America, recognizing that some works can establish themselves in literary history as quickly as they appear. Furthermore, to stretch one's modernity into the future is to draw out the length of one's contemporaneity, making an artist seem new for an indefinite period, though here Seldes extends it one generation. He reassures new writers that it is not contemptible 'to lag behind Joyce' since *Ulysses*, and by implication *The Waste Land*, is 'the only complete expression of the spirit' of its time.[4]

The second effect of high modernism's dual nature (revolution and reconciliation) is tied to this: as works become modern for all time, they become monuments much more quickly, so that even living writers held primary positions within 'the tradition'. The *preservation* of that which is new came to be associated with 'advanced' literature itself. Paul De Man would go so far as to define modernity as the discovery that being modern is in fact impossible.[5] One might like to change the notion of the impossibility of 'being modern' to that of 'remaining modern' when dealing with this period, though it is to some extent exactly what the high modernists succeeded in doing. It became clear to some contemporary commentators that high modernism's immediate self-preservation resulted in the creation of an art-less society – a period where art could no longer be produced – as did Wyndham Lewis.[6] But then Friedrich Nietzsche had pointed out half a century earlier that 'art flees if you immediately spread the historical awning over your deeds'.[7]

The writers coming straight after high modernism, as we have seen, felt this most strongly. The late modernist generation would, according to Seldes, inherit as contemporaries a group who were also their predecessors, remaining up to date despite having embalmed themselves (to use a favourite phrase of the late modernists) in history a decade or two earlier. In the four preceding chapters, we have seen how a number of different late modernists dealt with their apparent 'belatedness' – writing in the late 1920s and 1930s despite the fact that certain works of the 1910s and early

1920s still epitomized the modern. Yet it was not only a problem for those who came after. The high modernists themselves felt the effects of their own and their contemporaries' monumental achievements. Ezra Pound in *The Little Review* attempted to bring an end to the Christian Era, suggesting a new calendar to designate 1 November 1921 as the first day in Year 1 p.s.U. (that is, post scriptum *Ulysses*).[8] Pound's response to Joyce's novel not only illustrates contemporary regard for the text, but also outlines the modernist desire to begin again, not disregarding history, but renewing it. Even if the new calendar was meant only as a joke, it illustrates the fundamental problem of literary modernism, since it establishes everything written prior to *Ulysses* as part of the superseded, but simultaneously renders everything written after *Ulysses* incapable of superseding it in its turn, since these works find their place in the *Ulysses* era.

Pound was alone in making use of the calendar for a month or two, but the conception of *Ulysses* as a novel which had confirmed its date in the literary histories was widespread. Ford Madox Ford went on record in a contemporary review of the novel to say, 'If it does not make an epoch – and it well may! – it will at least mark the ending of a period.'[9] Despite (or because of) the emphasis placed upon it as an unsurpassably new work of art, a sense of its finality seemed to settle on the novel. It seemed so new a thing that it was difficult to imagine what could go further; thus it must (so the thinking went) be the last work of its kind. Pound, years later, spoke of 'the dead-end of "Ulysses"', by which he meant 'that "Ulysses" represents the end of a period or of a cycle of composition'.[10] Eliot, too, as Virginia Woolf remembered, had felt at the time that nothing more could be said after *Ulysses*: 'how could anyone write again after achieving the immense prodigy of the last chapter?'[11] Eliot, of course, in struggling with how to write in the wake of *Ulysses*, managed to compose his own monument, in turn leaving Pound to say of *The Waste Land*: 'Eliot's poem is very important, almost enough to make everyone else shut up shop.'[12] The statement was made, it must be said, in order to sell the poem to its eventual publisher, but even matters of commerce have their effect on the reputations of poets and create the shadows from out of which new poets must find their way. Pound himself would leave *The Cantos* which, though acknowledged by him as 'a botch' and finally left incomplete, would create one further modernist monument about which a younger poet would write:

> There they are, you will have to go a long way round
> if you want to avoid them.
> It takes some getting used to. There are the Alps,
> fools! Sit down and wait for them to crumble.[13]

These descriptions of monumentality, establishment and endurance, all used to describe markedly new and innovative works of art, reveal the sense of an ending that the high modernist generation brought about even just a few decades after the movement's first revolution.

Despite the obstacles such modernist monuments seem to raise up – despite the fact that many modernist contemporaries might have agreed with Georg Lukács when he says, 'We see that modernism leads not only to the destruction of traditional forms, it leads to the destruction of literature as such' – it is important to remember that literature did not stop dead after 1922, but continued to be written in a similar vein for two decades or longer.[14] The writers of this latter period have formed the subject of this study, which has investigated their attempts at the perpetuation of modernity even after the establishment of a new and sustained mode for the period. Some invested themselves in 'changing the changing', thereby setting themselves up as alternatives to the more accepted form of being modern – a new counter-countercurrent. In many ways, this simply returned them to the more radical prewar modernism. Others preferred to ignore the problem outlined by the high modernists themselves, maintaining that the only thing that mattered was the new works produced year by year. However, it was not an easy problem to ignore, as the problem of modernity began to challenge the very notion of a writer's vocation. Modernity, or newness, became simultaneously the only justification of the writer's career and the main challenge to him or her. The modernist latecomers could neither accept nor reject their predecessors' claims to modernity since the former would deprive them of making their mark and the latter, as De Man makes clear, would be simply repetitive and unoriginal.[15] Any claims to a new revolution in literature would simply repeat the claims of the high modernists themselves, responding to high modernism's 'make it new' with simply another 'make it new'. The high modernists had, to varying extents, defined themselves as being new and a break with this position would be no break at all. A more fundamental change was needed.

We have seen this desire for a more fundamental change in the writings of Lewis, who declared that the creation of something new simply for the sake of it being new is not enough. It has also been mentioned that Lewis, after first stating his case in *The Caliph's Design* in 1919, went seven years before publishing his next book, a length of time matched only by his more complete silence from 1941 to 1948.[16] This abstinence from book publication is not completely inexplicable. Lewis himself, as we have seen, suggested he had gone underground, waiting to see what would happen in the postwar period. It was an uneasy period for him for several reasons, not least of which was the ascendancy and establishment of his former allies. Lewis, it must be noted, would not have felt *forced* into a position of silence or marginalization. But he was not satisfied with the stylistic revolution fulfilled by Eliot, Pound, Joyce, Woolf, Marcel Proust and Gertrude Stein, and desired some kind of further, more fundamental, change to society before the really new art could be realized. Lewis struggled against his contemporaries for much of the last half of his life to bring about a more extensive revolution than had been consummated in 1922. His level of success is debatable.

Although Lewis perceived himself as a lone dissident – *the* enemy – he was not, as we have seen, a singular voice. His critical position in relation to ascendant modernism is perhaps most closely matched by that of Laura Riding, who stopped publishing poems herself about the same time as Lewis's second period of literary withdrawal. In Lewis's case, this latter silence is probably best attributed to the war, which fulfilled many of his prophecies, as well as making it materially difficult to carry on writing through its duration. It might be tempting to attribute the same cause to Riding, who also was forced to move back to North America during the war years. But with Riding we are left carefully described details of her reasons for the renunciation of poetry, which will be discussed in some detail shortly. But there is perhaps more than coincidence in the fact that both Lewis and Riding abandoned their careers (in Lewis's case for only a time). Other modernist latecomers reveal a similar trend. George Oppen, Carl Rakosi and Basil Bunting all left off writing poetry for a significant period. Barnes and Jean Rhys, both late modernist novelists, also took extended leave from their careers, only to return with new works produced late in life.[17] While neither universal among modernist latecomers nor identical in nature, it must be recognized that there was a general loss of faith in the production of literature within this group of writers during roughly the same period of time. Furthermore, it should be noted that the suspension of literary activity in most of these cases is of a different nature from that of, say, Pound sinking into fragments and suggestions of failure with the later *Cantos*. Pound was always considered a poet, even when he was not writing – one who simply could not bring off his masterpiece. Many of the late modernists appear to feel conflicted over the writer's vocation itself – a crisis of modernist literature which seems to have first been recognized with the maturity of the latecomer generation.

Apart from Lewis's time buried in the British Library, Oppen was one of the earliest of the modernist latecomers to suspend his poetic career.

In 1934 his first book of poems, *Discrete Series*, was published, his last act as a poet for nearly twenty-five years. Poetry seemed to him, in the Depression of the 1930s, an 'utterly inadequate' form of expression.[18] Oppen is not simply referring to his own poetry but to the high modernist approach in general. He mentions Pound, Eliot, William Carlos Williams and W. B. Yeats by name as examples of poets who seemed too detached from life as it was at that time, setting up the tradition in poetry from which he felt he had to turn away. Oppen's silence, then, had something to do with 'an act of conscience', a politically motivated shift from autonomous art to more practical action; but as Oppen himself relates, it was 'a poetic exploration at the same time', a recognition that poetry of the period was becoming so much noise when it should, where effective, 'be at least as good as dead silence'.[19] Rachel Blau DuPlessis thus argues that Oppen's literary withdrawal stems from an implicit criticism of modernist poetry as ineffective.[20] Oppen's belief that 'there are situations which cannot honorably be met by art' runs alongside the belief that art, in its turn, cannot be honourably met by a life sheltered from the world; or as Mary Oppen states: 'a life had to be lived out of which to write'.[21]

The criticism of high modernism that Oppen first forged by his silence in 1934 is not dissimilar from Lewis's critical attacks of the late 1920s and early 1930s; nor is the idea that one must first live in order to find new ways to write very far away from Henry Miller's problem of avoiding the literary affectations of the writer's vocation, seeking to build an oeuvre from the souvenirs and archives of his 'anecdotal life'.[22] Many late modernists, in fact, seem to share a desire for the end of what they call literature, even where that does not mean giving up writing. Oppen says that, during his twenty-five years of silence, 'I at no time thought I wasn't a poet', yet he also writes of his desire 'to be free from the career of poetry'.[23] Clearly, there are distinctions, though sometimes overlapping, between simply writing poems, *not* writing poems but considering oneself a poet, and having poetry as one's career. To have poetry as a career seems to mean for Oppen a subjection to the literary world of poetic institutions, groups and fashions, so for him it 'is necessary to have some stance outside Literature'.[24] Oppen's withdrawal is from 'literature' and, in order to reach that point, from poetic practice as well, though not from poetry itself. After his return to writing, Oppen would suggest to Robert Duncan, 'I write but cannot hope to live in what is written.'[25]

As we have seen, this would be a perennial problem faced by many late modernists: the shift away from officially endorsed literature which Jacques Derrida calls 'The End of the Book and the Beginning of Writing'.[26]

After the high modernist focus on the autonomy of art and the preeminence of form and innovatory style, the late modernists particularly would feel the difference between what Derrida labels good and bad writing: the good comes from within the writer, from life, and the bad comes from without, from a focus on 'technique' within the 'artful' pursuit of literature.[27] However, good writing is not so easily accomplished since any form of writing, no matter how involved in life, is set down in an institutional format and eventually becomes a historical document. It is the nature of writing that it cannot keep up with the present, as many modernists discovered. Yet for some reason, even perhaps after twenty-five years of silence, the writer feels compelled to return. The troubled relationship between life and art, between modernity and history, provided a continuing problem for the career of the late modernist, leading these writers away from writing but often back again.[28] The late modernists were aware of the limits of literature, and many of them struggled towards its end through withdrawal and renunciation; but many also returned after their silence, to continue writing even after the admission that the literary vocation, determined to put life to paper, is bound to fail.

Riding was a poet who did not return. Her decision to stop writing poetry, a gradual process centred (according to her own account) around 1942, coincides somewhat with Oppen's. Less political in nature, Riding's conviction that poetry could not convey truth led to her abandonment of writing and even, for a time, any reproductions of her poems.[29] However, there is significance in her eventual relenting to the republication of her poetry and in the fact that she continued to fight for her reputation as a poet through articles on literary history and canonicity. Clearly, Riding was finished with the institutional limits placed on poetry but had not necessarily given up her position as poet. As she would write in the preface to *The Telling* (1972) about that book, 'To speak as I speak in it, say such things as I say in it, was part of my hope as a poet. But, I have found, poetry imposes inhibitions upon the expressive faculties even while inducing expectation of new degrees of freedom of tongue, voice, mind, and all else that words live by.'[30] In other words, poetry had failed her, but she was still engaging in the pursuit of writing the things which poetry aimed, but failed, to express. The distinction, as far as it goes, seems to have more to do with poetic institutions, expectations and reception than with the aims of the writer herself.

Riding confirms this in her most important statement on the abandonment of poetry, the preface to her *Selected Poems: In Five Sets* (1970). Riding begins by saying, 'My history as one who was for long a devout advocate of poetry, and then devoutly renounced allegiance to it as a profession and faith in it as an institution, raises a question of consistency.'[31] There are two things to point out here. First of all, it is significant that Riding highlights both her devotion to poetry and, similarly, the devoutness of her renunciation, as if the two are somehow equal and opposite actions of a single poetic position.[32] Secondly, what Riding suggests she has renounced is not just the writing of poetry but her 'allegiance to it as a profession and faith in it as an institution' – thereby making her withdrawal from poetry a more specific withdrawal from the institutions of poetry, particularly in the context of what she calls 'mere period-modernism'. Throughout Riding's career, her developing sense of the injustice done to the poet's work by intrusions of criticism, biography, literary history and politics (as outlined earlier in this volume) might have contributed as much to her renunciation as her more philosophical position on poetry's inability to capture truth. When Riding describes how she became 'so much aware of a discrepancy, deep-reaching, between what I call the creed and the craft of poetry – which I might otherwise describe as its religious and its ritualistic aspects – that I perceived the impossibility of anyone's functioning with consistency in the character of poet', it becomes clear just how far her disillusionment is not with what poetry wants to accomplish but with the rules and techniques it is compelled to follow in this attempt.

Maurice Blanchot declared, 'The poet who renounces being one is still faithful to the poetic exigency, if only as a traitor.'[33] This statement, highlighting the role the traitor plays in sustaining the opposed institution even by acknowledging their antagonism, reveals the crucial dialectical role the late modernists sometimes came to play, even (perhaps particularly) in their silence and withdrawal from the literary vocation and its institutions. Riding was a highly devout traitor to poetry, faithful to the end of her life in her renunciation of poetry and, simultaneously, in her struggle to protect her poems from the literary institutions of academy and canon. As paradoxical as this position is, there is a certain consistency with her earlier critical programme, where she unwaveringly argued that poetry should be free of history, period fashions and the influence of self-criticism. We must remember that modernism, according to Riding, was over before it had begun simply because it had packaged itself within a historical and critical framework, thus binding poetry into a limited system that was no longer capable of full expression. Riding, while still writing poetry, would state that 'poetry is not literature', suggesting she blamed, along with many other late modernists, the common conception of the literary during the period for inhibiting expression (*CS* 14). Eventually, she realized that even poetry was bound by literary conventions, and a poet had to put poetry aside if they were to have a chance at writing truth.

The end of literature was a recurring topic for modernist latecomers. There seemed little hope for its continuation once it became clear that sustainable modernity – that quality which seemed most important in establishing the value of a work of art during the period – was an impossible goal. As soon as a thing was written, it was no longer modern; yet the modernist latecomers were writing in a period where the modern had grown established. Even to begin again was to be unoriginal. There seemed little alternative but to destroy art – as many avant-garde movements sought to do – or to sink into silence, either a complete renunciation of literature or a reprieve from it. Some late modernists were openly hostile to the high modernist literary values, while others rejected the high modernist notion of history by refusing to relegate the earlier group to the past. Some managed to reconcile the two, choosing like Miller to launch an attack on high art from the same elevated position he was criticizing – to paradoxically write and rewrite 'The Last Book' as a perpetual demolition of the literary institution that sustained it. The late modernist period, falling between the consummation of the high modernist revolution and the beginning, decades later, of a recognized postmodernist afterwards, seems to be the period where most emphasis was placed upon the idea of endings. T. J. Clark states that modernism's 'job turns out to be to make the endlessness of the ending bearable, by time and again imagining that it has taken place'.[34] In some ways, this ignores the emphasis on new beginnings at which the high modernists themselves excelled. But for every new beginning, there must be someone to call an end to what went before, and this was the modernist ambition: to establish a new beginning that might endure to the end. If the revolutionary modernist project has returned after a 'deferral', as Marjorie Perloff suggests, the literature of silence and exhaustion, in many ways begun by the modernist latecomers whether by direct antagonism or simply a general stocktaking, was a necessary step in setting the stage once more for the 'new' to emerge.[35] While the emergence of postmodernism in later decades might signal the successful, if ironic, movement beyond the end of the new – finding ways to speak after everything new has been said – it was the modernist latecomer who first recognized that the high modernist revolution might succeed in extending itself indefinitely by constantly reimagining that the end had already taken place.

The attempts by the high modernists to 'make it new' for all time only further convinced their immediate successors of the devaluation of newness, where surface innovations, literary fashions and manifesto-based groups, historical categories and subcategories, and the institutionalization of literature all contributed towards the illusion that modernity could be captured. Many modernist latecomers, because of the nature of their position, saw through these illusions and began the sometimes difficult process of bringing an end to the modernist vision of tradition, innovation, literary history and the literary field. The role of the literary latecomer is not limited to the modernist period, though it is perhaps made more obvious in an age where the up-to-date work became synonymous with that which would also endure beyond its own time. That postmodernism resulted from the recognition that the end of one mode of writing would not always result in a new advance in another – questioning, in fact, the very notion of progress – seems in this way directly related to the late modernist criticism of high modernist ideas of literary evolution, civilization and the institution of innovation. While strategies have sometimes changed in dealing with the vexed position of the innovative work in literary history, the modernist latecomers' engagement with the successful high modernist revolution reveals how early the problem first surfaced and how relevant are the questions raised by this often marginalized group for our own conception of the traditional and the new.

Notes

INTRODUCTION: THE MODERNIST LATECOMER
AND 'PERMANENT NOVELTY'

1. Ezra Pound, *ABC of Reading* (New York: New Directions, 1934), p. 29.
2. Thomas L. Scott and Melvin J. Friedman with the assistance of Jackson R. Bryer (eds.), *Pound/The Little Review: The Letters of Ezra Pound to Margaret Anderson* (London: Faber and Faber, 1988), p. 291.
3. For example, Matei Calinescu, *Five Faces of Modernity: Modernism, Avant-Garde, Decadence, Kitsch, Postmodernism* (Durham, NC: Duke University Press, 1987).
4. T. S. Eliot, 'Tradition and the Individual Talent', in Frank Kermode (ed.), *Selected Prose of T. S. Eliot* (London: Faber and Faber, 1975), p. 38.
5. Pound, *ABC of Reading*, pp. 13–14.
6. Chris Baldick, *The Modern Movement 1910–1940*, in Jonathan Bate (ed.), *The Oxford English Literary History*, 13 volumes (Oxford: Oxford University Press, 2004), vol. X, pp. 3–4.
7. W. B. Yeats, 'Introduction', in *The Oxford Book of Modern Verse* (Oxford: Clarendon, 1936), p. xxxvi.
8. Lawrence Rainey, *Institutions of Modernism: Literary Elites & Public Culture* (New Haven: Yale University Press, 1998), pp. 77–106.
9. Aaron Jaffe, *Modernism and the Culture of Celebrity* (Cambridge: Cambridge University Press, 2005).
10. Peter Nicholls, for one, uses the term 'hegemonic' to describe the Eliot/Pound strand of modernism while emphasizing that this was not the *only* strand, in *Modernisms: A Literary Guide* (Basingstoke: Macmillan, 1995), p. 167. Earlier, Fredric Jameson used the term to describe the modernist conventions Wyndham Lewis struggles against in *Fables of Aggression: Wyndham Lewis, the Modernist as Fascist* (Berkeley: University of California Press, 1979), p. 19.
11. Richard Aldington, 'The Poetry of T. S. Eliot', in *Literary Studies and Reviews* (London: Allen & Unwin, 1924), p. 182.
12. Pierre Bourdieu, 'The Field of Cultural Production, or: The Economic World Reversed', in Randal Johnson (ed.), *The Field of Cultural Production* (Cambridge: Polity Press, 1993), and Bourdieu, *Distinction: A Social Critique*

of the Judgement of Taste, trans. Richard Nice (Cambridge, MA: Harvard University Press, 1987). For modernism and markets, see also Kevin J. H. Dettmar and Stephen Watt (eds.), *Marketing Modernism: Self-Promotion, Canonization, Rereading* (Ann Arbor: University of Michigan Press, 1996); I. R. Willison, Warwick Gould and Warren L. Chernaik (eds.), *Modernist Writers and the Marketplace* (New York: St Martin's Press, 1996); Catherine Turner, *Marketing Modernism Between the Two World Wars* (Amherst: University of Massachusetts Press, 2003); and John Xiros Cooper, *Modernism and the Culture of Market Society* (Cambridge: Cambridge University Press, 2004).

13. Louis Untermeyer, 'Disillusion vs. Dogma', *Freeman* 6 (17 January 1923), p. 453.

14. Several critics have noted that *Ulysses* was more widely discussed than read, including Rainey, *Institutions of Modernism*, and Bruce Arnold, *The Scandal of Ulysses* (New York: St Martin's Press, 1992).

15. Noel Riley Fitch, *Sylvia Beach and the Lost Generation* (London: Penguin, 1985), p. 118.

16. Ford Madox Ford, '*Ulysses* and the Handling of Indecencies', reprinted in Robert H. Deming (ed.), *James Joyce: The Critical Heritage*, 2 vols. (London: Routledge, 1970), vol. I, p. 276.

17. Stuart Gilbert and Richard Ellmann (eds.), *The Letters of James Joyce*, 3 vols. (London: Faber and Faber, 1957–1966), vol. III, p. 69.

18. Ibid., p. 83.

19. The first version of the schema was sent to Linati 'for your personal use only'. See Gilbert (ed.), *The Letters of James Joyce*, vol. I, p. 146.

20. Deming (ed.), *James Joyce: The Critical Heritage*, vol. I, p. 261.

21. Unpublished letter, 25 November 1921, quoted by Richard Ellmann, *James Joyce*, revised edition (Oxford: Oxford University Press, 1983), p. 519.

22. Ellmann, *James Joyce*, p. 521.

23. Michael H. Whitworth, *Modernism* (Malden, MA: Blackwell, 2007), p. 23. See also Pericles Lewis, *The Cambridge Introduction to Modernism* (Cambridge: Cambridge University Press, 2007).

24. Gerald Graff, *Professing Literature: An Institutional History* (Chicago: University of Chicago Press, 1987), p. 124.

25. I. A. Richards, 'On TSE', in Allen Tate (ed.), *T. S. Eliot: The Man and His Work* (New York: Dell, 1966), pp. 2–6.

26. Alan Travis, 'Secret files expose Joyce fiasco', *The Guardian*, 15 May 1998. One Home Office official would write, 'Now that this work is to be the subject of a course of lectures for the English Tripos at Cambridge, there is sure to be a large demand for it … we should take steps to prevent the lectures taking place', p. 3.

27. Louis Menand, *Discovering Modernism: T. S. Eliot and his Context* (Oxford: Oxford University Press, 1987), p. 124.

28. Ibid., pp. 131–2.

29. Stan Smith, *The Origins of Modernism: Eliot, Pound, Yeats and the Rhetorics of Renewal* (New York: Harvester, 1994).

30. Ezra Pound, 'Date Line', in *Make It New* (London: Faber and Faber, 1934), reprinted in T. S. Eliot (ed.), *Literary Essays of Ezra Pound* (New York: New Directions, 1968), p. 80 (Pound's emphasis).
31. D. D. Paige (ed.), *The Letters of Ezra Pound: 1907–1941* (New York: Harcourt, 1950), p. 18. Monroe's question frames the title of her article in *Chicago Tribune*, 12 July 1912, p.11, as quoted in Claire Hoertz Badaracco, *Trading Words: Poetry, Typography and Illustrated Books in the Modern Literary Economy* (Baltimore: Johns Hopkins University Press, 1995), p. 40.
32. Ezra Pound, 'Harold Monro', *The Criterion* 11:45 (July 1932), p. 590.
33. Art Berman, *Preface to Modernism* (Urbana: University of Illinois Press, 1994), p. 64.
34. Michael H. Levenson, *A Genealogy of Modernism: A Study of English Literary Doctrine 1908–1922* (Cambridge: Cambridge University Press, 1984).
35. Bourdieu, 'The Field of Cultural Production', p. 60.
36. Eliot, 'Tradition and the Individual Talent', p. 38.
37. Pierre Bourdieu, *The Rules of Art: Genesis and Structure of the Literary Field*, trans. Susan Emanuel (Oxford: Polity, 1996), p. 214.
38. Edmund Wilson, *The Twenties: From Notebooks and Diaries of the Period*, ed. Leon Edel (New York: Farrar, Strans & Giroux, 1975), p. 49.
39. Harriet Monroe, 'Ezra Pound', *Poetry* 26 (May 1925), p. 97.
40. Both these points have been gratefully received from readers of early drafts of this work, the first from Robert Hampson and the second from an anonymous reader.
41. Whitworth, *Modernism*, p. 41.
42. Menand, *Discovering Modernism*, p. 9.
43. David E. Chinitz, *T. S. Eliot and the Cultural Divide* (Chicago: University of Chicago Press, 2003), p. 5.
44. Laura Riding and Robert Graves, *A Survey of Modernist Poetry* (London: Heinemann, 1927).
45. Frank Swinnerton, *The Georgian Literary Scene: A Panorama* (London: Heinemann, 1935), p. 513.
46. Richard Aldington, 'The Poetry of T. S. Eliot', in *Literary Studies and Reviews*, p. 181.
47. Malcolm Cowley, *Exile's Return: A Narrative of Ideas* (London: Jonathan Cape, 1935), pp. 121–2.
48. Michael Levenson, 'Introduction', in Levenson (ed.), *The Cambridge Companion to Modernism* (Cambridge: Cambridge University Press, 1999), p. 2.
49. See, for example, Cary Nelson, *Repression and Recovery: Modern American Poetry and the Politics of Cultural Memory, 1910–1945* (Madison: University of Wisconsin Press, 1989); Bonnie Kime Scott, *The Gender of Modernism* (Bloomington: Indiana University Press, 1990); Peter Nicholls, *Modernisms*; Ann Douglas, *Terrible Honesty: Mongrel Manhattan in the 1920s* (New York: Noonday, 1996); and Michael North, *Reading 1922: A Return to the Scene of the Modern* (New York: Oxford University Press, 1999).

50. See particularly the conclusion to Jane Tompkins, *Sensational Designs: The Cultural Work of American Fiction 1790–1860* (New York: Oxford University Press, 1985). Also, more fully devoted to this topic is Barbara Herrnstein Smith, *Contingencies of Value: Alternative Perspectives for Critical Theory* (Cambridge, MA: Harvard University Press, 1988).

51. David Trotter, *The Making of the Reader: Language and Subjectivity in Modern American, English and Irish Poetry* (London: Macmillan, 1984).

52. Bourdieu, 'The Field of Cultural Production', p. 42.

53. Letters from Pound to Thayer, 18 February and 9–10 March 1922, located at Beinecke Rare Book and Manuscript Library (*The Dial* Papers, Mss. 34, box 38, folders 1070–71), and quoted in Rainey, *Institutions of Modernism*, p. 83.

54. Letter to Felix Schelling, 8 July 1922, in Paige (ed.), *The Letters of Ezra Pound*, p. 180.

55. Cowley, *Exile's Return*, p. 122.

56. I have generally looked to use Bourdieu's model of the writer's position within respective cultural fields rather than the more psychological burden of influence as outlined by W. Jackson Bate, *The Burden of the Past and the English Poet* (London: Chatto & Windus, 1971), and Harold Bloom, *The Anxiety of Influence: A Theory of Poetry* (New York: Oxford University Press, 1973), not because influence studies are irrelevant here but because it seems the complexities of institutional and market-based relations between modernist writers in the late period have received too little attention.

57. Conrad Aiken, 'A Pointless Pointillist', *The Dial* 65 (October 1918), pp. 306–7.

58. Yeats, 'Introduction', *The Oxford Book of Modern Verse*, p. v.

59. Wyndham Lewis, *Time and Western Man*, ed. Paul Edwards (Santa Rosa, CA: Black Sparrow, 1993), p. 216.

60. Glenway Wescott, 'Review of *A Draft of Sixteen Cantos*', *The Dial* 79 (December 1925), pp. 501–3.

61. I am indebted to an anonymous reader for suggesting this view of modernist epics to me. Examples include W. B. Yeats's revisions of his poetry, Wyndham Lewis's *Tarr* 1918 and 1928, the openly suggestive ending of James Joyce's *A Portrait of the Artist as a Young Man* and the periodic public emergence of chapters of *Ulysses* or Ezra Pound's *Cantos*.

62. Edmund Wilson, *Axel's Castle: A Study in the Imaginative Literature of 1870–1930* (New York: Scribner, 1931), p. 1. See also Wyndham Lewis's characterization of Wilson's view in *Blasting and Bombardiering: An Autobiography 1914–1926*, revised edition (London: Calder, 1982), p. 256.

63. C. Barry Chabot, 'The Problem of the Postmodern', in Ingeborg Hoesterey (ed.), *Zeitgeist in Babel: The Postmodernist Controversy* (Bloomington: Indiana University Press, 1991), p. 34.

64. Levenson's text works well alongside Peter Bürger's work (translated into English the same year), *Theory of the Avant-Garde*, trans. Michael Shaw, (Minneapolis: University of Minnesota Press, 1984), distinguishing between the historical avant-garde and the fully distinct and more conservative modernism which is being discussed here as 'high' or counter-current modernism.

65. Matei Calinescu, 'Modernism, Late Modernism, Postmodernism', in Danuta Zadwarnoa-Fjellestad and Lennart Bjšrk (eds.), *Criticism in the Twilight Zone: Postmodern Perspectives on Literature and Politics* (Stockholm: Almquist & Wiksell, 1990), pp. 52–61.
66. Berman, *Preface to Modernism*, p. 82.
67. Tyrus Miller, *Late Modernism: Politics, Fiction, and the Arts Between the World Wars* (Berkeley: University of California Press, 1999), p. 10.
68. Alan Wilde, 'Surfacings: Reflections on the Epistemology of Late Modernism', *boundary2* 8:2 (Winter 1980), pp. 209–27. This essay is reprinted in Whitworth's *Modernism*, which also contains a brief introduction to 'late modernism' as a concept.
69. Fredric Jameson, *A Singular Modernity: Essay on the Ontology of the Present* (London: Verso, 2002), pp. 199–200.
70. Marjorie Perloff, *21st-Century Modernism: The 'New' Poetics* (Malden, MA: Blackwell, 2002), p. 3.
71. This perception is of course not entirely accurate, but it is a perception that began in the period and still exists. Richard Aldington would suggest of the high modernists, 'It is as if the poets had deliberately starved their art, condemned it to the malnutrition of a perpetual imitation, not of life, but of itself.' See 'The Poet and his Age', *Literary Studies and Reviews*, p. 221.
72. Tim Armstrong, *Modernism: A Cultural History* (Malden, MA: Polity, 2005), p. 11.
73. See Jameson, *A Singular Modernity*, p. 25.

CHAPTER I 'CHANGING THE CHANGING':
WYNDHAM LEWIS AND THE NEW MODERNIST ASCENDANCY

1. Wyndham Lewis, *Paleface: The Philosophy of the 'Melting Pot'* (London: Chatto & Windus, 1929), p. 120.
2. Matie Molinaro, Corinne McLuhan and William Toye (eds.), *Letters of Marshall McLuhan* (Toronto: Oxford University Press, 1987), p. 140.
3. The centrality of author-heroes to high modernism, as illustrated by Aaron Jaffe in discussing 'imprimateurs', is highly relevant here, and Lewis would fit nicely into his model – from his high modernist version of *Tarr* to his late modernist revisions regarding the value of the author myth. See Jaffe, *Modernism and the Culture of Celebrity* (Cambridge: Cambridge University Press, 2005).
4. David Trotter, *Paranoid Modernism: Literary Experiment, Psychosis, and the Professionalization of English Society* (Oxford: Oxford University Press, 2001), p. 289, calls Lewis a 'serial careerist' for his continual attempts throughout his life to redefine his position within cultural modernism.
5. Hugh Kenner, *Wyndham Lewis* (London: Methuen, 1954), p. xiv.
6. Fredric Jameson, *Fables of Aggression: Wyndham Lewis, the Modernist as Fascist* (Berkeley: University of California Press, 1979), pp. 4, 18.

7. SueEllen Campbell, *The Enemy Opposite: The Outlaw Criticism of Wyndham Lewis* (Athens: Ohio University Press, 1988), p. xv.
8. Toby Avard Foshay, *Wyndham Lewis and the Avant-Garde: The Politics of the Intellect* (Montreal: McGill-Queen's University Press, 1992), p. 4. Mark Perrino has lamented that Lewis is considered 'an inassimilable aberration of the modernist movement that he had helped to create' in *Wyndham Lewis's 'The Apes of God' and the Popularization of Modernism* (Leeds: Maney, 1995), p. 1.
9. This phrase is used purposefully to remind the reader of Pierre Bourdieu's idea of new writers 'making an epoch' for themselves, as discussed in the Introduction. See Bourdieu, *The Field of Cultural Production*, ed. Randal Johnson, (Cambridge: Polity, 1993). For more on the celebrity status of modernist authors, see Jaffe, *Modernism and the Culture of Celebrity*, as well as the second chapter of Chris Baldick, *The Modern Movement 1910–1940*, in Jonathan Bate (ed.), *The Oxford English Literary History*, 13 volumes (Oxford: Oxford University Press, 2004), vol. X.
10. David Peters Corbett, *The Modernity of English Art: 1914–1930* (Manchester: Manchester University Press, 1997), p. 44.
11. C. H. Collins Baker, 'Dry Bones', *Saturday Review*, 20 March 1915, quoted in Corbett, *The Modernity of English Art*, p. 44.
12. Robert Nichols, 'An Exposé of the Hun,' *The New Witness*, 6 September 1918.
13. Tyrus Miller, *Late Modernism: Politics, Fiction, and the Arts Between the World Wars* (Berkeley: University of California Press, 1999), p. 28.
14. Wyndham Lewis, 'What Art Now?', *The English Review* 28 (April 1919), pp. 334–8, reprinted in Paul Edwards (ed.), *Creatures of Habit and Creatures of Change* (Santa Rosa, CA: Black Sparrow, 1989), p. 46.
15. Lewis, 'What Art Now?', p. 49. For further discussion of Lewis's shifting relationship with modernism and revolution, see Andrzej Gasiorek, *Wyndham Lewis and Modernism*, gen. ed. Isobel Armstrong, *Writers and their Work* (Tavistock, Devon: Northcote House Publishers, 2004).
16. Wyndham Lewis, *The Caliph's Design: Architects! Where is your Vortex?*, ed. Paul Edwards, (Santa Rosa, CA: Black Sparrow, 1986), p. 9.
17. Foshay, *Wyndham Lewis and the Avant-Garde*, p. 21.
18. Peter Bürger, *Theory of the Avant-Garde*, ed. Michael Shaw, (Minneapolis: University of Minnesota Press, 1984).
19. Lewis, *The Caliph's Design*, p. 79.
20. Ibid.
21. Renato Poggioli, *The Theory of the Avant-Garde*, trans. Gerald Fitzgerald, (Cambridge, MA: Belknap Press, 1962), p. 25.
22. Lewis, *The Caliph's Design*, p. 91.
23. Ibid., p. 93.
24. Ibid., p. 96.
25. Ibid., p. 109.
26. Ibid., p. 111.

27. Ibid., pp. 112–13.

28. Ibid., p. 53.

29. Wyndham Lewis, 'The Children of the New Epoch', *Tyro: A Review of the Arts of Painting, Sculpture and Design* 1 (1921), p. 3.

30. Wyndham Lewis, 'Editorial', *Tyro* 2 (1922), p. 6.

31. Wyndham Lewis, 'The Long and the Short of It', in Edwards (ed.), *Creatures of Habit*, pp. 80–2.

32. Jeffrey Meyers, *The Enemy: A Biography of Wyndham Lewis* (Boston, MA: Routledge, 1980), p. 105. Meyers's book has recently been supplemented by Paul O'Keeffe's more comprehensive *Some Sort of Genius: A Life of Wyndham Lewis* (London: Jonathan Cape, 2000).

33. The book sold 'probably no more than 1500' copies according to Reed Way Dasenbrock, 'Afterward', *ABR* 433.

34. Lewis recants some of his criticisms of democracy in *TWM* 25.

35. From the typescript of *The Art of Being Ruled* in the Poetry Collection at the State University of New York at Buffalo, included in the Black Sparrow edition of *ABR*, pp. 288–91.

36. Pierre Bourdieu, *The Rules of Art: Genesis and Structure of the Literary Field*, trans. Susan Emanuel, (Oxford: Polity, 1996).

37. Norbert Elias, 'The Kitsch Style and the Age of Kitsch' is reprinted in Johan Goudsblom and Stephen Mennell (eds.), *The Norbert Elias Reader* (Oxford: Blackwell, 1998), p. 28.

38. Ibid., p. 32.

39. For an investigation into how Lewis's move from *Mrs. Dukes' Million* to *Tarr* reflects his conception of what makes a 'modernist career', see Geoffrey Gilbert, 'Intestinal Violence: Wyndham Lewis and the Critical Poetics of the Modernist Career', *Critical Quarterly* 36:3 (Autumn 1994), pp. 86–125.

40. Reed Way Dasenbrock, 'Afterword', *ABR* 433–4.

41. T. S. Eliot, 'A Note on Poetry and Belief', *The Enemy: A Review of Art and Literature* 1 (January 1927), p. 17.

42. Wyndham Lewis, 'Editorial', *The Enemy: A Review of Art and Literature* 1 (January 1927), p. ix.

43. Ibid., p. iv.

44. Jameson, *Fables of Aggression*, p. 19.

45. Poggioli, *The Theory of the Avant-Garde*, p. 66.

46. Harry Levin, *James Joyce: A Critical Introduction*, revised edition (New York: New Directions, 1960), p. 89.

47. T. S. Eliot, 'Tradition and the Individual Talent', in Frank Kermode, ed., *Selected Prose of T. S. Eliot*, (London: Faber and Faber, 1975), pp. 38–9.

48. Wyndham Lewis, 'Editorial', *The Enemy: A Review of Art and Literature* 2 (September 1927), pp. xxxiii–iv.

49. Ibid., p. xxxiv.

50. Ibid., pp. xxxv–vi.

51. Wyndham Lewis, *Paleface,* p. 120.

52. Ibid., p. 123.

53. Ibid., pp. 122–3.

54. Corbett, *The Modernity of English Art*, p. 142.

55. Richard Ellmann, *James Joyce*, revised edition (Oxford: Oxford University Press, 1983), p. 596.

56. Paul Edwards, 'Afterword', *TWM*, p. 477.

57. Joyce said, 'I've put in so many enigmas and puzzles that it will keep the professors busy for centuries arguing over what I meant, and that's the only way of insuring one's immortality,' quoted in Ellmann, *James Joyce*, p. 521.

58. Ezra Pound, *ABC of Reading* (New York: New Directions, 1934), p. 29.

59. Adorno's article 'Perennial Fashion—Jazz' is in many ways an elaboration of two paragraphs in Lewis's 'Appendix to Book One', which include Lewis's label *'permanent novelty'* applied specifically to jazz. See Theodor W. Adorno, *Prisms*, trans. Samuel and Shierry Weber, (London: Neville Spearman, 1967).

60. Max Horkheimer and Theodor W. Adorno, *Dialectic of Enlightenment: Philosophical Fragments*, ed. Gunzelin Schmid Noerr, trans. Edmund Jephcott, (Stanford, CA: Stanford University Press, 2002), p. 108.

61. F. R. Leavis's desire to teach the novel even before it was allowed into Britain, is revealed in Alan Travis, 'Secret files expose Joyce fiasco', *The Guardian* (15 May 1998), pp. 1, 3.

62. Anon., 'James Joyce: Genius Becomes Legal', *Vanity Fair* (March 1934), p. 17.

63. O'Keeffe, *Some Sort of Genius*, pp. 265, 278.

64. See Peter Nicholls's discussion of the relationship between a satire and its object, particularly in the context of *The Apes of God*, in *Modernisms: A Literary Guide* (Basingstoke: Macmillan, 1995), p. 270.

65. Paul Edwards draws parallels between characters in *The Apes of God* and contemporary personages in his 'Afterword', *AG* 635.

66. Geoffrey Wagner, *Wyndham Lewis: A Portrait of the Artist as the Enemy* (London: Routledge, 1957), pp. 170–1. Also, Mark Perrino suggests that, although Ratner is modelled on Rodker, his 'aesthetic implies an eclectic dilution of the major modernists', in *Wyndham Lewis's 'The Apes of God'*, p. 62. Paul Edwards sees the subjects of the novel as minor characters in the art history of the period, but considers that it broadly suggests 'a general failure in Modernism,' in *Wyndham Lewis: Painter and Writer* (New Haven: Yale University Press, 2000), p. 343.

67. Perrino, *Wyndham Lewis's 'The Apes of God'*, pp. 2, 3.

68. Interview with Wyndham Lewis, 'Author As His Own Publisher', *Star*, 9 June 1930, p. 18.

69. Marshall McLuhan first used the phrase in 1958 at the National Association of Educational Broadcasters Convention. See Paul Benedetti and Nance DeHart (eds.), *Forward Through the Rearview Mirror* (Cambridge, MA: MIT Press, 1997).

70. Perrino, *Wyndham Lewis's 'The Apes of God'*, p. 152.

71. Wyndham Lewis, *Men Without Art*, ed. Seamus Cooney (Santa Rosa, CA: Black Sparrow, 1987), pp. 57, 67.

72. Lewis, *Men Without Art*, p. 165.

CHAPTER 2   LAURA RIDING, MODERNIST FASHION
AND THE INDIVIDUAL TALENT

1. Laura (Riding) Jackson, *The Poems of Laura Riding* (Manchester: Carcanet, 1980), p. 173.
2. Laura Riding, *Anarchism is Not Enough*, ed. Lisa Samuels (Berkeley: University of California Press, 2001), p. 64.
3. Ibid., p. 72.
4. Laura (Riding) Jackson, 'What, If Not a Poem, Poems?', *Denver Quarterly* 31:1 (Summer 1996), p. 26. Originally written in 1974.
5. Hugh Kenner, 'Introduction', in Barbara Adams, *The Enemy Self: Poetry and Criticism of Laura Riding* (Ann Arbor: UMI, 1990). K. K. Ruthven, 'How to Avoid being Canonized: Laura Riding', *Textual Practice* 5:2 (Summer 1991), pp. 242–60. See also Jo-Ann Wallace, 'Laura Riding and the Politics of Decanonization', *American Literature* 64:1 (March 1992), pp. 111–26, and Peter S. Temes, 'Code of Silence: Laura (Riding) Jackson and the Refusal to Speak', *PMLA* 109:1 (January 1994), pp. 87–99.
6. Louise Cowan, *The Fugitive Group: A Literary History* (Baton Rouge: Louisiana State University Press, 1959), p. 9.
7. Thomas Daniel Young and George Core (eds.), *Selected Letters of John Crowe Ransom* (Baton Rouge: Louisiana State University, 1985), p. 150.
8. 11 October 1923, quoted by Cowan, *The Fugitive Group*, p. 132.
9. Cowan, *The Fugitive Group*, p. 184.
10. These views are shared with Tate in a 1923 letter from Riding, as paraphrased by Deborah Baker, *In Extremis: The Life of Laura Riding* (New York: Grove, 1993), p. 85.
11. Laura (Riding) Jackson, 'Literary News as Literary History', *Massachusetts Review* 21:4 (Winter 1980), p. 672.
12. Laura Riding Gottschalk, 'A Prophecy or a Plea', *Reviewer* 5 (April 1925), pp. 1–7. This is also available through the website of the English department at the University of Illinois at Urbana-Champaign, 'Modern American Poetry', ed. Cary Nelson, www.english.uiuc.edu/maps.
13. T. S. Eliot, 'Tradition and the Individual Talent', in Frank Kermode (ed.), *Selected Prose of T. S. Eliot* (London: Faber and Faber, 1975), p. 40.
14. Jeffrey Walsh, 'Alternative "Modernists": Robert Graves and Laura Riding', in Gary Day and Brian Docherty (eds.), *British Poetry 1900–1950: Aspects of Tradition* (New York: St Martin's Press, 1995), p. 140.
15. Laura Riding, 'Marginal Themes', *Epilogue: A Critical Summary* II (Summer 1936), pp. 223–4.
16. I. A. Richards, *Practical Criticism: A Study of Literary Judgement* (London: Routledge, 1929). Riding was not the only late modernist to appreciate this approach. Louis Zukofsky in 1948 adopted a similar approach and methodology in his *A Test of Poetry* (Hanover, NH: Wesleyan University Press, 2000), as cited in the fourth chapter of this study.
17. (Riding) Jackson, *The Poems of Laura Riding*, p. 137.

18. John Crowe Ransom letter to Allen Tate (1922) as quoted in Cowan, *The Fugitive Group*, p. 92.
19. Allen Tate letter to Davidson as quoted in Cowan, *The Fugitive Group*, p. 205.
20. As quoted by Cowan, *The Fugitive Group*, p. 199.
21. Ruthven, 'How to Avoid being Canonized', p. 246.
22. The criticism was a piece entitled 'The H. D. Legend', which Eliot did not accept, yet which was incorporated into *A Survey of Modernist Poetry*, as we shall see. See Paul O'Prey (ed.), *In Broken Images: Selected Letters of Robert Graves 1914–1946* (London: Hutchinson, 1982), p. 162.
23. Letter from Graves to Eliot, 16 February 1926, O'Prey (ed.), *In Broken Images*, p. 164.
24. Letter from Graves to Eliot, 18 September 1926, O'Prey (ed.), *In Broken Images*, pp. 168–9.
25. See Hans Robert Jauss, 'Modernity and Literary Tradition', trans. Christian Thorne, *Critical Inquiry* 31 (Winter 2005), pp. 329–64. See also Stan Smith, *The Origins of Modernism: Eliot, Pound, Yeats and the Rhetorics of Renewal* (New York: Harvester, 1994), where an overlap between modernism and postmodernism is suggested.
26. Paul de Man, 'Literary History and Literary Modernity', *Daedalus* 99:2 (Spring 1970), p. 388.
27. Ibid., p. 401.
28. See Barbara Herrnstein Smith, *Contingencies of Value: Alternative Perspectives for Critical Theory* (Cambridge, MA: Harvard University Press, 1988), p. 50.
29. Since 'jazz' as a verb had first been used only some ten years before *A Survey*, it is worth noting its presence here, particularly in describing passing fashions in the poetic arts. In particular the phrase might be read in the context of Theodor Adorno's essay 'Perennial Fashion – Jazz' in which he recognizes that the jazz craze never passed away, even while remaining, he claims, mere fashion. See Adorno, *Prisms*, trans. Samuel and Shierry Weber (London: Neville Spearman, 1967), pp. 122–3.
30. See Wyndham Lewis's assertion that for each fashion the exact opposite should count as equally fashionable, in 'The Long and the Short of It', in Lewis, *Creatures of Habit and Creatures of Change*, ed. Paul Edwards (Santa Rosa, CA: Black Sparrow, 1989), pp. 80–2.
31. T. S. Eliot, 'The Function of Criticism', in Kermode (ed.), *Selected Prose of T. S. Eliot*, p. 69.
32. Smith, *The Origins of Modernism*.
33. The letters are both to Sassoon, December 1926 and September 1927, O'Prey, *In Broken Images*, pp. 174, 176.
34. No author, 'Contemporary Poetry', *Times Literary Supplement* (5 April 1928), p. 254.
35. Eliot, after receiving and answering a negative review in the *Times Literary Supplement* for this piece, modified his statement months later in 'The Perfect

'Critic', simplifying it to say that philosophical critics are philosophers and historical critics are historians. What this makes the poetic critic is left implicit. See Kermode (ed.), *Selected Prose of T. S. Eliot*, p. 58.

36. Patrick Parrinder, *Authors and Authority: English and American Criticism 1750–1990* (Basingstoke: Macmillan, 1991).

37. Riding's frustration with *Ulysses* and *The Waste Land* for being destructive is perhaps due to their nature as, in Louis Menand's words, 'works that create some of their effects by ridiculing their own artistic pretensions. This is the side of modernism that points to the end of the high-culture line, that presents itself as the cautionary object of history's lesson.' See Menand, *Discovering Modernism: T. S. Eliot and His Context* (New York: Oxford University Press, 1987), p. 112.

38. Matthew Arnold, *Culture and Anarchy*, ed. Samuel Lipman (New Haven: Yale University Press, 1994), p. 102.

39. Ibid., p. 103.

40. Kermode (ed.), *Selected Prose of T. S. Eliot*, pp. 68–9.

41. Anne Ferry, *Tradition and the Individual Poem: An Inquiry into Anthologies* (Stanford, CA: Stanford University Press, 2001) investigates many of these topics, though she gives Graves little credit for identifying them much earlier and virtually edits Riding out of the collaboration.

42. Michael Roberts (ed.), *The Faber Book of Modern Verse* (London: Faber and Faber, 1936); Gwendolen Murphy (ed.), *The Modern Poet* (London: Sidgwick & Jackson, 1938), in which Riding is allowed several pages in the endnotes to justify herself as a unique voice in poetry just before her renunciation; and C. Day Lewis and L. A. G. Strong (eds.), *A New Anthology of Modern Verse 1920–1940* (London: Methuen, 1941).

43. Riding and Graves are listed as having 'refused permission' in W. B. Yeats (ed.), *The Oxford Book of Modern Verse 1892–1935* (Oxford: Clarendon Press, 1936), p. xlii. The other poet mentioned is Pound, who was underrepresented because his fees were too high.

44. Janet Adam Smith, 'The Making of *The Faber Book of Modern Verse*', *Times Literary Supplement*, 18 June 1976, reprinted in Michael Roberts (ed.), *The Faber Book of Modern Verse* (London: Faber and Faber, 1982).

45. Smith, 'The Making of *The Faber Book*', p. xxviii.

46. Ibid., pp. xii–xiii.

47. Eliot letter dated 11 July 1935, quoted by Smith, 'The Making of *The Faber Book*', p. xii.

48. Smith, 'The Making of *The Faber Book*', p. xiii.

49. Aaron Jaffe points out that Edith Sitwell included a press cutting in the fifth *Wheels* anthology of 1920 claiming, 'The publication of "Wheels" is regarded by all right-minded people as more of a society event than a literary one.' For a discussion of the modernist anthology, see Jaffe's fourth chapter in *Modernism and the Culture of Celebrity* (Cambridge: Cambridge University Press, 2005), pp. 137–68.

50. Smith, 'The Making of *The Faber Book*', p. xiv. This idea is pursued in terms of Riding's career in Ella Zohar Ophir, 'The Laura Riding Question: Modernism, Poetry, and Truth', *MLQ* 66:1 (March 2005), pp. 85–114.
51. (Riding) Jackson, 'Literary News as Literary History', p. 676.
52. Ibid., pp. 676–7.
53. Ibid., p. 669.
54. Ibid., p. 664.
55. Ibid., pp. 669–70.
56. Ibid., p. 678.
57. Paul writes in the Paris *Tribune* of 1926, as quoted in Baker, *In Extremis*, p. 182.
58. (Riding) Jackson, 'Literary News as Literary History', pp. 678–9.
59. Ibid., p. 678.
60. Ibid., p. 679.
61. Laura (Riding) Jackson, 'Introduction for a Broadcast', *Chelsea* 12 (1962).

CHAPTER 3   THE IMMOLATION OF THE ARTIST: HENRY MILLER AND THE 'HOT-HOUSE GENIUSES'

1. Henry Miller, *Tropic of Cancer* (London: Calder, 1963), p. 133.
2. Early printings of the Obelisk Press editions of *Tropic of Cancer* position high praise from both Eliot and Pound on the front cover. Eliot wrote, 'A very remarkable book, with passages of writing in it as good as any I have seen for a long time'; Pound wrote, 'At last an unprintable book that is fit to read.' See Henry Miller, *Tropic of Cancer*, 3rd printing (Paris: Obelisk, 1938).
3. Aaron Jaffe, *Modernism and the Culture of Celebrity* (Cambridge: Cambridge University Press, 2005), p. 39.
4. Robert McAlmon, *Being Geniuses Together: 1920–1930*, revised version by Kay Boyle (London: Hogarth Press, 1984), p. 282.
5. See Barbara Will, *Gertrude Stein, Modernism, and the Problem of 'Genius'* (Edinburgh: Edinburgh University Press, 2000).
6. Draft from the Henry Miller Collection at UCLA, quoted in Jay Martin, *Always Merry and Bright: The Life of Henry Miller* (Santa Barbara, CA: Capra Press, 1978), p. vii.
7. Henry Miller, 'Un Etre Etoilique', in *The Cosmological Eye* (New York: New Directions, 1939), p. 270.
8. Lawrence Lipking, *The Life of the Poet: Beginning and Ending Poetic Careers* (Chicago: University of Chicago Press, 1981), p. viii.
9. Roland Barthes, 'Authors and Writers', in *Critical Essays*, trans. Richard Howard (Evanston, IL: Northwestern University Press), p. 149.
10. Barthes, 'Authors and Writers', pp. 144, 146.
11. Jacques Derrida, *Of Grammatology*, corrected edition, trans. Gayatri Chakravorty Spivak (Baltimore: Johns Hopkins University Press, 1997), p. 17.
12. Erica Jong, *The Devil at Large* (London: Chatto & Windus, 1993), p. 88.

13. Gunther Stuhlmann, 'Introduction', in *Henry Miller: Letters to Anaïs Nin*, ed. Gunther Stuhlmann (London: Peter Owen, 1965), p. 7.
14. Robert Ferguson, *Henry Miller: A Life* (New York: Norton, 1991), pp. 106, 147.
15. Ibid., p. 39.
16. Steven Watson, *Strange Bedfellows: The First American Avant-Garde* (New York: Abbeville Press, 1991), p. 231.
17. Ibid., pp. 231–2.
18. Miller, *Tropic of Cancer*, p. 1.
19. Mary V. Dearborn, *The Happiest Man Alive: A Biography of Henry Miller* (London: HarperCollins, 1991), p. 133.
20. Martin, *Always Merry and Bright*, p. 238.
21. Henry Miller, 'An Open Letter to Surrealists Everywhere', in *The Cosmological Eye* (Norfolk, CT: New Directions, 1939).
22. See Peter Nicholls, *Modernisms: A Literary Guide* (Basingstoke: Macmillan, 1995), p. 287. See also Caroline Blinder, *A Self-Made Surrealist: Ideology and Aesthetics in the Work of Henry Miller* (New York: Camden House, 2000).
23. Miller, *Tropic of Cancer*, p. 2.
24. Ibid., p. 243.
25. Ibid., p. 6.
26. Ibid., p. 26.
27. Stuhlmann (ed.), *Letters to Anaïs Nin*, p. 93.
28. Henry Miller, 'The Universe of Death', reprinted in Lawrence Durrell (ed.), *The Henry Miller Reader* (New York: New Directions, 1959), p. 203.
29. Ian S. MacNiven (ed.), *The Durrell–Miller Letters 1935–1980* (London: Faber and Faber, 1988), p. 68.
30. Miller, 'Universe of Death', pp. 204–5.
31. Ibid., pp. 222, 224.
32. Ibid., p. 205.
33. Ibid., p. 204.
34. George Orwell, 'Inside the Whale', in *Inside the Whale, and Other Essays* (London: Gollancz, 1940), reprinted in *England Your England* (London: Secker & Warburg, 1953), pp. 93–142.
35. For a useful discussion of archives and modern time, see Mary Ann Doane, 'Temporality, Storage, Legibility: Freud, Marey, and the Cinema', *Critical Inquiry* 22:2 (Winter 1996), pp. 313–43.
36. Dearborn, *The Happiest Man Alive*, p. 13, for instance, discusses his 'lack of critical judgment in publishing virtually everything he wrote, no matter how negligible'.
37. Alfred Perlés and Lawrence Durrell, *Art and Outrage: A Correspondence about Henry Miller* (London: Village Press, 1973), p. 53.
38. Ibid., p. 32 (emphasis Miller's).
39. Ibid., p. 32.
40. Ibid., p. 41.
41. Ibid., p. 40.

42. Ibid., p. 53. Ferguson, *Henry Miller*, p. 376, is one critic who agrees with Durrell that Miller's main contribution is to bridge a gap between 'high art' and the common reader.

43. Lawrence Durrell, 'The Happy Rock', in Bern Porter (ed.), *The Happy Rock: A Book about Henry Miller* (Berkeley: Packard, 1945), p. 1.

44. Norbert Elias, 'The Kitsch Style and the Age of Kitsch', in Johan Goudsblom and Stephen Mennell (eds.), *The Norbert Elias Reader* (Oxford: Blackwell, 1998), p. 32.

45. Alison Pease, *Modernism, Mass Culture, and the Aesthetics of Obscenity* (Cambridge: Cambridge University Press, 2000).

46. Elias, 'The Kitsch Style', p. 28.

47. Theodor W. Adorno, 'The Position of the Narrator in the Contemporary Novel', in Rolf Tiedemann (ed.), *Notes to Literature*, trans. Shierry Weber Nicholsen, 2 vols. (New York: Columbia University Press, 1991–2), vol. I, p. 31.

48. Durrell, 'The Happy Rock', p. 5.

49. Adorno, 'The Position of the Narrator', p. 31 (emphasis Adorno's).

50. See Will, *Gertrude Stein*, pp. 81–2.

51. James Olney, *Memory & Narrative: The Weave of Life-Writing* (Chicago: University of Chicago Press, 1998), p. 339.

52. Wilhelm Dilthey, 'Drafts for Volume II of the Introduction to the Human Sciences', in Rudolf A. Makkreel and Frithjof Rodi (eds.), *Selected Works*, trans. Jeffrey Barnouw and Franz Schreiner, 6 vols. (Princeton: Princeton University Press, 1985–1989), vol. I, p. 300.

53. 'Solar plexus' and 'big shots' *LE* 105. It is the Surrealists that Miller describes as 'highly conscious'. See MacNiven (ed.), *The Durrell-Miller Letters*, p. 15. 'Aware' comes from Stuhlmann (ed.), *Letters to Anaïs Nin*, p. 69.

54. Henry Miller, *My Life and Times* (London: Pall Mall, 1972), p. 52.

55. Henri Bergson, 'Intellectual Effort', in *Mind-Energy: Lectures & Essays*, trans. H. Wildon Carr (London: Macmillan, 1920).

56. Miller, 'Un Etre Etoilique', pp. 287–8.

57. Paul De Man, 'Literary History and Literary Modernity', *Daedalus: Journal of the American Academy* 99:2 (Spring 1970), p. 392.

58. Henry Miller, *Tropic of Capricorn* (London: Calder, 1964), p. 294, emphasis Miller's.

59. Paul John Eakin, *Fictions in Autobiography: Studies in the Art of Self-Invention* (Princeton: Princeton University Press, 1985), p. 181.

60. Ibid., p. 195.

61. Stuhlmann (ed.), *Letters to Anaïs Nin*, p. 180.

62. Originally published in 1936: Gertrude Stein, 'What are Masterpieces and Why are There So Few of Them?', in *What are Masterpieces?* (New York: Pitman, 1970), p. 92.

63. Derrida, *Of Grammatology*, p. 25.

64. Nicholls, *Modernisms*, p. 288.

65. The first quotation is from MacNiven (ed.), *The Durrell-Miller Letters*, p. 16. The second is from Nicholls, *Modernisms*, p. 284.

66. De Man, 'Literary History and Literary Modernity', pp. 396–7.

67. John Sturrock, *The Language of Autobiography: Studies in the First Person Singular* (Cambridge: Cambridge University Press, 1993), p. 6.

68. Paul De Man, 'Autobiography as De-Facement', in *The Rhetoric of Romanticism* (New York: Cambridge University Press, 1984), p. 67.

69. Eakin, *Fictions in Autobiography*, p. 3.

70. Philip Rahv, *Image and Idea: Fourteen Essays on Literary Themes* (New York: New Directions, 1949), reprinted in Edward Mitchell (ed.), *Three Decades of Criticism* (New York: New York University Press, 1971), p. 27.

71. Richard Clement Wood (ed.), *Collector's Quest: The Correspondence of Henry Miller and J. Rives Childs, 1947–1965* (Charlottesville: University Press of Virginia, 1968).

72. Ferguson, *Henry Miller*, p. 354.

73. See for example, Lawrence Rainey, *Institutions of Modernism: Literary Elites & Public Culture* (New Haven: Yale University Press, 1998).

74. Ferguson, *Henry Miller*, p. 300.

75. Orwell, 'Inside the Whale', p. 141.

76. Bern Porter (ed.), *Henry Miller Miscellanea* (San Mateo, CA: Greenwood Press, 1945). The book was limited to 500 copies, each including an original holograph.

77. Ferguson, *Henry Miller*, p. 326.

78. Jong, *Devil at Large*, p. 186.

79. Ibid., p. 46.

80. Ibid., p. 50.

81. Miller, 'Un Etre Etoilique', p. 278.

82. Miller, *Tropic of Capricorn*, p. 258.

CHAPTER 4   INVESTING IN THE MODERNIST LEGACY:
OBJECTIVIST ADVENTURES IN THE 'POUND TRADITION'

1. Stephen Fredman, '"And All Now Is War": George Oppen, Charles Olson, and the Problem of Literary Generations', in Rachel Blau DuPlessis and Peter Quartermain (eds.), *The Objectivist Nexus: Essays in Cultural Poetics* (Tuscaloosa: University of Alabama Press, 1999), p. 287.

2. Hugh Kenner, *The Pound Era* (Berkeley: University of California Press, 1971). Also see Marjorie Perloff, *Dance of the Intellect: Studies in the Poetry of the Pound Tradition* (Cambridge: Cambridge University Press, 1985).

3. Louis Zukofsky, 'Bottom: A Weaver', in *Prepositions: The Collected Critical Essays of Louis Zukofsky*, expanded edition (Berkeley: University of California Press, 1981), pp. 170–1.

4. Michael Heller, *Conviction's Net of Branches: Essays on the Objectivist Poets and Poetry* (Carbondale: Southern Illinois University Press, 1985), p. xi.

5. Fredman, '"And All Now Is War"', p. 287.

6. Andrew Crozier, 'Zukofsky's List', in DuPlessis and Quartermain (eds.), *The Objectivist Nexus*, p. 275.

7. Crozier, 'Zukofsky's List', pp. 275–6.
8. Also on this topic, see Ron Silliman, 'Third Phase Objectivism', *Paideuma* 10:1 (Spring 1981), pp. 85–9.
9. Lisa Pater Faranda (ed.), *'Between Your House and Mine': The Letters of Lorine Niedecker to Cid Corman, 1960 to 1970* (Durham, NC: Duke University Press, 1986), p. 164.
10. L. S. Dembo, 'The "Objectivist" Poet: Four Interviews', *Contemporary Literature* 10:2 (Spring 1969), p. 179.
11. Ibid., p. 197.
12. Ibid., p. 160.
13. Christopher Beach, *ABC of Influence: Ezra Pound and the Remaking of the American Poetic Tradition* (Berkeley: University of California Press, 1992), p. 44.
14. Dembo, 'The "Objectivist" Poet', pp. 196–7.
15. Heller, *Conviction's Net of Branches*, p. 104.
16. Dembo, 'The "Objectivist" Poet', pp. 180–1.
17. D. D. Paige (ed.), *The Letters of Ezra Pound 1907–1941* (London: Faber and Faber, 1951), pp. 160–1.
18. Peter Makin, *Bunting: The Shaping of his Verse* (Oxford: Clarendon Press, 1992), p. 25.
19. Basil Bunting, 'Mr. Ezra Pound', *The New English Weekly*, 1932, reprinted in Carroll F. Terrell (ed.), *Basil Bunting: Man and Poet* (Orono, ME: National Poetry Foundation, 1981), p. 254.
20. This letter is undated, though we can place it in May or June of 1923, while Margaret Anderson and Jane Heap were visiting Europe. This excerpt was quoted in the catalogue *Basil Bunting: A Collection*, Special List Number 2 (Hadley, MA: Waiting for Godot Books, [n.d.]), no pagination.
21. Paige (ed.), *The Letters of Ezra Pound*, pp. 160–1.
22. See Makin, *Bunting*, pp. 99–100.
23. See John Harwood, 'Pound, Eliot and "The Waste Land"', in Andrew Gibson (ed.), *Pound in Multiple Perspectives* (London: Macmillan, 1993).
24. See Lawrence Rainey, *Institutions of Modernism: Literary Elites & Public Culture* (New Haven: Yale University Press, 1998).
25. Bunting himself said that Pound 'did for my "villon" exactly what he'd done for Eliot in *The Waste Land*', as quoted in Barbara E. Lesch, 'Basil Bunting: A Major British Modernist', unpublished PhD thesis, University of Wisconsin, Madison (1979), p. 29.
26. A portion of 'Faridun's Sons', *The Criterion* 15:40 (April 1936), pp. 421–3.
27. Bunting is most critical of Eliot in 'English Poetry Today', *Poetry* 39:5 (February 1932), p. 266. In the same year he wrote praising *The Waste Land* in 'Mr. T. S. Eliot', *The New English Weekly* 1:21 (8 September 1932), pp. 499–500.
28. Cited in John Seed, 'Irrelevant Objects: Basil Bunting's Poetry of the 1930s', in DuPlessis and Quartermain (eds.), *Objectivist Nexus*, p. 129.
29. Russell Banks, 'Going to the Source: A Lesson in Good Manners', in Jonathan Williams (ed.), *Madeira & Toasts: For Basil Bunting's 75th Birthday* (Highlands, NC: The Jargon Society, 1977), no pagination.

30. See Keith Alldritt, *The Poet as Spy: The Life and Wild Times of Basil Bunting* (London: Aurum Press, 1998), p. 68.

31. Recorded in a television programme, 'Measure of Words', on 21 July 1983 and 19 April 1985, quoted in Victoria Forde, *The Poetry of Basil Bunting* (Newcastle: Bloodaxe, 1991), p. 56.

32. Lesch, 'Basil Bunting', pp. 182–3.

33. Bunting's copy of *Guide to Kulchur* is in the possession of Tom Pickard. The marginalia are reproduced by several critics, in this case by Makin, *Bunting*, p. 150.

34. Quoted by Alldritt, *The Poet as Spy*, p. 95.

35. Alldritt, *The Poet as Spy*, p. 96.

36. Bunting in conversation with Eric Mottram, 1975, a small selection of which is reprinted in Terrell (ed.), *Basil Bunting: Man and Poet*, p. 286.

37. Bunting's 'Open Letter to Louis Zukofsky' appeared in the local Rappallo newspaper, *Il Mare*, on 1 October 1932. Bunting sent an English language translation to him, now at the University of Texas. Reprinted in Dale Reagan, 'Obiter Dicta', in Terrell (ed.), *Basil Bunting: Man and Poet*, pp. 240–1.

38. Reagan, 'Obiter Dicta', p. 242.

39. Makin, *Bunting*, pp. 76–7.

40. Basil Bunting, 'The Poet's Point of View', in Richard Caddel (ed.), *Three Essays* (Durham: Basil Bunting Poetry Centre, 1994), p. 34.

41. Interview with Peter Quartermain and Warren Tallman, 'Basil Bunting Talks About *Briggflatts*', *Agenda: Basil Bunting Special Issue* 16:1 (Spring 1978), p. 18.

42. Basil Bunting, 'A Note on *Briggflatts*' (Durham: Basil Bunting Poetry Archive, 1989), n.p.

43. Bunting's obituary, *The Times*, 19 April 1985, p. 14.

44. Peter Makin (ed.), *Basil Bunting on Poetry* (Baltimore: Johns Hopkins University Press, 1999), p. 116.

45. For an indepth treatment of Zukofsky's life, see Mark Scroggins, *The Poem of a Life: A Biography of Louis Zukofsky* (Emeryville, CA: Shoemaker and Hoard, 2007).

46. Robert Creeley, 'For L. Z.', in Carroll F. Terrell (ed.), *Louis Zukofsky: Man and Poet* (Orono, ME: National Poetry Foundation, 1979), p. 75.

47. Pierre Bourdieu, 'The Field of Cultural Production, or: The Economic World Reversed', in Randal Johnson (ed.), *The Field of Cultural Production*, trans. Richard Nice (Cambridge: Polity, 1993), p. 60. Other generational models, such as W. Jackson Bate, *The Burden of the Past and the English Poet* (London: Chatto & Windus, 1971), and Harold Bloom, *The Anxiety of Influence: A Theory of Poetry* (New York: Oxford University Press, 1973), seem less applicable to the Objectivist position, given the eagerness of the younger poets to *engage* with the fathers. Yet even Bourdieu's pattern, as we will see, is subverted in this case.

48. Ezra Pound, 'Introductory Preface', in Pound (ed.), *Active Anthology* (London: Faber and Faber, 1933), p. 24.

49. Bourdieu, 'The Field of Cultural Production', p. 32.
50. In 1933 Pound claims to be with Eliot 'in agreement, or "belong to the same school of critics", in so far as we both believe that existing works form a complete order which is changed by the introduction of the "really new" work', in Pound, 'Introductory Preface', *Active Anthology*, p. 9. Compare this with the statement, 'Each author, school or work which "makes its mark" displaces the whole series of earlier authors, schools or works'. See Bourdieu, 'The Field of Cultural Production', p. 60.
51. Robert Kern, 'Composition as Recognition: Robert Creeley and Postmodern Poetics', *boundary2* 6:3 (1978), pp. 211–32, quoted in Michael H. Whitworth, *Modernism* (Malden, MA: Blackwell, 2007).
52. See Carla Billitteri, 'William Carlos Williams and the Politics of Form', *Journal of Modern Literature* 30:2 (Winter 2007), pp. 42–63.
53. No stated author, 'Notes', *Poetry: A Magazine of Verse* 37:5 (February 1931), p. 295.
54. Harriet Monroe, 'The Arrogance of Youth', *Poetry: A Magazine of Verse* 37:6 (March 1931), p. 328.
55. Louis Zukofsky, 'Program: "Objectivists" 1931', *Poetry* 37:5 (February 1931), p. 269.
56. Monroe, 'The Arrogance of Youth', p. 329.
57. Marjorie Perloff, '"Barbed-Wire Entanglements": The "New American Poetry," 1930–1932', *Modernism/Modernity* 2:1 (April 1995), pp. 147, 170.
58. Ibid., p. 146.
59. Louis Zukofsky, 'American Poetry 1920–30', reprinted in Zukofsky, *Prepositions,* p. 138.
60. René Taupin, *L'Influence du Symbolisme Français sur la Poésie Américaine (de 1910 à 1920)* (Paris: H. Champion, 1929).
61. Zukofsky, 'American Poetry 1920–1930', p. 137.
62. Louis Zukofsky, 'Influence', reprinted in Zukofsky, *Prepositions*, p. 135.
63. Bourdieu, 'The Field of Cultural Production', p. 31.
64. Heller, *Conviction's Net of Branches*, p. 5.
65. Louis Zukofsky, *A Test of Poetry* (Hanover, NH: Wesleyan University Press, 2000), p. 45.
66. Makin, *Bunting*, p. 324. The link between fear of illness and of influence is reinforced by the shared etymology of influenza and influence, as Tim Armstrong has reminded me.
67. Carroll F. Terrell, 'Louis Zukofsky: An Eccentric Profile', in Terrell (ed.), *Louis Zukofsky: Man and Poet*, p. 69.
68. Louis Zukofsky, 'Recencies', in Zukofsky (ed.), *An 'Objectivists' Anthology* (Le Beausset, France: TO Publishers, 1932), pp. 16, 25.
69. Zukofsky, 'Recencies', p. 16.
70. See Peter Nicholls, 'Lorine Niedecker: Rural Surreal', in Jenny Penberthy (ed.), *Lorine Niedecker: Woman and Poet* (Orono, ME: National Poetry Foundation, 1996).

71. Lorine Niedecker, letter to Harriet Monroe (1933), reprinted in 'Letters to *Poetry* Magazine, 1931–1937', in Penberthy (ed.), *Lorine Niedecker: Woman and Poet*, p. 178.

72. See Rachel Blau DuPlessis, 'Lorine Niedecker, the Anonymous: Gender, Class, Genre and Resistances', in Penberthy (ed.), *Lorine Niedecker: Woman and Poet*, and Marjorie Perloff, 'Canon and Loaded Gun: Feminist Poetics and the Avant-Garde' in Perloff, *Poetic License: Essays on Modernist and Postmodernist Lyric* (Evanston, II: Northwestern University Press, 1990).

73. Faranda, *'Between Your House and Mine'*, p. 49.

74. Ibid., p. 141.

75. Edwin Honig, 'A Memory of Lorine Niedecker in the Late '30s', in Penberthy (ed.), *Lorine Niedecker: Woman and Poet*, pp. 45–6.

76. All poems from Jenny Penberthy (ed.), *Lorine Niedecker: Collected Works* (Berkeley: University of California Press, 2002), p. 157.

77. See Penberthy (ed.), *Collected Works*, pp. 291, 194–5, 197.

78. DuPlessis, 'Lorine Niedecker, the Anonymous', p. 113.

79. Faranda, *'Between Your House and Mine'*, p. 153.

80. Regarding the publication of 'A' in 1957, she wrote, 'You will be the most discussed figure in the writing world, do you realize that?' (*NCZ* 240).

81. Faranda, *'Between Your House and Mine'*, p. 59.

82. Pierre Bourdieu, 'The Long Run and the Short Run', in Johnson (ed.), *The Field of Cultural Production*, p. 97.

83. DuPlessis, 'Lorine Niedecker, the Anonymous', p. 118.

84. Niedecker writes to Corman that if it is true, then 'one could almost faint over it', in Faranda, *'Between Your House and Mine'*, p. 102.

85. Faranda, *'Between Your House and Mine'* (ellipsis Niedecker's).

86. Ibid., p. 77.

87. See *P/Z* xviii or *NCZ* 102.

CHAPTER 5   THE LAST WORD: OR HOW TO BRING
MODERNISM TO AN END

1. Patrick Parrinder, *Authors and Authority: English and American Criticism 1750–1990* (Basingstoke: Macmillan, 1991), p. 216.

2. Djuna Barnes, *Nightwood* (New York: New Directions, 1937), p. 90.

3. Gilbert Seldes, 'Nineties – Twenties – Thirties', *The Dial* 73 (November 1922), p. 577.

4. Ibid., pp. 578, 577.

5. Paul De Man, 'Literary History and Literary Modernity', *Daedalus* 99:2 (Spring 1970), p. 385.

6. See Wyndham Lewis, *Blasting and Bombardiering: An Autobiography 1914–1926*, revised edition (London: Calder, 1982), pp. 260–1.

7. Friedrich Nietzsche, *On the Advantage and Disadvantage of History for Life*, trans. Peter Preuss, (Indianapolis, IN: Hackett, 1980), p. 28.

8. Ezra Pound, 'The Little Review Calendar', *The Little Review* 8 (Spring 1922), p. 2.
9. Ford Madox Ford, 'A Haughty and Proud Generation', *Yale Review* 11 (July 1922), p. 714.
10. Ezra Pound, 'Augment of the Novel', *Agenda* 7:3/8:1 (Autumn/Winter 1969–70), p. 55.
11. Anne Olivier Bell (ed.), *The Diary of Virginia Woolf*, 5 vols. (London: Penguin, 1985), vol. V, p. 353.
12. Letter from Pound to Thayer, 18 February 1922, quoted in Lawrence Rainey, *Institutions of Modernism: Literary Elites & Public Culture* (New Haven: Yale University Press, 1998), p. 83.
13. Basil Bunting, 'On the Fly-Leaf of Pound's Cantos', in Bunting, *The Complete Poems* (Oxford: Oxford University Press, 1994), p. 114.
14. Georg Lukács, 'The Ideology of Modernism' in Arpad Kadarkay (ed.), *The Lukács Reader* (Oxford: Blackwell, 1995), p. 209.
15. De Man, 'Literary History and Literary Modernity', p. 400.
16. See David Peters Corbett (ed.), *Wyndham Lewis and the Art of Modern War* (Cambridge: Cambridge University Press, 1998), pp. 99–153.
17. Oppen will receive more attention in the pages to come. Rakosi stopped writing poetry between 1939 and 1965 in order to pursue his work in psychotherapy. Bunting was silent between 1941 and 1947, and between *The Spoils* in 1951 and *Briggflatts* in 1965. Djuna Barnes's *Nightwood* (1937) was succeeded only by *Antiphon* in 1958. Similarly, Jean Rhys followed *Good Morning, Midnight* in 1939 with *The Wide Sargasso Sea* in 1966.
18. Burton Hatlen, 'Poetry and Politics: A Conversation with George and Mary Oppen', in Hatlen (ed.), *George Oppen: Man and Poet* (Orono, ME: New Poetry Foundation, 1981), p. 25.
19. Ibid., pp. 25, 123.
20. Rachel Blau DuPlessis, '"The Familiar/Becomes Extreme": George Oppen and Silence', *North Dakota Quarterly* 55:4 (Fall 1987), pp. 18–36. See also Peter Nicholls, *George Oppen and the Fate of Modernism* (Oxford: Oxford University Press, 2007).
21. Rachel Blau DuPlessis (ed.), *The Selected Letters of George Oppen* (Durham, NC: Duke University Press, 1990), p. 65. The latter quotation was spoken at a San Diego Conference on George Oppen, May 1986, as recorded by DuPlessis, '"The Familiar/Becomes Extreme"', p. 24.
22. Miller did not enter his period of silence until his roughly book-a-year output ended during the last sixteen years of his life, but, born seventeen years before Oppen, the 'life' from which he might write was lived *before* 1934, the year of his first publication.
23. L. S. Dembo, 'The "Objectivist" Poet: Four Interviews', *Contemporary Literature* 10:2 (Spring 1969), p. 175, and in Rachel Blau DuPlessis (ed.), 'The Philosophy of the Astonished', *Sulfur* (Fall 1990), p. 210.
24. David Young (ed.), 'Selections from George Oppen's *Daybook*', *The Iowa Review* 18:3 (Fall 1988), p. 7.

25. DuPlessis, *The Selected Letters of George Oppen*, p. 183.

26. Jacques Derrida, *Of Grammatology*, corrected edition, trans. Gyatri Chakravorty Spivak (Baltimore: Johns Hopkins University Press, 1997), p. 6.

27. Ibid., p. 17.

28. De Man, 'Literary History and Literary Modernity', p. 399.

29. For the similarities between Oppen's and Riding's careers and a useful theoretical discussion of poets giving up poetry, see Thomas Harold Fisher, 'Poetry's Forfeiture: The Case of Laura Riding and George Oppen', unpublished PhD thesis, State University of New York at Buffalo (2000).

30. Laura (Riding) Jackson, *The Telling* (London: Athlone Press, 1972), p. 1.

31. Laura (Riding) Jackson, *Selected Poems in Five Sets* (New York: Norton, 1973).

32. See Fisher, 'Poetry's Forfeiture', p. 20.

33. Maurice Blanchot, 'The Final Work', *The Infinite Conversation*, trans. Susan Hanson (Minneapolis: University of Minnesota Press, 1993), p. 285.

34. T. J. Clark, *Farewell to an Idea: Episodes from a History of Modernism* (New Haven: Yale University Press, 1999), p. 373.

35. The term 'deferral' is borrowed from Marjorie Perloff, *21st-Century Modernism: The 'New' Poetics* (Malden, MA: Blackwell, 2002).

Index